KV-437-288

Improving learning

Improving learning

Professional practice in secondary schools

Derek Glover and Sue Law

Open University Press
Buckingham · Philadelphia

Open University Press
Celtic Court
22 Ballmoor
Buckingham
MK18 1XW

email: enquiries@openup.co.uk
world wide web: www.openup.co.uk

and
325 Chestnut Street
Philadelphia, PA 19106, USA

First Published 2002

Copyright © Derek Glover and Sue Law

All rights reserved. Except for the quotation of short passages for the purpose
of criticism and review, no part of this publication may be reproduced, stored
in a retrieval system, or transmitted, in any form or by any means, electronic,
mechanical, photocopying, recording or otherwise, without the prior written
permission of the publisher or a licence from the Copyright Licensing Agency
Limited. Details of such licences (for reprographic reproduction) may be
obtained from the Copyright Licensing Agency Ltd of 90 Tottenham Court Road,
London, W1P 0LP.

A catalogue record of this book is available from the British Library

ISBN   0 335 20912 2 (pb)   0 335 20913 0 (hb)

Library of Congress Cataloging-in-Publication Data
Glover, Derek.
   Improving learning: professional practice in secondary schools / Derek
Glover and Sue Law.
      p. cm.
   Includes bibliographical references and index.
   ISBN 0-323-20913-0 (hardcover) – ISBN 0-335-20912-2 (pbk.)
      1. High school teaching–Great Britain. I. Law, Sue. II. Title.
LB1607.53.G7 G56 2002
373.1102–dc21

                                                          2001054511

UNIVERSITY OF
CENTRAL ENGLAND

Book no. 3287646 7

Subject no. 373.1102 Glo

LIBRARY SERVICES

Typeset by Graphicraft Limited, Hong Kong
Printed in Great Britain by Biddles Limited, Guildford and King's Lynn

Contents

Acknowledgements

This book has grown from an extensive programme of research aimed at finding out what students of all ages in 10 secondary schools think about the context and the process of their learning experience. We have then reflected on their perceptions and attempted to discover what works and what doesn't work in securing effective teaching and even more effective learning. What follows is a distillation of the good practice that we have been privileged to see in action. Our thanks go first and foremost to the 3000 students who, willingly or not, gave us their opinions of the subject they were studying at the time of the initial investigation. Without them, and the staff who taught them, we would have been working on hunch rather than objective evidence. The staff then shared with us their views on practice in the classroom and allowed us to collect exemplars of good practice. The leaders of subject areas or of schools allowed us to share in their assessment of the context of their work and we are grateful for their help in enabling us to understand how, at times in very difficult socio-economic circumstances, schools were making a difference to learning. We have been privileged to share in the enthusiasm, determination to succeed, and the sheer joy of learning that has been evident in some of the subject areas, and in some of the schools. It is significant that all the schools, anonymized in the book, have contributed something to the material. They have been positive and adventurous in the most difficult circumstances.

We have enjoyed sharing thoughts and working with the research team. Beryl Miles, Steve Garnett and Peter Landau worked hard to collect the contextual material and to support schools during the process of involvement and they have given us unstinting advice as the book has emerged. Rob Bray helped with the development of material on gender. Without the dogged persistence and patience of Mark and Unni Glover we would not have had consistent and coherent statistical returns for each school. Shona Mullen, Anita West and the Open University Press team have given us unfailing support and encouragement and helped us to feel that others do want to share our journey of discovery. Finally our thanks go to our respective families, who have shown interest, given support and made allowances during the research and preparation of this book. Needless to say, all errors of both fact and judgement remain ours alone.

Derek Glover and Sue Law

The research team

Our concern has been with the student experience of their classroom life. The research team have been or still are secondary classroom teachers. They have all become interested in the context within which effective teaching and learning can take place, and they have shared the successes and problems of the schools with whom they have worked. Each member of the team was responsible for negotiation with headteachers, the collection of data, and the reporting back for two or three schools. Each member prepared a report on the context and culture of 'their' schools and then collected a range of materials demonstrating good practice in action.

Derek Glover is a visiting professor of education at Nottingham Trent University, and honorary professor in the Education Department at Keele University. After 18 years' experience as the head of a large community school in Oxfordshire with boarding and agricultural units attached, he completed his PhD with the Open University and is now well into his 'second career' – teaching on postgraduate courses, researching, and writing extensively. His interests have been in school organization, financial management and the management of school reputation. He and Sue Law have previously co-written *Managing Professional Development in Education* and *Educational Leadership and Learning*.

Sue Law is Professor of Education and Head of the Department of Secondary and Tertiary Education at Nottingham Trent University. After teaching in schools and colleges for 20 years, she became Director of Continuing Professional Development at Keele University, where she established innovative distance-learning MBA and MA educational management programmes. She now balances the leadership responsibilities of a large university department with researching and publishing on teachers' professional development, education management and educational policy-making.

Steve Garnett is currently head of humanities at Garibaldi School, Mansfield, Nottinghamshire. Over the past four years he has become very involved in the development of efficient and effective learning techniques and in identifying best practice within schools. As a member of a team of senior colleagues he has undertaken regular curriculum reviews and planned subsequent improvement strategies. His secondment as a part-time teacher fellow at Nottingham Trent University has enabled him to become more fully involved in development work and student-centred learning.

Peter Landau retired in 1999 from a Gloucestershire comprehensive school after 22 years as its head. Under his leadership the school developed a large all-ability sixth form, became one of the first community schools in the county and as a grant-maintained school it became a magnet for innovative secondary education. For him, headship was more about people than paper, and more about leadership than management.

Beryl Miles was educated at Wimbledon School of Art and the Institute of Education, University of London. She has taught art and design in a wide range of schools and is currently Head of the Arts Faculty at an 11–18 comprehensive school in Derbyshire. In 1998 she was seconded for a short period to the Derbyshire Advisory Service and in 1999–2000 she worked with Nottingham Trent University as a schoolteacher fellow. She has wide-ranging interests in teaching and learning in the creative arts field and was one of the Best Practice Research Scholars in 2000.

The authors relied heavily on the advice and experience of **Rob Bray** for their work on gender. Rob was educated at Warwick University and is currently deputy headteacher of an 11–18 comprehensive school in Derbyshire. He has a special interest in raising the achievement of boys and is a co-author of the Secondary Heads Association publication *Can Boys Do Better?*

Abbreviations

AL	accelerated learning
ALIS	Advanced Level Information System
BEI	British Education Index
BIDS	Bath Information and Data Services
CAME	Cognitive Acceleration through Maths Education
CASE	Cognitive Acceleration through Science Education
CAT	Cognitive Ability Test
DfEE	Department for Education and Employment (until June 2001)
DfES	Department for Education and Skills (since June 2001)
ERIC	Educational Resources Information Centre
GCSE	General Certificate of Secondary Education
HMI	Her Majesty's Inspectorate
ICT	information and communications technology
INSET	in-service training
LEA	local education authority
NFER	National Foundation for Educational Research
Ofsted	Office for Standards in Education
PDC	professional development coordinator
PGCE	Postgraduate Certificate in Education
PHSE	personal, health and social education
QCA	Qualifications and Curriculum Authority
SATs	Standard Assessment Tasks
SCAA	School Curriculum and Assessment Authority
SMART	specific, measurable, achievable, realistic and time bound
TGAT	Task Group on Assessment and Testing
TQM	total quality management
TTA	Teacher Training Agency

Preface

We have noticed that there has been a sharp change of focus in the nature of demands for continuing professional education since 1997. No longer are matters of management such as finance and appraisal to the fore. Rather schools are seeking help with improvement strategies that focus on teaching and learning. At the same time action research has developed within schools as teachers reflect on their practice and undertake limited experiments to improve their effectiveness in the classroom. The research team includes practitioners for whom deeper understanding of approaches to teaching has underpinned their attempts to secure livelier and more motivational experience for their students. At the same time there has been an increased interest in learning style differences and the need to provide stimulation related to the needs of the learner rather than to the predilections of the teacher. This has prompted a pincer movement and increasingly efforts have been made to match teaching style to learning need. This book charts some of this work

Teaching and learning do not, however, occur in isolation. There is clear evidence that schools are affected by the socio-economic and physical contexts of the school and classroom. To this end we have looked at two features of context – the environment for learning and the culture within which teaching and learning take place. Culture, and hence attainment, may be affected by the nature of relationships between teachers and taught. In Chapters 1 and 10 we have attempted to set the improvement of teaching and learning into this growing theoretical framework drawing upon the ever-growing body of literature. Our hope is that this will provide a basis for understanding and a starting point for those who want to follow some aspects further.

We have outlined the basic research methodology and findings of the work. The approach has been that of asking the students to rate their experience and then to relate these measures to the evidence for the nature of context and practice within the schools. Chapter 2 sets out the background to the research and outlines some of the tenets of action research as a starting point for those who might be interested in establishing their own research agenda. Chapters 3 to 8 summarize the findings on the environment, challenge, practice, relationships and overall educational attainment arising from a variety of approaches to teaching and learning. Chapter 9 outlines some of the developmental work being undertaken to equalize attainment between the genders although we recognized that this was integral, rather than discrete as a factor within the classroom.

Because we felt that colleagues would gain most from having data available for their own study we have included the major findings in Chapter 2 and presented these in table form in the Appendix. The statements of the learning audit are thus available for schools to develop their own approaches and undertake their own work as often as they choose. The figures from the complete cohort offer some benchmarks for those who want to use comparative data. To name or not to name the schools who had helped us posed a problem. Opinion varied: some felt that they would have moved on from the time of the investigation to publication, others felt that they were happy to share their good practice but less willing to share their difficulties. In the belief that it is the content of the findings that counts, rather than any associated gossip, we have taken a walk in the woods and anonymized all participants. This in no way diminishes our gratitude to them.

Within each chapter we have included some examples of good practice, mainly as cameos, to stimulate response among policy-makers within schools and subject areas, and we have presented some commentary as the basis of professional development discussion. Further reading is suggested for the topics in each chapter. When the work was begun we included a full reference list of the web sites visited in the course of the writing of this book. Within twelve months we have realized that this is a constantly changing feature of life – some have sunk without trace, some have changed site details, and some have been further developed. Inclusion of all this material would, we thought, lead to frustration rather than resourcing! Accordingly we have included some of the key sites currently yielding worthwhile research trails and would commend the Department for Education and Employment (DfEE) now Department for Education and Skills (DfES), Bath Information and Data Services (BIDS), Educational Resources Information Centre (ERIC) and Education Online web sites as starting points for much highly valuable discussion. Electronic Journals On Line now offer a good range of international thinking on teaching and learning, and because so much of the work has been used commercially, web sites on, for example, accelerated learning (AL) yield much practical material including audit, assessment and prompts for use by teachers for individuals, or within a class or school group.

The book has been designed to meet the needs of a range of users within education. Governors and general readers may find that it offers a background to the main focus of school improvement and effectiveness. In the belief that it will serve primarily as an introduction to those entering the profession, or to classroom practitioners, we have included discussion points to prompt reflection on practice. We have also included check points as arguments have been developed. On the top line of these are three descriptors and on the bottom line are three suggested questions to move practice to a newer and (we would argue) more effective level. Facile typologies have had their day but we do conclude with a suggested matrix demonstrating how the elements of effective learning relate to each other. At that point we recognized that there was more work to be done especially in understanding how the component elements are themselves affected by culture and context . . . and so the study goes on.

1 The context of learning

Background

During the intense debates which surrounded the Education Reform Act 1988, two key perspectives on school improvement emerged. On one side, there were those favouring changes which would enable schools to become self-governing organizations (see, for example, Caldwell and Spinks 1988, 1992; Beare et al. 1989; Ranson 1994). On the other side were those stressing the importance of the secretary of state's powers to ensure improvement through thinly veiled centralist control (see, for example, McClure 1989; Bowe et al. 1992; Ball 1994; Smyth 1995).

Over a decade later, central government control over education and the 'improvement agenda' has been strengthened by the School Standards and Framework Act 1998 and influenced by educational research (see, for example, Barber 1996), albeit within the context of the continuing semi-autonomous nature of school governance.

As part of the centralizing agenda, governments during the 1990s progressively tightened requirements on local education authorities (LEAs) to utilize development strategies capable of bolstering school improvement within the context of the attainment of national objectives. Commentators like Tooley (1999) have attempted analyses of the twin tensions of centralization and local autonomy, and their interactions – as exemplified through the drive of the National Curriculum and national assessment systems in the context of the growing devolution of responsibilities to governing bodies. These tensions emerge, for example, where governors may favour an exclusion policy in relation to student discipline which is at odds with national guidance directed at keeping miscreants within schools. These tensions also impact on the ways in which teachers plan, deliver, assess and monitor their classroom work because of the need to adhere to nationally published subject guidelines.

During the 1990s, research findings into school effectiveness have increasingly informed and sometimes even underpinned national policies for educational improvement. This is evident, for example, in pressures for wider use of school development planning (for example, Hargreaves and Hopkins 1994; Fidler 1996), the application of cultural change mechanisms (for example, Beare et al. 1989; Meyerson and Martin 1997) and enhanced participation in school policy development (for example, Myers 1996). While the drive for an 'improvement agenda' has become more widely accepted, concerns remain over the ways in which universal panaceas are offered. School staff consider that many of these are at variance with the more bespoke needs of individual schools. Moreover, meeting the particular needs of students can be problematic in such a setting (Slee and Weiner 1998).

The process of integration of numerous interrelated school improvement issues into a national educational development policy is illustrated by the report of the House of Commons Select Committee on Education and Employment (1999) into the role of headteachers. The committee agenda incorporated many of the issues already identified by teachers and heads as a high priority for enhanced teaching and learning. The combination of both external and internal pressures to achieve educational improvement means that many schools now face a multiplicity of tasks and responsibilities, leading to 'innovation overload' (Power and Whitty 1999; Tooley 1999), not to mention 'initiative fatigue'. The need for schools to take time to plan and then implement policy changes impacts on and, ironically, may threaten, their capacity to plan and implement teaching and learning strategies effectively.

The successful management and balancing of priorities requires a strong emphasis on both learning and leadership – whether at school or classroom levels (Law and Glover 2000). This precise balancing of priorities depends on the extent to which those leading change at school and classroom levels have the capacity and opportunity to interpret and translate – in a shared and coherent language – national policies into local action, and then, importantly, prioritize often competing demands in agreed ways.

The pressure on schools to both conform and succeed in relation to external agendas inevitably, to a lesser or greater degree, determines their internal agenda for organizational change. There is some evidence in, for example, Office for Standards in Education (Ofsted) school inspection reports (produced by independent inspectors using a notionally consistent framework), that schools labelled as 'failing schools' have proved themselves unable to conform to national requirements – in other words, unable to accommodate the external national agenda. While for many, adverse comment was initially focused around an inability to provide an acceptable moral, spiritual and religious education, often largely for technical (such as available space) reasons, other schools have been deemed failing because of much more fundamental weaknesses in leadership and management, in the expectations of attainment by both staff and students, and in limited responsiveness to community and parental criticism.

The most significant element facing schools, however, is the need to maintain student numbers and thus retain adequate financial resourcing. This, however, is often possible only where schools have a good local reputation. The criteria by which the public is frequently encouraged to judge a school's success are first, examination success and second, the local impression created by its Ofsted report (Glover 1992; Foskett 1998). This situation leads to three sets of tensions that affect approaches to teaching and learning.

External pressures for improvement	versus	Internal awareness of the limitations of a school's socio-economic context
The school leader's perception of the potential for improvement	versus	The class teacher's ability to motivate students to establish change
The class teacher's role as a subject specialist	versus	The class teacher's role as a pastoral support for students (for example, when pressured by other subject staff)

These tensions impact upon teachers at all levels, both those leading school change and those leading classroom change. The impetus for change is underpinned by Ofsted's guidance to inspectors (Ofsted 1995) which emphasizes the need to focus on continuing improvement and was developed in order to reduce bureaucratic, and possibly limiting, slant of some of its initial guidance (Ofsted 1992). In further modifications made in 1998, with the guidance on evaluating school improvement, Ofsted shows increasing concern for context as a factor in establishing future change, as the following extract indicates:

Questions which you need to consider are:

- what change could reasonably be expected?
- how much change has there been?
- how does the change compare with what might be expected?
- how have the changes been brought about?

You must also look to the future and decide:

- how well the school is placed to continue to improve or maintain high standards
             (Ofsted 1998: section 6.1 – Evaluating School Improvement)

This stimulates an important question. What does this guidance mean for teachers?

Consider, for example, the following extract from a class teacher's work diary, written in her third year of teaching at Beech School:

7.45 Arrive at school, coffee; to my classroom to sort out materials for this morning's lessons.
8.00 Begin replacing display of Natural Disasters on one of the display boards in advance of visit by LEA adviser but short of backing paper and so had to recycle display from another board – subsequent problem because this then showed some graffiti which can't be covered without some more materials – selected an [Ordnance Survey] map and put that up in the hope that it will be of interest.

8.20 First of the form group come in. James wants to tell me about continuing problems at home but as he starts the others come in and we arrange to meet later in the day – I want to help but know that there will be problems over confidentiality.

8.25 Complete register and notify office of 'third day absentees'. Prepare to take group to Assembly but notice that three of the girls have gone into non-regulation top-coats and so have to hold them back.

8.30 Assembly reminders for House Drama competition entries by lunch time, and repeated warning from the Head about unsuitable top-coats – helps me in some ways but means that I can't let anything go.

8.45 Start teaching 7Y but then minutes into lesson there is a note from the Deputy Head wanting details of the exam requirements for Year 9 tests – tell class to get on with an exercise while I find this data – I am sure that I have given it to Jim, head of department, already.

15.30 Dismiss 10 (2) and then attempt to tidy the room before the cleaners come in – should be more able to organize the students for this but not always possible especially if you want to set some extra work for the borderline group.

15.40 Go via the staffroom to collect a coffee en route to the staff meeting – contact with the rest of the subject department is helpful and we arrange a social evening with partners after the school's Presentation Evening next week.

15.45 Staff meeting concerned with the forthcoming audit of key skills teaching throughout the school – currently looking like a great deal of work for very little return, and heated discussion on the professional development opportunities for the coming year with the usual pressure to get more money for subject based work. The head seems to have an agenda which is not the agenda we want.

16.45 Back to my room to mark the work from 7Y. Particular problem in tracking the records needed for the completion of the Individual Development Plans for two students with special needs.

And so it goes on . . .

DISCUSSION POINT

- At what points do internal and external tensions impinge on this teacher's work? How could the load be lightened?
- And how would this 'lightening of the load' affect the quality of education provided in this particular classroom?

Good schools, improving schools

The diary extract shows the ways in which school/societal pressure impact on the quality of education offered to students in the classroom. There is evidence (Reavis et al. 1999) that so-called 'good schools' are able to manage the tensions outlined in ways which impact positively on the student experience and their achievements.

Much of this book is concerned with the ways in which those leading schools – whether at organizational or classroom levels – seem to be able to establish a learning and teaching environment conducive to effective teacher–student interaction which in turn maximizes student successes. It is also concerned with the ways in which decisions about learning and teaching strategies at classroom level are able to further enhance student success.

Some schools are readily successful while others, despite huge efforts by school staff, sometimes find it problematic – even in 'good socio-economic areas' – to aid student progress, at least in terms of national achievement norms. There is, however, strong evidence which indicates that social deprivation lowers the level of results attained because schools do not work alone: they are able to provide only so much of the support needed by socially and culturally deprived students (Glover and Law 1999). Schools in socially deprived areas are often inhibited by a range of strong external influences which Mortimore and Whitty (1997) argue are not capable of modification by the school alone. Gilroy and Wilcox (1994) contend that many of the criteria being used for the evaluation of schools are imprecise and subjective.

The contextual factor most focused upon by government is the proportion of a school population making application for and entitled to free school meals. Levačić and Glover (1994) noted a 42 per cent correlation within secondary schools between the number of students excluded from school and free school meals. The authors also concluded that 22 per cent of the variation in the achievement of a favourable judgement of learning quality is attributable to the free meal context, suggesting that a poverty of attitude in relation to the benefits of education and a paucity of resources within the home environment frequently inhibits student progress overall. This prompts important questions about the ability of schools to be deemed 'successful' when they are fighting at best, limited or low levels of interest and help in the home. As Randall (1996) has shown, schools confronted by such a negative counterculture, frequently find that home and parental views can seriously inhibit students' behaviour improvement. There is also a hidden underclass in that many parents, whether through ineptitude or to avoid possible investigation by social agencies, fail to make application for free school meals. The real level of entitlement in many schools may therefore be much higher than the official figures suggest.

Many schools are fully aware of the limitations imposed by contextual factors and are extremely active in attempting to overcome these problems – through close community work, integrating parents into the student learning process, and developing an atmosphere high on self-esteem and low on unnecessary criticism. Payne et al. (1996: 9) summarize the difficulties inherent in this approach: 'Deprivation has a class connected but independent existence, because it is a way of life'.

Some schools do, however, break through these deprivation barriers – often with a mixture of determined and/or charismatic leadership, an exceptionally committed and dedicated staff, generous resourcing and a community will for the school to succeed (Myers 1996). Mortimore and Whitty (1997) have stressed that schools can be helped to make significant improvement if three elements are present. For them, the importance of extra commitment by leaders within the school, sustained hard work by teachers and support staff, and a maintained effort in securing improvement across the total environment of the school, cannot be minimized.

Successful schools

Much has been written on the nature of successful schools and the way in which educational improvement and effectiveness can be achieved. Scheerens (1992), one of the foremost researchers in the more objective analysis of school effectiveness, has compared research findings from various national contexts and suggests that most research outcomes indicate a concern with

- pressure for achievement
- aspects of teaching and learning
- recruiting and retaining qualified staff
- the ability of the school to consider its own progress towards goals
- the financial and material characteristics of the school
- the organization of the school
- the school climate ('the way we do things here').

All these elements usually figure in the preparation for and investigation of school effectiveness – although there is a longstanding concern that such a 'menu' simplifies complex issues (Teddlie and Reynolds 2000). Indeed, this kind of analysis has led to what is labelled as a 'list perspective'.

Rutter et al.'s (1979) seminal research in the area of school effectiveness also produced a list indicating that effective schools demonstrated

- a good school ethos
- good classroom management
- high teacher expectation
- teachers as positive role models
- positive feedback and treatment of students
- good working conditions for teachers and students
- responsibility given to students
- shared staff–student activities.

This list indicates the importance of two leadership levels: at school level (head and senior staff who create the culture within which other staff work) and at classroom level (where teachers lead the learning process).

The range of 'effectiveness elements' have been reviewed and consolidated in Sammons et al.'s (1995) review of research findings for Ofsted, which stresses that although research indicates particular features as characteristic of effective schools, the existence of one or more on their own is unlikely to lead to effectiveness. Because promoting effective education is a complex process, it is the synergy that counts! Sammons et al. draw attention to features which, for example, have been recognized in Ofsted's (1995) framework and a good many school improvement initiatives developed by government:

- professional leadership – firm, participative and leading professional
- shared vision and goals – unity of purpose, consistency of practice and collegiality and collaboration
- a learning environment – orderly, attractive and calm
- concentration on teaching and learning – not only across the day but also in every lesson
- purposeful teaching – well organized, planned in advance, well structured and having clear objectives based on differentiated learning styles which are communicated to students
- high expectations – communicated to enhance student self-esteem
- positive reinforcement – achieved through the use of praise as well as correction
- monitoring progress – to provide and attain targets
- student's rights and responsibilities – based on mutual respect and developing responsibility
- home–school partnership – in a spirit of cooperation
- a learning organization – both teachers and students are learners in the process of educational development.

Culture

An alternative (but far less measurable) perspective on what constitutes 'school effectiveness' can be found in the work of researchers like Lightfoot (1983), Rosenholtz (1989) and Barth (1990). For example, Barth's view of school effectiveness is not dependent only on examination/test scores, performance indicators, or lists of characteristics. Like Rosenholtz, Barth's model of effectiveness looks at schools not as places 'for important people who do not need to learn and unimportant people who do', but as settings where 'students discover, and adults rediscover, the joys, the difficulties and the satisfactions of learning'. This is a model focused on the concept of school culture – where school effectiveness is more dependent on the creation of 'a community of learners' or, in Rozenholtz's terms, the building of 'learning enriched' as opposed to 'learning impoverished' environments.

School culture may be defined as the sum total of all the aspirations, relationships and practices within a school. Commenting on pilot work in Washington DC, Deal (1985) writes of culture as 'the way we do things here'. Prosser (1999) sees it as a 'black hole or fertile garden' and demonstrates the complexity of cultural influences and their impact on teachers and students. Improvement leading to enhanced learning and teaching outcomes requires strategic and tactical planning, as well as the kinds of development planning which Hargreaves and Hopkins (1991) suggest will empower schools. Policies cannot be developed and implemented without some recognition of the cultural context.

Early work to identify models of organization led Blake and Mouton (1964) to see culture as the result of a tension between concern for people and

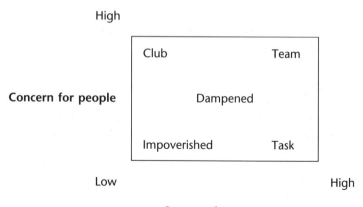

High

Concern for people

Club	Team
Dampened	
Impoverished	Task

Low   High

Concern for outcomes

Figure 1.1   Orientations on the people and outcomes continua
Source: after Blake and Mouton (1964)

concern for outcomes (Figure 1.1). Think of this in terms of the tension between students' needs and whole school targets.

• high concern for people and low concern for outcomes leads to a 'country club' atmosphere
• high concern for people and high concern for outcomes promotes a 'team' orientation
• low concern for people and low concern for outcomes leads to an 'impoverished' organization
• low concern for people and high concern for outcomes leads to a 'task' orientation
• a midway point in both respects may lead to a 'dampened' organization.

Another aspect of culture is the relationship between leaders and led. Building on Harrison's work, Handy (1993) has characterized differences in organizational culture or orientation in the following ways:

• *power culture*: exemplified as intricate networks of micropolitical groupings (characterized as a form of spider's web)
• *task culture*: exemplified as a matrix organizational structure, where largely ad hoc, project teams 'get the work done' (characterized as a net)
• *role culture*: exemplified as a bureaucractic, hierarchical and role-driven structure (characterized as a greek temple)
• *person culture*: exemplified by those who are 'a law unto themselves' – with a highly individualist, high profile emphasis and organizational structures which take second place, do not exist or are subservient to the concerns of the individuals concerned (characterized as a 'galaxy' or 'milky way' of individual stars).

While Handy's classification may apply to or within areas of almost any organization, Hargreaves (1995) articulates culture as the particular interplay of social control (rule and regulation mentality) and social cohesion (team spirit) within a school. He characterizes the following school cultures, arguing that the midpoint on each axis leads to a position of balance with 'effectiveness' predominating:

a traditional culture	high control and low cohesion
a hothouse culture	high control and high cohesion
an anomic culture	low control and low cohesion (nothing happens)
a welfarist culture	low control and high cohesion

This suggests that we can move from a descriptive view of 'what is' to an analytic view of 'what might be' achieved through some change. This leads to a view of culture as a reflection of attitudes within the school. Stoll and Fink (1996) take this dynamic aspect further by looking at the whole organization in relation to the achievement of organizational objectives. For Stoll and Fink:

- effective and improving organizations = 'moving'
- effective but declining organizations = 'cruising'
- ineffective and improving organizations = 'struggling'
- ineffective and declining organizations = 'sinking'.

For them the midpoint is the 'strolling' school – increasingly targeted in national improvement policies and much of the effort in schools is focused at the management of change so that more educationally productive cultures can be developed. The problem is that 'reculturalization' of classes and schools cannot be achieved easily if past influences remain too strong and 'the way we do things here' remains fixed by past images of what the organization is all about (Hannay 1996).

DISCUSSION POINT

- Analyse the culture of a school known to you according to the descriptors of culture outlined above.
- Think also of the culture of a classroom – perhaps yours – and attempt to assess 'cultural mismatch'.
- Has any mismatch been recognized? How might it be addressed?

Leadership

Effective leadership is crucial to the drive to raise school standards. The best school leaders establish a shared vision of school improvement;

inspire students, staff, parents and all those in the wider school community; plan and monitor progress; empower and develop teachers and other school staff; and refresh the vision, setting new goals for continuing and continuous improvement.

(DfEE Teaching Reforms web site 2000)

The above quotation emphasizes the centrality of leadership and in particular, the leadership of heads and senior staff. However, so much leadership is readily applicable to classroom settings – particularly in the context of the national school improvement agenda. A brief excursion into some elements of leadership demonstrates the way in which teachers are helped or hindered by the context within which they are working. This is fundamental to the development of government support for those schools that are said to be 'failing'. The four elements of strong leadership, effective management, clear planning and committed teachers intent on improvement, all highlight the key factors in securing change (DfEE 1999) and offer a background to our understanding of what happens in classrooms.

Strong leadership

Leadership is displayed in a variety of settings. For example, Bush (1995; 2000) suggests six 'types' are apparent:

- *bureaucratic*: hierarchical and systems bound
- *collegial*: cooperative and consensual with pragmatic features
- *political*: dependent upon varying micropolitical power groups
- *subjective*: lacking cohesion and dependent upon individuals
- *ambiguity*: where the rhetoric and reality are mismatched
- *cultural*: where the emphasis is on informal features of coexistence within the organization.

Our concern here is to highlight the ways that leadership features are influential over and may be supportive of effective classroom practice. A school leader with a clear vision for development who also welcomes the participation of colleagues as part of a moving/changing culture offers considerable benefits in terms of motivation and encouragement – by contrast with those where no sense of direction exists, structures are inhibiting or even repressive and people are 'left to their own devices'. For example, a review of the diary extract which began this chapter indicates the impact of leadership – or more precisely its absence, on the part of both school leaders and subject leaders.

So how is leadership exercised in schools? A traditional model, often known as 'scientific' or 'rational' management – in itself a significant alternative to leadership – perpetuates the view that human beings need to be driven to meet objectives and are efficient in their work only if they are managed, controlled and supervised in ways that secure required organizational outputs. A contrasting approach is based on encouraging human endeavour within a systemic framework where work is organized with minimum control. Here, the emphasis is on enabling staff to feel they actively contribute to organizational success or failure (Cuthbert and Latcham 1979). Mintzberg (1990) argues that leaders need to draw upon both rational and systems approaches, suggesting that some of the leadership work is based around the cerebral application of rationality as well as the insightful (based on the development of vision and encouraging of others).

Where tensions exist between teachers and school leaders, between colleagues, or between departments and other interest groups, school improvement and development is inhibited. Headteachers may choose to handle the complex interpersonal relationships and the attainment of aims and objectives by focusing on the achievement of a task (for example, the imposition of a whole school student assessment system). This will be transactional – a requirement of employment as the bottom line. Alternatively, they may adopt a more transformational focus, more concerned with the empowerment of people within the establishment so that movement towards a vision for the school is a shared experience.

Transactional leadership is marked by clear definition of role and responsibility, performance measurement against targets and an implied transaction between leader and led. By contrast, transformational leadership functions as a staged process with two elements – empowering those being led so that they can then carry out their roles with maximum effectiveness and minimum monitoring. Educational improvement research (Stoll and Fink 1996) indicates that within a dynamic organization, a transformational style permits and encourages more effective relationships between professionals.

Leadership is also concerned with the management of change – whether in the school overall or classrooms. This is not to suggest that instability prevails. However, it does reflect the need for awareness of the ways in which improvement can be initiated and sustained. Knowing what to change and when to change contributes to leadership expertise. Fielding (1997) maintains that it is necessary to contextualize change and suggests that the effective management of change requires an understanding of:

- *timeline*: proposals are made, discussed, implemented and reviewed
- *experience*: participants feel able to undertake the change
- *commitment*: the 'ownership' of the change is assessed before participants are driven forward
- *culture*: participants are aware of the way in which the culture will help or inhibit change
- *structures*: participants consider the ways in which change has been successfully implemented previously and build on these
- *conditions*: the extent to which participants are involved in inquiry and reflection, staff development, collaborative planning, policy involvement, coordination and leadership.

Nadler (1993) offers a systems model for analysing organizations. At the core of this is the belief that planning is more likely to secure effective change – whatever its nature. While inputs include the environment, the resources to be used and the views held about goals, the change process involves developing a common understanding of the focus, the role of participants, the organizational structure and the cultural possibilities. Outputs include the achievement of goals, effective use of resources, and the impact of participating on both individuals and groups. Dalin et al. (1993) suggest that the successful change management demands requires an understanding of four 'barriers':

- *values barriers*: where there is a fundamental disagreement over the values system for example, in the establishment of a rewards-based discipline system
- *power barriers*: where those in favour of change are those who also benefit
- *psychological barriers*: where change challenges basic personal security
- *practical barriers*: where change is constrained by fundamental inability to do what is required.

In short, successful change is dependent on an understanding of change within context. Although this brief summary sets the process within a framework of successful teaching and learning, the complexity of change leadership has been explored in depth by Fullan (1991), who stresses the importance of three stages – initiation, implementation and institutionalization – and by Morrison (1998), who offers considerable evidence that success is premised on consultation and involvement.

Effective management

In the previous section, we hinted at differences between leadership and management. Leadership may be characterized as knowing what needs to be done, and how to get it done, while management is about putting plans into practice in effective ways. This implies a false dichotomy in many respects, since the reality in schools is, that all leaders are managers and the downward delegation of tasks and responsibilities affects both staff and students. One way of looking at this is to consider Hersey and Blanchard's (1988) idea of 'situational leadership'. Building on the 'task' and 'relationship' focus between leader and led, manager and managed, they identified four leadership styles:

Delegating	Low relationship, low task – the leader passes responsibility for a role or function to a member of staff and then does little to support them
Participating	High relationship, low task – the leader maintains a strong link with the member of staff and may offer support but still does not become involved in the actual work
Selling	High relationship, high task – the leader supports the member of staff but offers constant attention to the work in hand according to his or her ideas
Telling	Low relationship, high task – the leader insists on the achievement of targets whatever the impact on the person undertaking the work

In addition, Hersey and Blanchard identify the 'maturity' level of followers as a key factor which leaders need to consider when determining the specific tasks and level of delegation involved.

The cameo illustrates this at work in the classroom.

Jeremy Snaith is seen as a highly successful art teacher at Oak Grove School. When shown a copy of Hersey and Blanchard's (1988) analysis at an INSET day which was looking at the link between differentiation and student self-esteem, he agreed to see if it was helpful in his classroom. He reported back to the curriculum committee as follows:

> I thought all this was so much hot air until I talked about it with 9R. They're not an easy group and although you can keep them going they're a pretty disillusioned lot. The long and the short of it was that I looked at the group and made a note of how actively I thought each of them were progressing. But before long I realized I was actively 'delegating' to the best – they had their tasks to do and although we looked at their work from time to time, they had sufficient get up and go to manage their own learning. Then again, for some of the group 'selling' was the best approach: they were pretty keen, but lacked confidence and I spent a lot of the time proving that they could get to where I wanted them to go. You could almost guess who needed 'telling' – but, somehow, although I couldn't let up at all they pretty soon came to realize that if they got on with the job properly I was more ready to relax.

DISCUSSION POINT

● Has Jeremy, and 9R, gained from this approach or is it what cynics suggest teachers have always done? Whatever your thoughts it is clear that Jeremy had to plan what he was going to do with the students. Good management requires that this is undertaken in a systematic and planned way.

Clear planning

In addition to developing ideas about whole school ethos and culture, a good deal of attention has been paid to the way schools plan and allocate their financial and human resources. However, such planning should not be undertaken in isolation. A significant outcome of Ofsted inspections has been the fact that schools increasingly work to a strategic plan, allocating resources according to the ways they consider their stated aims can best be achieved (Levačić 1995). This impacts on class teachers because there is a need to plan what is to be taught, with what resources, and how successfully. Development planning is the process by which school aims can metamorphose into action plans. Hargreaves and Hopkins (1991) emphasize that the 'empowered school' is one that undertakes strategic and longer term planning, identifies priorities and then sets out a clear resourcing and training programme in order to achieve its aims. According to Hargreaves and Hopkins, a development plan

- articulates the organization's strategic aims
- builds long and medium term plans which enable strategic aims to be met
- produces an annual plan based on the prioritization of objectives
- establishes action plans, including details of objectives, resource needs, supervision, and success criteria
- monitors the progress of action plans and their outcomes
- evaluates the contribution of outcomes to overall organizational aims as a prelude to review and replanning.

The class teacher's role is to plan, deliver, monitor and communicate teaching and learning resource needs to those planning for their department and the school as an entity. This is identified as rational planning because the attainment of aims is the driving force for resource management. However, the problems of planning can be recognized even at classroom level. Weindling (1997) argues that members of organizations may be unable to plan effectively because of a limited knowledge base or because they are constrained by power-groups that inhibit open discussion.

Bailey and Johnson (1997) suggest that strategic planning develops in different ways and argue that unless it is values driven and supported by the people within the organization, it is unlikely to be realistic and effective. Mintzberg (1994) claims that many organizations have developed a planning process with great concern for the future to the detriment of the present. The reality is that the nature and impact of planning will vary from department to department, and from school to school (Glover et al. 1996). However, for individual teachers, classroom planning is an essential prerequisite for day-to-day existence as well as the longer term acquisition of resources.

The planning system in use at Sycamore High, locally regarded as the most successful of four schools serving a dormitory town in the Midlands, shows how plans can be a force for the maintaining of standards. Planning within the school occurs at three levels: classroom, department and whole school.

- *The classroom*: during the closing weeks of the previous Summer term every member of staff is asked to outline his or her teaching programme for each class to be taught in the coming year. This is recorded in a consistent style with reference to teaching content and targets for each term, the establishment of success criteria and the resources to be used. The subject teacher also completes a section of the record listing likely problems of resourcing and organization in the coming year.

- *The department*: at the start of the Autumn term the subject leader discusses the teaching programmes with the individual members of the department and some revision in the light of General Certificate of Secondary Education (GCSE) results is noted. All the subject staff then discuss the problems which were previously noted and a departmental list of priorities for teaching and learning, and resource and training needs forms the substance of a subject development plan.
- *The whole school*: during the second half of the Autumn term each subject leader has a meeting with the headteacher and the so-called 'finance deputy'. This is to review the departmental progress towards objectives which had driven the programme in the previous academic year and to establish aims and objectives, together with resource needs, for discussion in the preparation of the school improvement plan and subject and whole school targets.
- At the start of the Spring term senior management produce the draft plan for the ensuing academic year. This brings together the agreed priorities and needs of the subject meetings and reconciles these to whole school objectives and targets for attainment. The draft is discussed at subject meetings and by governors. Once approved, this plan provides the basis for the allocation of resources to departments and allocation to subject staff follows.

DISCUSSION POINT

- What are the advantages and disadvantages of this type of planning for classroom teachers?
- Do plans inhibit action?

You may conclude that there has to be a balance between flexibility and structure in planning, so that teachers can cope with the day-to-day classroom pressures. In short, teachers need to act as 'professionals' without being caught up in bureaucratic systems.

Committed teachers

The history of teaching and state education in the United Kingdom reveals a continuing debate about the nature of teachers' work and how far it constitutes a profession. Lawn and Grace's (1987) collection of papers shows that traditional definitions of professionalism are inconsistent with the nature of their work, attitudes to gender, and teacher unionization. The 1990s demonstrated a further shift which has underpinned the notion of 'legitimized professionalism' which exists by the grace of central government rather than because of the inherent self-governing nature of the group concerned in the way of medicine and the law. McIntyre and Hagger (1992) claim that a distinctive body of professional knowledge is established by those in their first teaching post. This is then reviewed at a later stage as they stand back from their practice, building on Schön's (1983) view of 'reflection in action'.

While teachers are considered by some to have the autonomy accorded to professionals, their work has become increasingly constrained by the combined impact of target-formed teaching (some may say 'teaching to the test'), by the framework of Ofsted inspections, and by the development of performance-related pay and promotion. Arguably, teacher commitment needs to be greater than ever, because survival in a highly controlled professional environment depends on the teacher's ability to manage and balance pressures, which condition the way in which teaching and learning is organized. An analysis of the pressures (Glover and Law 2000) indicates four main areas of staff discussion in schools:

- *national policy issues*: school inspection; target setting for year on year school improvement; and policies aimed at securing improved home–school links
- *classroom practice issues*: the expectations of groups and individuals; the effect of student groupings and differentiated teaching; teaching styles and strategies; lesson content and variation in activity; homework setting, assessment and the monitoring of teaching effectiveness
- *resource management issues*: LEA relationships including support and funding; student recruitment within an 'open market'; the adequacy/condition of buildings; the adequacy/suitability of teaching and learning resources; and school organization vis-à-vis the school day/school year
- *professional development structures and conditions of service*: influencing teacher attitudes, morale and remuneration matters, including performance review and promotion opportunities. Teachers tend to be most concerned with the ways in which policies affect what happens directly within their classrooms and are most comfortable when they feel changes are 'owned' rather than imposed. This has implications for senior leaders in schools – particularly in the way that professional development activities are planned, problems are dealt with, and policies developed.

What, then, is the view of a committed teacher? Hay McBer (2000) produced a model of teacher effectiveness for the DfEE which articulates the government's expectations of teachers as agents of educational improvement. Hay McBer suggest that educational improvement is dependent on openness to good practice (for example, from other schools) and to critical evaluation of teaching (such as by colleagues within the same school). In order to initiate change senior managers and teachers need an awareness of the impact that methods of selection, career planning, performance management, and professional development can have on school effectiveness. To this end, they suggest that teachers may significantly influence student progress through

- *teaching skills*: reflected in the time on task and the flow of the lesson and practised through expectations, planning, methods and strategies, student management, time and resource management, assessment and the use of homework

- *professional characteristics*: defined as 'deep-seated patterns of behaviour' reflected in overall confidence and ability to work with others; leadership which offers flexibility, accountability and managing students; relationships with others; thinking capacity and planning and setting expectations for self and students
- *classroom climate*: the perceptions of students about what it means to be in a particular teacher's room including purpose, order, standards, fairness, participation, support, safety, interest and the nature of the physical environment.

Hay McBer's model offers a system for developing and assessing teaching competence, which appears to be universally applicable for all teachers: this may, however, underplay the importance of contextual factors like social deprivation, which impact on teacher 'performance' (Cullingford 1999). It also appears to offer solutions to classroom management problems, which may not be effective in some situations for example, when a student has such a low self-esteem that praise is seen to be patronizing.

Harris (1996) has demonstrated that individual staff development within a supportive organizational context is one of the key components of improving schools in difficult circumstances. Glover and Law (1996) repeated previously that much professional development post-1968 was delivered on a whole staff basis in an attempt to deliver training for national objectives through a 'cascade' model of lectures or workshops. Much of the current work within schools is managed by professional development coordinators (PDCs) who make use of appraisal/performance review reports and targets to develop a more refined needs analysis for each member of staff, and who then seeks a variety of opportunities.

Wilson and Easen (1995) point to the problems that arise when teachers express 'wants' but schools have a different 'needs' agenda. Resources must balance the needs of individual teachers, subject areas and the school as an entity (Adey and Jones 1997): for this reason, most schools link school development plans with professional development programmes (Broadhead et al. 1996). Many schools now recognize that 'in school' development opportunities through, for example, the shared experience of teaching the same class, good practice dissemination, action research and other investigative work (supported by senior staff or an external 'critical friend') may minimize disruption while maximizing opportunities for productive reflection (Halsall 1998).

Our aim so far has been to outline the context in which teaching and learning takes place. However, the process of reflection may highlight differences in viewpoint between teacher and taught. Although the assumption has been that if teachers got things right then success followed, the problem is that students' perceptions may be at variance with teachers'. The research, which underpins this book utilizes the views of the school students, and articulates their perceptions of good teaching and effective learning. Our research findings, we hope, will contribute to the reflective process undertaken by teachers charged with establishing effective strategies and techniques for school improvement.

● Further reading

This chapter has offered a very broad brush overview of the tensions faced by teachers in the teaching and learning process. The following readings may help to develop the picture.

For a recent general survey of leadership and its impact on learning:

Law, S. and Glover, D. (2000) *Educational Leadership and Learning*. Buckingham: Open University Press.

For a more specific introduction to leadership and the management of change:

Morrison, K. (1998) *Management Theories for Educational Change*. London: Paul Chapman.

An overall survey of school culture is given in:

Prosser, J. (1999) *School Culture*. London: Paul Chapman.

The implementation of cultural change is fundamental to discussion in:

Stoll, L. and Fink, D. (1996) *Changing our Schools*. Buckingham: Open University Press.

Joyce, B., Calhoun, E. and Hopkins, D. (1999) *The New Structure of School Improvement*. Buckingham: Open University Press.

The process of reflection is shown in a very practical way in:

Pollard, A. and Triggs, P. (1997) *Reflective Teaching in Secondary Education*. London: Cassell.

Finally the issues in school improvement and effectiveness are fully set out in:

Teddlie, C. and Reynolds, D. (2000) *The International Handbook of School Effectiveness Research*. London: Falmer.

And to start the internet trail we suggest you go to the DfES web sites on school improvement. Start with http://www.dfes.gov.uk/index.htm. Also look at Ofsted for research reports on school improvement in action, the British Education Index for abstracts, using the keywords – school improvement, school effectiveness, and school culture. The commercial sites offer leads into all elements of leadership and management for example, by searching for culture, transformational leadership, or performance management, and considerable help is available from Emerald at the University of Bradford.

2 Perceptions

Measuring progress

The improvement of teaching and learning is fundamental to national policies to secure a more certain economic future for the United Kingdom. Problems may arise where guidelines and standards offered to secure such improvement by national bodies such as Ofsted and the Teacher Training Agency (TTA) may not be successful because of problems arising from the socio-economic context of student and school, and unsuitable leadership and pedagogy in some schools and classes. Reid et al. (1987: 22) have argued that 'while all reviews assume that effective schools can be differentiated from ineffective ones there is no consensus yet on just what constitutes an effective school'. There are signs, however, of growing consensus regarding appropriate methodologies for investigating and assessing school effectiveness (McPherson 1992; Sammons et al. 1995: MacBeath and Mortimore 2001). Despite the tendency to conflate various terms associated with the effective schools movement, Mortimore (1991: 9) suggests that an effective school is 'one in which pupils progress further than might be expected from consideration of its intake', while Sammons et al. (1995: 3) suggest it is one which 'adds extra value to its students' outcomes in comparison with other schools serving similar intakes'.

This brief summary indicates that there are several sources of information that a school can provide to give an indication of the progress being made towards stated objectives and targets. These so-called performance indicators fall into two groups: objective data and subjective data.

Objective data

Objective data are based upon measurable (quantifiable) information such as test results, external examination results and attendance rates. They are either presented as 'raw' data or refined to take account of contextual and other process factors. The most frequently quoted examples of objective approaches are the studies by Coleman et al. (1966) who attempted to relate educational success to the social conditions of students throughout the USA, and the study by Rutter et al. (1979) of the experience of students in a group of Inner London schools who were assessed according to the nature of their background, their experience while at school and the outcomes which resulted. While Rutter's work established the use of accurate, valid and reliable statistical data developed from school processes rather than outcomes it was subject to criticism from those who felt that the analysis was too simplistic. This issue was considered by Mortimore et al. (1988) in their evaluation of the impact of classroom and whole school experiences for a similar group of primary schools. Here the measurable material, for example, mathematics achievements, was analysed against the organizational data, for example, class teaching group arrangements which, although not as readily measurable, could be categorized according to stated criteria of size and learning arrangements. This work has led to analysis of improvement by individuals or groups against a cohort as a whole. Gray et al. (1999) and Thomas et al. (2001) provide examples of the use of these types of data.

The way in which data may be generated is diverse. Frequency of occurrence of a feature of learning or behaviour related to known background factors is the most readily available statistic for the classroom teacher. Much can also be gained from grouping a set of frequencies related to, for example, student satisfaction, or parental perception. A fundamental evaluative point is that the existence of one set of data which appears to equate with another is not necessarily a reflection of causality and analytic techniques have been developed to ensure that where relationships are suggested they are statistically significant and not simply a matter of chance. This has led to refined mathematical processes based upon the predictability value of a set of objective data and the establishment of relationships which might indicate how students normally perform in given situations. In other words, are we able to suggest what might happen if a particular course of action is taken in similar circumstances?

Objective data may be collected in many ways and are concerned with either individual pupil performance or the aggregate performance of the school as a whole – the so-called 'benchmarking'. Much analysis has been concerned with the changes over a period of time and matching performance against an anticipated level knowing the background and previous achievement of the pupil. This is the basis of the value-added approach by which the performance of pupils is measured on entry and at various stages of a school career to ascertain whether improvement is below, at the expected level, or above that level. Gray et al. (1995) have applied this multilevel analysis technique in an assessment of potential outcomes over time in different schools. Deviations from the normal pattern and the eventual outcomes stemming from a group of educational processes led to the use of more complex, but easily computed, regression analysis by which a variety of causal factors can be separately analysed so that their individual impact may be evaluated. Among the statistical concepts used for analysing objective data are:

- *variance*: this considers the difference in performance between different groups of students, or by the same group at another time in their educational history

- *correlation*: this indicates the relationship between two or more factors under review
- *regression analysis*: this indicates the effect of one factor isolated from the other influencing factors
- *covariance*: this indicates the behaviour of one factor when considered against another.

Levačić and Glover (1997) have used these techniques to ascertain the impact of measurable context factors on educational outcomes and found that the only really significant data currently available – for all its imperfections – is the free school meals take-up for any school.

Subjective data

Subjective data are based upon less readily measurable elements such as attitudes and perceptions including student behaviour, personal development and parental views of the school. It is qualitative rather than quantitative although results may be quantifiable. The criticism levelled at reports that actually describe what is happening within a school or classroom is that they are affected by the uniqueness of the context and the lack of measurability. One frequently used approach to this work is through case studies which, however effective they may be in setting the context for the research being undertaken, are dependent upon a 'double subjectivity'. This is because the description of what is happening is being interpreted by the researcher, and the response of the participants may be conditioned by the knowledge that research is taking place.

Recognition that such double subjectivity may occur is frequently the key to presenting assessment in a way that meets the possible criticisms. This is demonstrated in much of the work from the late 1980s to the present where the popularity of ethnographic evidence – that based upon what people actually say and the precise events they are involved in – has been set into its context and analysed in a more precise way. This may involve analysis based upon dissection of a response phrase by phrase and then the build up of frequency tables based upon a classification of the comments or 'descriptors' given. Because of the relationship to context and the time needed to undertake subjective data collection, analysis and review, many of these studies are comparatively small scale. They do, however, provide evidence of the way in which much curriculum work has been assessed – and often the role of an external adviser has been to ensure that the monitoring is consistent and that the evaluation is valid and reliable. The importance of such work is precisely that it can be undertaken on a small scale and by teachers within their own classroom situation. This has led to much action research where a teacher or group of teachers have attempted to develop greater effectiveness through a particular programme of work or approach to learning. Our description of objective and subjective approaches might suggest that there is a clear distinction between the two types of data but the classroom teacher often has to deal with a process by which the qualitative is made quantitative.

At Oak Grove School the headteacher had been concerned by the increasing amount of petty misbehaviour in classrooms and felt that much of this was due to readiness on the part of some staff to accept standards which, by being allowed to persist, were undermining discipline in the school as a whole. There had not been any increase in so-called 'major' misdemeanours but there had been a significant increase in 'the type of silliness which leads staff to send a student out of the classroom or to a senior member of staff, or which, worse still, allows the students to remain unchecked'.

At a staff meeting where these problems were discussed, it was decided to attempt to monitor the level of misbehaviour. Some of the staff doubted whether this would be possible except for the obvious data arising from the official detention statistics. Others suggested that a more positive approach would be to look at the way in which the commendation or reward system of house points was used to counter misbehaviour by recognizing student contribution to the class. Both approaches were felt to be flawed because they did not define the criteria by which behaviour could be judged as good or bad.

A working party was set up with the precise task of defining expectations of behaviour in the classroom and the school. This began its work with a brainstorming session at which staff pooled their ideas of 'acceptable' and 'unacceptable' behaviours and then it took evidence from students at all stages in the 11–16 school to ascertain their views of what disturbed progress in the classroom. Three common elements were defined:

- *talking out of turn*: 'tooting' was seen as the initial stage of misbehaviour because it broke the continuity of lessons and prevented the teacher from working with all members of the class
- *disruption*: 'nuisancing' was redefined as 'anything that impedes the learning of yourself or other students' and it was agreed that this should include the silent behaviours which can lead to classroom teasing
- *cooperation*: 'supporting others' was seen as the only criteria for reward and commendation.

The working party reported back to the staff as a whole, to the School Council, and to the governors. Some cynicism persisted among those who felt that the system was being built on a simplistic combination of behaviour and assessment, and those who felt that the 'zero tolerance' policy, while theoretically acceptable, would impede any progress in the more difficult teaching groups. It was agreed that the standards would be explained to students during the first week of the succeeding term and this would be followed by a week of demonstrating how the system would work – and then it would operate.

The headteacher was concerned also to see that infringements meant action and that positive contributions merited praise. Staff were issued with blue and pink report slips which were completed in the course of a lesson and then handed to the senior member of staff responsible for data collection. Three blue slips became the basis of an after-school detention, and three pink slips merited mention in assembly in the following week. This enabled the senior management to identify those lessons where disruption was a problem and then to follow this through with class management support, and also led to immediate action when misbehaviour that might have gone unchecked in different subjects now became obvious as a pattern requiring attention.

DISCUSSION POINT

• What are the problems associated with introducing a behaviour manage-ment system of this sort into a classroom if it is not part of the policy for the school as a whole?
• What is the value of attempting to measure behaviour management statistics?

Action research

The group of staff involved in the working party described above were un-dertaking a piece of action research. Action research has become a subject in its own right both as a methodology and as a means of promoting effect-ive educational practice. Some definitions help to establish the principles that underpin the development of the subject and something of its history. Kemmis, writing in 1983, established the purpose and method very suc-cinctly as a form of self-reflective inquiry undertaken by participants in a social (including educational) situation in order to improve the rationality and justice of

• their own social or educational practices
• their understanding of these practices
• the situations in which these practices are carried out.

While his definition fits all forms of action research the significance to the teacher is revealed by Hitchcock and Hughes (1995) in suggesting that action researchers are concerned to improve a learning situation through active intervention and in collaboration with all the parties involved so that 'prac-titioner relevant' information is evolved. The process of action research is broadly cyclic based upon

• problem identification
• fact-finding and analysis
• action to plan and secure change
• evaluation of data collection and policy impact
• the movement into a second cycle of action.

This pattern stems from the work of Kurt Lewin (1946), who is regarded as the founder of the movement in social science research in North America.

The application of these principles to the classroom situation owes much to two writer-practitioners. Stenhouse (1975) believed firmly that curriculum research and development belonged to the teacher. He argued that successful change in the practice of teaching and learning required that teachers became reflective about their approach to teaching, modified their teaching approaches to respond to this reflection, redefined their teaching objectives, and then moved to assess the impact of changes. His concern was with the process of action research rather than precise methodology and his work has been subject to criticism because of the method, or process orientation, rather than with the rigour of collection and analysis of research findings. He did much to encourage collaborative work, an enthusiasm for reflection and the assessment of innovative approaches. The term 'reflection' is now one of the educational buzzwords – simply it implies that we should think about what we are doing, how we do it, why we do it, and how we could do it more effectively!

A later writer, John Elliott (1991), has met some of the general criticism of Stenhouse's work by sharpening the focus of the reflective process, by stressing the need for reflection based upon the daily practice in the classroom, by arguing that teachers need to have the tools for self-reflective assessment, and by stressing the value of the action research process for the professional development of teaching staff.

The school improvement movement, as summarized by Hopkins et al. (1994), is moving increasingly from the 'being done to' to the 'doing' mode and teachers are becoming increasingly aware of the part they play in securing change. It is significant that in their assessment of practice the importance of staff development is linked to involvement, inquiry and reflection, leadership, coordination and collaborative planning. In all of these the opportunity for teachers to utilize opportunities for research is evident. Often this is action research because teachers are using the data alongside their daily work. This is exemplified in the way in which data already known in the school were analysed as the basis of planning to secure coherent approaches to personal education in one school – the process of analysis offered the opportunity for reflection. A further example is offered in the way in which one school approached quality improvement by asking individuals to chart new practices within subject groups and then sharing their findings at departmental meetings. The senior staff of the school believed that success was built upon:

- motivation which lay with the team
- leadership which empowered the team
- vision-building generated by all participants
- the allocation of time for the project
- clear objectives for developing practice
- focus on outcomes for students
- time for staff reflection leading to new targets.

Hopkins (1993) sets research more fully into its 'improving' context by elaborating the process of school or college improvement through

- *self-evaluation*: knowing where we are
- *curriculum evaluation*: knowing how the curriculum is contributing to this situation
- *teacher appraisal*: knowing what is needed by staff to ensure that we have confidence in reflection even when it may not always be positive
- *development planning*: knowing how we can build on our findings.

Much of the effective professional development work within our schools has taken note of method and impact to ensure that action research is both resourced and given priority in school development.

The use of action research does, however, pose some problems. Hurrell (1995) has demonstrated that teachers consciously or unconsciously discriminate against students on the basis of social class, ethnicity or gender and this could affect the implementation of change processes and the interpretation of data. Looking from another perspective, Follman (1995) has pointed to particular problems where student perceptions used as the basis of data collection may be coloured by their views of the staff concerned. To minimize such problems, classroom researchers are reminded that they should investigate only after considering a framework of ethics for research. Hopkins (1993) offers a summary of ethics based upon earlier work by Kemmis and McTaggart (1988) which includes the following:

- observe protocol – seek the necessary permissions
- involve participants – to help them shape the work
- negotiate with those affected – taking care to avoid putting on others
- report progress – this keeps participants aware and ready to meet changes
- obtain explicit authorization before you observe – it invades professionalism
- obtain explicit authorization before you use confidential material
- negotiate participants' involvement – let them challenge your approach
- negotiate accounts of others' points of view – allow fair amendment
- obtain explicit authorization before using quotations – they are personal
- negotiate reports for release – differing audiences
- accept responsibility for confidentiality – trust is the price of involvement
- retain the right to report your work – it is not otherwise worthwhile
- make your principles of procedure known and binding.

These principles are all acceptable and commonplace although it is possible to argue that they are not all applicable in all situations. For example, how far is it necessary to obtain permission if you wish to investigate learning processes which will be used within your classroom, with your students and for your own agenda. Fraser (1997) illustrates the dilemmas which arise in more detail. She speaks of the need to ask 'uncomfortable' questions, and the need to manage situations so that these do not inhibit worthwhile research.

DISCUSSION POINT

- How applicable are the ethical questions listed by Hopkins (1993) relevant to classroom research?
- Are the issues overstated?

Surveys by questionnaire

This is not the place to develop the processes and techniques of planning for an investigation in any detail (see Hopkins 1993; Atweh et al. 1998), but the research upon which this volume is based owes much to the use of surveys as a means of presenting quantified data about teaching and learning to classroom teachers. Hutton (1990) explains the survey method in depth and points to the essential characteristics of the use of a questionnaire with preformulated questions in a predetermined sequence which are used with a sample of people. The advantages of such an approach are that answers can be quantified, can be representative of the population as a whole and can be repeated at a future date to secure some evidence of longitudinal change. The success of the survey does, however, depend upon the way in which the questions have been formulated in order to elicit the same set of responses from every member of the sample. Are the questions clear, unambiguous, capable of gaining the information that is needed from every respondent, and with the potential to yield data which is generalizable in similar situations? McNiff et al. (1996) argue that questionnaires should be used only if no alternative is available and are of greatest value to find out information which would not otherwise be obtainable, and when it is inappropriate to seek information by alternative techniques such as interview.

DISCUSSION POINT

• Do you agree with McNiff's view?
• What are the advantages of an interview compared to a questionnaire?

The value of questionnaire surveys as a means of reaching large numbers of respondents has been realized in education where students in similar, but differing school environments, have been questioned to provide a basis for developmental work. They may be asked about their school experiences (as in a survey of 4500 students by Glover and Cartwright 1998), about their attitudes to school in general (with 32,000 students through the Keele Successful Schools Project 1991 to present) or about their attitudes to specific subject study (as in the Advanced Level Information System – ALIS, University of Durham). All this material is of value to the participating schools because they have their own data to compare with the aggregated data of the sample as a whole and mathematical refinements now allow separation of component parts, for example, by gender, year, ethnicity and subject to prompt yet more questions to provoke improvement (FitzGibbon 1996).

These questionnaires have all been used to ascertain student attitudes in some form. They involve the use of closed questions requiring the selection of one of a number of specific responses, and of open questions seeking opinion expressed in the respondent's own way. Usually reports based upon questionnaire surveys identify the closed and open responses. One of the advantages of the use of a standard questionnaire is that it can be used consistently either across time with the same groups of students, or with differing samples. Whatever the approach it is to be hoped that investigation leads to reconsideration of policy and practice and eventual classroom improvement. Powney and Hall (1998) demonstrate, however, that much of the 'feedback' when students are asked about their learning experiences has little impact on future delivery of courses or learning styles.

Nottingham Trent research

Following a broader investigation of the relationship between student achievement and socio-economic context, efforts were made to develop a questionnaire which could be easily used and processed to yield data to help teaching staff to reflect on their practice and the learning process in their classrooms as perceived by the students in their care. The value of this was believed to be that it offered teaching staff an indicator of the perceived stimulation and motivation offered by alternative teaching and learning strategies in three ways.

- The impact of particular teaching approaches to a topic can enable the teacher to discard less effective practice.
- It can also help to establish the way of working which suits a particular group of students, for example, where a previous experience of group learning has been unsatisfactory and where alternative approaches may be needed.
- Lesson evaluation of this sort can also be used as the basis of measurement of the implementation and the impact of changed whole-school policies, for example, in the use of in-class assessment.

Such an investigative tool can be developed only within certain parameters.

- It must be capable of easy completion and measurable analysis.
- It must be usable without fear of adverse staff reaction to the views of either individuals or groups.
- It must offer an insight into aspects of teaching and learning which can help staff to meet student needs more effectively.
- It must offer a means of repeated assessment.
- It must offer a view of teaching and learning which is capable of comparison, for example, between staff, between classes and over a period of time.

To this end a Learning Effectiveness Audit was developed. This asks students to rate their agreement with 30 statements which reflect 6 aspects of teaching and learning. These are based upon curriculum theory and current thinking on reflective teaching as well as the structure and content of the Ofsted reports written for 31 secondary schools within a single LEA (Law and Glover 1999). The 6 aspects were

- The learning context – concerned with the way in which the classroom stimulates students to learn through the arrangement of furniture, the quality of displays and the availability of learning resources.

- Challenge and pace in learning – based upon the way in which students perceive the tasks which they have to complete and the way in which these stretch them.
- The use of a variety of approaches and activities including the use of a range of learning strategies and resources including information technology.
- Lesson planning and structure to provide stimulation, pace and progression building upon understanding.
- Teacher involvement and feedback to ensure that the student is aware of diagnostic assessment and support in securing individual improvement.
- Student perception of the acquisition of knowledge, skill and understanding in the course of the lesson.

About 2900 students in 10 co-educational comprehensive secondary schools serving communities with diverse socio-economic backgrounds have used the Learning Effectiveness Audit. Administration of the audit took about 15 minutes per class – students were asked to indicate whether the statement given was 'usually', 'sometimes' or 'rarely' true of teaching in the subject under review. Processing of data has been achieved by the use of the Sphinx programme. Schools were invited, following negotiation, to use the audit in a way that would most help their own development programme and data was reported according to an agreed format. Two schools used it with students at a given time in the week to get a whole-school survey; three used it with year groups to ascertain the relationship between the teaching and learning experience and achievement problems; two used it randomly in an attempt to see how students reacted to differing teaching styles; three offered it to staff who were interested in student reaction to their teaching. Each school was provided with a commentary on results according to gender, age and subject area compared with those of the total cohort. There were approximately equal numbers of male and female respondents in the cohort overall. The detail of the response levels for perceptions of what is 'usually true' of the lessons surveyed according to gender, subject and secondary year group is given in the appendix. This may help schools to attempt their own surveys and to consider them against the findings to date. At this stage we are outlining our overall findings as a basis for the discussion in the following chapters.

It is recognized that effective pedagogy requires differing approaches according to maturity, subject area and objectives as explored in detail by contributors to Olson and Torrance (1998), and it was unlikely that teachers would use all the elements of the analysis in every lesson but the analysis has been subject to tests of statistical significance and it is suggested that where a response is below 40 per cent 'usually' or above 10 per cent 'rarely' the school might like to consider the implications for teaching and learning further and consider the nature of the learning culture (Tuohy 1999) that might offer explanations for some of the results. Further where the difference between male and female responses is in excess of 10 per cent this might indicate some gender-related issues.

There are problems with this type of survey (Rosier 1988) and these emerged in the course of our analysis. To ask for comment on a situation 'usually, sometimes, or rarely' offers scope for student misinterpretation, and for selective memory. Recognizing this, staff were, however, prepared to accept that student opinion had something to offer. This prompted the use of the study as a developmental tool for the schools rather than as a pure research activity (McNiff et al. 1996). Similarly, despite the care taken at the pilot stage, the statements upon which reaction was sought were also capable of differing interpretation according to maturity, ability and experience. Again, this was met by offering analysis to schools with the details of age, gender and subject to facilitate reflection by staff who might, in a subsequent, school-based analysis, look towards further refinement and adaptation. With these shortcomings in mind the analysis of all responses was offered as some sort of normative statement against which responses in an individual school can be assessed. All elements are discussed in detail in subsequent chapters.

Environment

The setting for teaching and learning has not been neglected previously (Bowring-Carr and West-Burnham 1997; Caldwell and Spinks 1998) and the Ofsted Framework has highlighted the importance of the classroom environment (Ofsted 1992, 1995). Ofsted reports often point to schools and subject areas where less attention has been paid to the learning environment than is conducive to good student involvement (Ramsden et al. 1989; Samdal et al. 1999). To ascertain how far teachers were able to manage the physical and resource environment students were asked to comment upon five characteristics that reflected the care taken by teaching staff to organize their rooms in such a way that learning could be enhanced. The results are shown in Table 2.1.

The need for attractive, changing and stimulating displays still occurs in about half the subject lessons that were commented upon, and students' reactions shows a similar proportion who feel that the layout of the room may not suit their learning needs. The suggestion that one-quarter of students cannot see the board or teacher may well be related to the layout question but two of the participating schools commented upon the problems inherent in the 'wide but not very deep' classroom which characterized much school architecture of the 1970–80 period. The problem has been exacerbated by the use of grouped tables to allow maximum student circulation to access resources. Resources are fundamental to the availability of equipment within the classroom, and of books for homework. Our evidence suggests that students fare better with the former but less than one-half believes that they have the necessary homework resources.

Table 2.1 Percentage responses to aspects of the learning environment (n = 2600)

	M usually	F usually	M rarely	F rarely	Range of 'usually'
There is a lot to look at in the room	51.4	49.0	12.5	12.7	33.8–64.2
I can see the teacher's desk and the board	76.1	76.2	4.2	4.5	63.4–82.1
The classroom is arranged to help us work	52.7	56.9	10.0	7.1	38.4–62.5
The classroom is well equipped for the subject	67.0	73.6	6.3	6.1	39.6–80.0
We have books and resources for homework	48.9	48.7	19.1	16.0	25.7–62.8

● **Challenge**

School improvement and effectiveness research (for example, Joyce et al. 1999; Teddlie and Reynolds 2000) shows the importance of high expectations as the basis of effective teaching and learning. This is not that students are set targets beyond their reach but they are helped to maximize their individual potential as investigated by Elliott (1999) and Warrington and Younger (1996). Several pointers to the nature of challenge were investigated in the research to develop the view that school improvement has to be classroom based (MacGilchrist et al. 1997). The results are shown in Table 2.2.

If three-quarters of students feel that they are coping with the work they are being set, it might be argued that teachers are finding the right level in their demands consistent with the achievement of self-confidence but it might also be argued that ability to cope may indicate that targets are being set too low. Seeking the extent to which students perceived that their work was differentiated according to ability then tested the basis of this assumption and this presented another dilemma. Do the very high figures of students who believe that their work is undifferentiated not recognize that basic assessments are being undertaken by staff, or is the general classroom experience homogeneous? Where attempts have been made to use individual target setting it appears that students are more aware of individualized learning activity (Beresford 1999). Students do, however, recognize that staff use a variety of approaches to ensure understanding and check that effective learning has taken place. Throughout the research we have endeavoured to see how teachers introduce variety into the resources, approaches and activities used – only one-third of students appear to learn in situations where teachers are changing activities to ensure 'pace' in lessons.

Table 2.2   Percentage responses to aspects of student expectations (n = 2600)

	M usually	F usually	M rarely	F rarely	Range of 'usually'
I can cope with the work I am given	73.3	74.5	2.0	1.3	58.4–81.0
We have different tasks matched to our ability	18.3	17.2	49.4	54.1	10.7–27.3
The teacher changes activities so that we concentrate	36.2	30.6	17.2	19.0	24.8–53.5
The teacher uses different ways to ensure understanding	58.9	60.9	7.2	6.9	40.6–65.4
The teacher checks that we all understand	68.4	70.4	5.6	5.5	45.3–86.5

● **Teaching and learning styles**

Pace of learning requires the use of a variety of teaching and learning approaches and styles. This has been documented by others, for example, Dixon and Woolhouse (1996), Joyce et al. (1997) and Tuohy (1999). The statements used in the Learning Effectiveness Audit were arranged according to the broader issues of style and approach, as well as the more restricted features of lesson planning, and were designed to offer a view of the way in

Table 2.3 Percentage of response to elements of teaching and learning style (n = 2600)

	M usually	F usually	M rarely	F rarely	Range of 'usually'
We have opportunities to work in groups	29.2	33.9	24.0	24.6	5.4–45.0
We make notes of what we have done	25.5	28.0	34.9	35.1	16.8–41.2
We use computer programs in this subject	9.3	9.9	61.8	66.3	3.9–15.2
There are times when we are left to work alone	52.5	53.7	7.6	5.1	41.5–68.2
A variety of books etc. are available in this subject	36.8	35.5	24.7	24.9	19.8–56.7
Homework instructions are clear	62.7	69.6	6.9	3.3	37.7–73.6
I can understand how lessons fit together	56.0	56.7	5.5	5.5	34.9–64.7
We do different things in the lesson	28.4	25.3	19.0	20.4	15.1–47.5
My work record is shown in my subject notebook	70.9	77.8	8.2	6.3	46.5–83.3
There is a balance between being talked to and doing things	53.2	60.2	6.8	6.1	32.7–67.7

which teaching and learning styles are recognized and used in the classroom. This work builds upon previous findings by Tuomey (1998) and Lawrence and Veronica (1997). The results are given in Table 2.3. Each of the elements in this part of the questionnaire raised issues for teaching staff in the participating schools. For example, group work is not applicable to all subjects; notemaking may not be a desirable practice and could indicate preference for a didactic pedagogy; information and communications technology is demanding on time and resources and while it may be desirable it may not be possible, and individual work may be essential in the period before public examinations. The research team had made it clear that these were all reasonable arguments but that student perception might help further consideration by staff of the way in which they approached their planning. The lesson planning data show that instructions are usually clear and that a work record is retained but only half the students recognized the progression between one lesson and the next and the balance between being spoken to and doing things in the course of the lesson. Once again the proportion reporting variety in the lesson is less than one-third of the complete cohort.

Teacher–student relationships

Teacher–student relationships are fundamental to effective learning and have been investigated as a fundamental to school improvement particularly where the culture of the school may have promoted antagonistic interaction (Scanlon 1999). In all respects the rating for 'usual' behaviours is less than two-thirds and there are indications that bad relationships mar the learning experience for some students – with a great range between responses in the same school. The summary results are shown in Table 2.4.

Some students may not have readily understood the diagnostic use of subject reports and the 'challenge' issue emerges again with students feeling that they usually have to work hard just over half the time. The apparent absence of monitoring for group activities also poses questions about the effectiveness of some work organized in this way. Similarly low figures for

Table 2.4 Percentage responses to aspects of teacher–student relationships (n = 2600)

	M usually	F usually	M rarely	F rarely	Range of 'usually'
My teacher makes me work hard	54.6	53.4	5.9	8.0	37.7–64.2
The teacher uses subject reports to help us	35.4	34.8	21.9	22.8	18.9–43.5
Our teacher knows what we are doing in groups	63.5	65.5	8.6	8.9	34.9–83.3
We know how well we are doing	54.7	53.8	7.8	8.9	38.6–58.7
We are encouraged as individuals and groups	62.1	63.5	7.4	6.6	33.0–73.3

the perceptions that the teacher knows the progress being made, and only marginally better recognition of teacher encouragement, have been a matter of concern in those schools that have already received their results.

The broader curriculum

Throughout this work we have been aware of three pressures upon teachers in attempting to develop the learning experiences of students. Concern with Ofsted reporting and national league tables has led to concentration on examination outcomes as a result of which elements which could produce a variety of learning approach and experience have been lost. The necessity to follow National Curriculum requirements is cited as a reason for the apparently circumscribed nature of teaching, and the pressure on time in an overloaded curriculum has led to concentration on the completion of courses in a didactic manner (Nixon et al. 1996). All these are demonstrated in Table 2.5. This attempted to explore the way in which teaching and learning are related to the broader curriculum of interdisciplinary knowledge, the acquisition of key skills and understanding and are based upon aspects of curriculum theory (Kelly 1989).

The most worrying aspect for those concerned with the deeper purposes of education may be that the relevance of learning to life is minimized and even the use of skills and the debate of issues is seen as normal in less than half the subjects reported upon. There could be some explanation in that these qualities may emerge only after students have had time to reflect upon the long-term impact of their learning experience.

Table 2.5 Percentage responses to aspects of the broader curriculum (n = 2600)

	M usually	F usually	M rarely	F rarely	Range of 'usually'
We have to learn a lot of facts	55.7	56.3	7.9	8.1	44.6–66.7
We discuss how what we are doing affects our lives	17.7	15.3	41.9	45.9	4.2–25.3
We practise what we have learnt	47.6	47.7	11.8	12.1	26.4–59.9
We discuss issues related to our work	48.5	49.6	10.1	13.2	32.1–60.1
The teacher goes back through things even if it holds us up	54.2	54.8	9.0	8.2	40.6–74.7

Gender, age and subject differences

The generalized results presented in the tables above mask the great variation between gender, age and subject within each school. These confidential results have been used to some effect in promoting staff development activities. In one school the boys have consistently scored 8 per cent below the girls in each of the groups of characteristics outlined above and 15 per cent below in aspects of student–teacher relationships. In another where there has been a deliberate policy of supporting male students, the greatest divergence is 4 per cent above that of the girls in believing that they work under challenge. While these may be attributed to adolescent attitudes there is a clear relationship to local macho cultures when the results are set into the socio-economic context; it is a problem for schools in the industrial heartland taking part but not evident as such in more suburban, and heavily oversubscribed, schools.

Consideration of the responses by age shows that there is a general decline in positive responses between Year 7 and Year 11. This may reflect adolescent disenchantment, emergent critical ability and increasing self-sufficiency, for example in elements that assess relationships with staff, or the classroom environment. Of the Year 7 responses 63.6 per cent are usually aware of interest in the room, and feel that teachers know them well, but by Year 11, the positive responses fall respectively to 41.6 per cent and 47.3 per cent. The relentless pressure for examination success may explain the evidence for decreasing variety of approach and activity, and the increasingly fact-bound nature of learning by Year 11. On entry 37.9 per cent of students usually perceive variety in the learning activities, but this drops to 27.9 per cent by Year 11 while the notemaking approach is recognized as usual by 24.1 per cent of Year 7 and 44.6 per cent of Year 11. Within the overall picture of declining satisfaction, there is a dip in satisfaction in many elements in Year 8 including the interest of the classroom environment, the ability to cope, the level of encouragement by teachers and awareness of progress. This improves slightly in Year 9 with an increase from 67 per cent to 79.8 per cent in those who feel that they are coping with the work and in some respects in Year 10 where positive responses on the availability of books and equipment emerge coincident with GCSE preparation.

Given the general nature of the questionnaire it is to be expected that there will be some subject-related differences, for example, in French 40.6 per cent believe that there are usually a variety of activities, and 64.2 per cent of the students are aware of changes in the resources used. For maths, the corresponding figures are 31.9 per cent and 18.1 per cent. There are also variations in the way in which the broader curriculum is integrated into subject teaching with 60.2 per cent of students agreeing that they discuss issues related to their work, while this is only true of 43.1 per cent in science. Overall there is a tendency for greater variety of approach, content and resources with the humanities subjects scoring more positively in student rating than sciences and mathematics as illustrated in Table 2.6.

Perhaps surprisingly, the use of computers is higher in geography (7.1 per cent) than in science (3.5 per cent), and the use of notemaking is lower in both history (26.2 per cent) and geography (11.3 per cent) than in science (44.6 per cent). While there are differences in matters of teaching style and

Table 2.6   Percentage positive responses by subject

Audit element	Geography	History	English	Science	Maths
Approaches	43.3	39.2	27.1	28.5	31.7
Resources	64.9	60.8	39.1	40.3	18.1
Activities	60.8	58.5	58.3	54.2	55.7

learning processes particular to each subject there is little difference in responses concerned with relationships, coping and understanding progression and progress in subject work. Much depends upon the interaction
between student and teacher rather than the subject being taught.

School differences

The nature of this interaction may explain the marked difference in the figures
for the schools taking part in the research. The teaching and learning culture
is revealed where similar positive response rates emerge whatever the subject
within the same school, for example, in one school, rated highly by Ofsted and
with a 68 per cent 5 A–C GCSE pass rate in 1999, the overall subject deviation is plus or minus 6 per cent from the norm for all elements. In another,
currently under special measures following an adverse Ofsted report, the
variation between subjects is much greater with a deviation of 18 per cent
from the norm and evidence of some poor relationships, routinely didactic
lessons, and inhibiting learning environments. When all elements are considered, the aggregate positive response rate is 54 per cent in the first school
but this falls to 34 per cent in the second school. The external pressures to
achieve examination improvement in this school is, perhaps mistakenly,
reflected in the low scoring for indicators of variety, and the broader curriculum. By contrast the first school has more positive responses than the nine
other schools for the elements of relevance, the practice of skills and the
discussion of issues in lessons. The figures also reflect the paucity of resourcing
experienced by some schools. Three, although scoring well overall, from 'cash-
strapped' LEAs have less than 30 per cent of students responding positively
to the availability of books for homework, while three from socially deprived
areas but with considerable additional Standards Funding have over 40 per
cent of students usually having books for homework. The first three schools
do, however, make the most of what they have with good scores for the learning environment elements compared with those who have been more gener-
ously funded who report low scores for interest, and layout in their classrooms.
  The Learning Effectiveness Audit was only part of the investigation in each
school. Researchers also interviewed staff and pupils using a structured questionnaire in order to develop an evaluation of leadership and management
structures and styles within the school. This facilitated comparative analysis
of the data. Each school was also asked to identify at least one example of
good practice to illustrate their changing attitudes to teaching and learning.
These, together with the full school-based data, form the evidence used in
much of the work which follows.

● Further reading

For those wishing to further their understanding of the use of evaluative techniques, and in addition to the references given in this chapter, we suggest that you look at:

Scheerens, J. (1992) *Effective Schooling*. London: Cassell.

Willms, J.D. (1992) *Monitoring School Performance*. London: Falmer.

Fitz-Gibbon, C.T. (1996) *Monitoring Education*. London: Cassell.

MacBeath, J. and Mortimore, P. (eds) *Improving School Effectiveness*. Buckingham: Open University Press offer much material grounded in educational research.

The process of researching is widely covered but

Halsall, R. (1998) *Teacher Research and School Improvement*. Buckingham: Open University Press deals with this from the classroom perspective, and

Blaxter, L., Hughes, C. and Tight, M. (1996) *How to Research*. Buckingham: Open University Press show how findings can be used to maximum effect.

And to start the internet trail we suggest you go to the DfES Research Briefs and the Ofsted site for research reports on school improvement in action. There is a lot of material on Action Research if you begin with the online journal of Action Research at http://www.scu.edu.au and the Collaborative Action Research Network at http://www.uea.ac.uk/care/carn.

3 The teaching and learning environment

Environment

The term 'environment' is capable of differing definitions. To Hoy and Miskel (1987) it was the external environment by which they meant the combination of geographical and socio-economic factors which affects the school's relationship to its community, either as a market from which pupils come or as the resource base for the school. This interrelationship between school and its so-called market affects teaching and learning because pupil recruitment is increasingly linked to the perceived success, or otherwise, of the school (Hammond and Dennison 1995; Levačić and Woods 2000). But there is also an internal environment, the bricks and mortar of the building and the availability of resources for the teaching and learning task.

Lackney (1999) suggests that there are three elements in the internal environment – health and safety, ambient environment, and curriculum-based factors. From the viewpoint of the pupil and teacher these are manifest in the general state and standards of care of the building, the suitability and appearance of the classroom, and the availability and quality of learning resources.

Ash Grove is considered by the community to be one of the best comprehensive co-educational schools serving the suburban area on the fringe of a Midlands industrial city. It is successful in that over 60 per cent of the students gain at least five A–C GCSE grades, and the large sixth form consistently has 95 per cent of the entry gaining three Advanced level passes. All students wear uniform, attendance rates are high and the contribution to the community in sport, music, drama and the sharing of facilities, is acknowledged as 'superb'.

But therein lies a problem. Because it is deemed to be so successful it is extremely popular, estate agents sell houses on the basis of nearness to the school, and each year over 100 students are refused entry because the school is oversubscribed. In the early 1990s the school was a grant-maintained school and used its greater freedom to admit pupils both as a means of satisfying local demand and to ensure that high-level funding would continue. Ofsted inspectors visited the school in 1995 and wrote in glowing terms of the ethos, outcomes and organization of the school. A further visit in 1999 was however, less commendatory and referred to 'the obvious problems arising from the pressures on space on a restricted campus'.

The governors were concerned that adverse comments would have an impact on student recruitment but the headteacher argued that 'a self-correcting mechanism was at work' and that some fall in numbers would not be detrimental to the long-term development of the school. Her comments prompted further discussion among governors and staff, who argued the merits and demerits of recruitment policies and, for the first time, recognized that some 'strategic view' was essential if the school was to use its facilities in a way which would maximize recruitment but minimize pressure. At this point one of the governors suggested that there should be an audit of accommodation and the way in which it was used and it was agreed that the work would be undertaken by one of the deputy headteachers, two governors and two of the staff.

The first part of the audit involved consideration of the way in which accommodation was used for the school timetable. Three facts emerged:

- Subject allocation of rooms had not been reviewed since 1992 and the size and disposition of subject suites was now inappropriate, for example, the Modern Languages Department retained a hold on a room which had been the language lab. This was now being used for teaching small sixth form groups and resources storage but was unoccupied for 20 of the 35 lessons each week.
- The 5 design technology rooms had been developed in the late 1980s to provide for a range of traditional craft activities and while these rooms were underused they were no longer appropriate for design technology teaching or flexible enough to be used for associated craft or information and communications technology (ICT) activities.
- Of the 48 rooms, 22 had been designed for small GCSE and A level groups and could not accommodate more than 24 students.

It was hardly surprising that only 78 per cent of lessons were thought to be taught in appropriate rooms, that overcrowding of smaller rooms was the norm, and that the limitations imposed by narrow corridors and the need to use the hall and dining rooms for social activities had been identified by the heads of year as a cause of minor bullying and intimidatory behaviour in Years 7, 8 and 9. All this had been recognized by the Ofsted inspection team but they had also been critical of the manifestations of overcrowding with areas of litter, limited and often 'tatty' displays and noisy lesson changes.

The audit team concluded that the school had sufficient teaching rooms for its roll of 1200 students but that a radical rethinking was necessary to use the resources more effectively and to reduce the pressures on both teaching and circulation space. To this end they proposed:

- a critical re-examination of the subject suites as they had developed within the school
- a review of the teaching group sizes which had been allowed to develop at GCSE and A level
- a re-examination of arrangements for the beginning and end of lessons
- reconsideration of the availability of specialist ICT facilities
- reconsideration of the display policy throughout the school.

As might be anticipated, opposition to changes came from the subject heads who had been using the same areas for many years and who 'felt threatened' by the re-examination of teaching and learning arrangements in the senior school, and year heads who were sceptical of the likely success and anxious about the 'disciplinary fall-out' of more open display policies.

In the event minimal changes to rooming have occurred – ICT and Design Tech now use the same area of the school, Modern Languages has lost its so-called resource-room, and the humanities subjects now share what was the history, geography, religious education and economics areas. A standard form of display board with polyacrylic covers in the corridor areas has been accepted and these are being maintained by designated subject staff; a review is underway to examine and implement improved storage for resources in all rooms.

DISCUSSION POINT

- To what extent can an audit of this sort produce tangible changes in the teaching and learning environment?
- What would be the inhibiting factors in a school known to you?

There are a number of issues to be considered. The problem of popularity leading to pressure on accommodation is particularly challenging where the school has grown piecemeal and classrooms and circulation space are no longer appropriate for current approaches to teaching and learning. For governors this poses the problem of allowing growth to meet demand, and thus enhance funding, or limiting it to ensure that the building is not overfull. Add to this the difficulty of staffing stability in long established and popular schools and the resulting pride of possession which leads to a room becoming seen as 'mine'. This has been an inhibiting factor in managing change where senior managers have failed to convince colleagues that the learning needs of the students may be more important than the predilections of the staff. The history of the 1970s, 1980s and 1990s is one of great change in both the pedagogy and content of learning. Particularly in science and design and technology subject areas, there has been need for flexibility but the resourcing to make change and re-equipment a possibility has lagged behind. It may be that strategic planning has been lacking at Ash Grove and the school needs to be more responsive to change. The fundamental difficulty of optimizing accommodation use is that building adaptations take time to materialize and teachers become disillusioned when they cannot respond to student needs as they would wish to do.

These problems are mirrored in countless schools which have been adapted piecemeal since the early 1960s. 'Suiteing' subject areas by placing all teaching of the same subject in adjoining rooms has maximized the use of teaching and learning resources, and increased the ease with which the staff concerned can work together in activities such as team teaching. It has also enhanced the possibilities of informal professional development. During the 1990s, with greater openness between teaching staff and readiness to share experiences and practice, there has also been a significant development in the monitoring and evaluation of work undertaken by teaching colleagues in subject departments (Leask and Terrell 1997; Joyce et al. 1999). Where timetable arrangements have been constructed in such a way that half or whole year groups are in the same area of accommodation at the same time setting by ability has been more flexible and students have not been destined to spend all of the time between one assessment and the next within the same group and classroom. This underpinned much of the 'open plan' organization of teaching areas in schools built during the 1970s. These schools have suite-type accommodation but originally had few dividing walls and minimal doors – prompting problems of class management, incompatible activities and teacher stress. That said, current changes in those schools that are developing individualized learning require enhanced provision in library, media and ITC resources. The changing role from teacher to learning facilitator will require teaching space that offers the ability to supervise and support learning in a very flexible manner (Caldwell and Spinks 1998; Lackney 1999).

It could be argued that individual teachers can do little to change the environment within which they work, especially where pupils may show negative attitudes to the care of premises and where low levels of resourcing have inhibited decorative improvement and the purchase of quality furniture and fittings for the teaching areas. This is not so, and there is considerable evidence that improvement of the environment can result in improvement of pupil attitude and learning. Many of the first round of Ofsted reports referred to the poor decorative state of buildings and lack of care on the part of users but the second reports on these schools speak of enhanced accommodation, furnishings and use (Gray et al. 1999). The importance of the enhancement of the environment and the development of a positive culture of improved use underpins much of the original work on school effectiveness (for example, Rutter et al., 1979; Lightfoot 1983; Barth 1990) and subsequent strategies for school improvement (for example, Louis and Miles 1990; Stoll and Fink 1996; Teddlie and Reynolds 2000). The authors of the latter volume stress the importance of the 'buffer' between the school and the prevailing cultures of its environment and demonstrate the importance of positive and caring attitudes to the physical environment within the school. This is an important element of Ofsted inspection reports as shown in the following comment:

> The society outside the school often overspills onto the site. Even with a full-time security officer, on occasions intruders come onto the site climbing over the high fences. On other occasions difficulties within the school invoke quick response from family members, unaware of the full situation, to come onto premises and further inflame delicate situations. The community must be encouraged to have more confidence in the effective, sensible, and caring manner in which the senior managers of the school deal with difficult situations. In this they have been aided by supportive responses from agencies including the police.

Our evidence is that the standard of care is variously perceived by the pupils within the same class and school and that effective management of the classroom environment also depends upon the attitude, practice and management skills of the teacher concerned. Problems are more evident when the same room is used by several teaching staff – ownership is fundamental to the culture of care. Where the physical environment is rated as good and there is an awareness of a policy of care for the environment within the school at large, pupils are more likely to be positive in their ranking of other features of the teaching and learning process.

● The classroom

The extent to which teacher and taught can improve the classroom environment is controlled by the basic architecture, the potential for alternative arrangements and attitudes to the care of property and equipment. Architecture may have to be taken as a given – we have already alluded to the limitations imposed by 'wide and shallow' and 'deep and narrow' rooms. Teachers who are aware of the problems of such a structure can occasionally check sight lines, readjust furniture and provide opportunities for those who might have some difficulty in seeing the teacher or the board – and reflective whiteboard surfaces are a real problem here! Sight-line checking is a particular problem where furniture is fixed, as for example in science and design technology laboratories. This has been frequently noted in comments by Ofsted on the arrangement of ICT rooms which, with equipment arranged on outer walls, results in students having their backs to teachers and there is a consequent requirement for a very clear set of instructions so that students turn to watch the teacher during exposition and discussion sessions. Hasan and Wagner (1996) have pointed out that students are being prepared for a much more individualized learning situation in the future and that it may not be disadvantageous if the teacher becomes a servicing agent of the learner. This requires flexibility in both the arrangement of furniture and facilities, and in the management of the learning process. McSporran (1997) stresses that hearing as well as seeing are vital to student interaction and argues that there may be pockets of diminished sound that inhibit learning.

Check point and possible action		
All students have an uninterrupted view of the teacher	Some students have an impaired view for some teaching activities	The room is built in such a way that some students cannot see the teacher clearly
How is this monitored for each teaching group?	Is it possible to replan the activity or move the students?	Can rearrangement of furniture or a platform for the teacher assist in improving this?

Duke (1998) has considered the research evidence for the impact of the learning environment on outcomes and although there is a positive correlation between school condition and test scores, this is limited. He shows that air quality, temperature, lighting and noise absorption all have the potential to affect outcomes but stresses that there is a difference between individual and group reactions which have still not been investigated and concludes that the effect of environmental aesthetics is difficult to research because it affects each student differently. The importance of ventilation has been stressed in teaching guides since the early twentieth century. While the need for fresh air or for turning on lights is not doubted, the potential for problems where students open windows at will, or where a general request from the class teacher for the opening of windows results in a dangerous free for all, has to be recognized and developed as a fundamental of the rules for the use of the room.

The extent of overcrowding within a room is usually beyond the control of the individual teacher but it is a factor in raising stress levels that are detrimental to the learning situation. Blatchford and Martin (1998) investigated the impact of class size on the attainment of students and concluded that where accommodation is under pressure, learning is affected because of lack of flexibility in arranging grouping and the tendency of teachers to revert to more didactic approaches. This has an impact on learning because:

● students are more likely to be distracted
● noise levels proportionate to cubic area rise
● both students and teachers feel more stressed by the crowded environment.

This can be managed, most frequently by the arrangement of the furniture in a way that facilitates student groupings, particularly where a variety of learning tasks are simultaneously underway. However, there is clearly a need for circulation by both students and teachers, especially where a variety of resources are being used. Problems arise when the arrangement of furniture for one lesson is incompatible with the needs of another teaching group, and this is exacerbated when there is a change of teacher using the room. Lightweight and easily moved furniture is available in some schools; others insist that a standard layout should be followed, either in all rooms, or in subject areas. For many schools the standard arrangement of rows facing the board is indicative of good order but this can have an adverse impact on learning situations requiring collaborative or group work.

Fisher et al. (1995) have demonstrated that once students have been made aware of the imperfections of a room which they may have taken for granted over a period of time, and are asked to contribute to plans for its improvement, there is a tendency for student-driven positive change – attitude enhances learning. This has also been demonstrated by Shore (1998), who realized that the general expectations of accommodation care and use in a large high school were heightened when each member of staff worked with each class to secure environmental improvement and that the most significant factor in change was the personalization of the approach being made to students. Lackney (1999) stresses the importance of comfort, security, visibility, space and personal space, and interest. Hay McBer (2000) also highlight these elements from the viewpoint of the students, who should feel stimulated to learn and appreciative of a comfortable, organized, clean and attractive physical environment. The quality of display is fundamental to this.

Check point and possible action		
Displays are relevant, lively, current and stimulating	Displays are maintained as examples of student work in progress	Displays are used as wall covering to make the room brighter
Do they show a balance between student and commercially produced input?	Are the displays changed sufficiently frequently to maintain interest?	How can they be adapted to stimulate learning?

Effective display work is an art form and most teachers feel that they are already under such pressure that displays, unless their contribution to enhanced teaching and learning is certain, fall low in the list of priorities. In the course of our work we have found examples of senior students from within the subject area being trained and then allowed to cope with displays, and of sixth form design students being allocated to subject departments to maintain specified display areas. It appears that the fundamental requirements are the use of quality materials, the use of mounting to give a consistent standard, and the use of an agreed computer-generated labelling system to enhance appearance and interest.

At Oak Grove discussion in the staffroom led to an approach being made to all the double glazing firms in the area served by the school. They were each invited to place an opening display unit of standard size made in white uPVC (unplasticized polyvinyl chloride) on one of the internal walls in the main school corridors. It was agreed that a small plaque, no more than 30 × 10 cm could be attached, with the name of the donating firm. The greatest problem was that of encouraging one or two firms to start – once that was done and a photograph appeared in the local paper, six other firms agreed to take part in the scheme. Displays are now of a much higher standard, within closed units, and it has become a matter of competition between the subject departments to ensure both freshness and originality including the celebration of students' achievements with a student artist, writer and designer each half-term.

We began this chapter by recounting the problems encountered by one school in attempting to rationalize accommodation and then to improve the learning environment. The principles for the display policy at Oak Grove provide an example of the way in which change in the quality of the learning environment can be secured.

Oak Grove School display policy
1 'Display' is to be an agenda item for the first and third of the four departmental meetings held each term.
2 Every subject department is to have a designated 'display' coordinator for associated corridor areas and every class teacher is to be responsible for displays within his or her own room.
3 A tutor group information board will be provided for each room. All other display space is to be used for subject associated materials.
4 It is to be hoped that all staff will be able to change their classroom displays every three weeks, either using a rotation system or by changing all displays at the same time.
5 Corridor displays are to be changed each half-term according to a programme agreed by the subject department.
6 Because of the variation in available materials, no hard and fast guidance can be given to the amount of 'commercial' and the amount of 'student developed' material used either in classrooms or corridors.
7 Where student-developed material is used, it is expected that it will meet the criteria set down in the conventions for the cross-curricular key skills used by all departments, and that it will be a reflection of pride and self-esteem by individuals and groups.
8 It is recognized that good displays take time to plan and arrange. Arrangements have been made for the design technician to be available for each of the ten subject areas for three hours each half-term.
9 Student attitudes have to change to accept that displays are part of the learning process for all. Please act immediately and decisively if any instances of defacing or destruction occur.
10 The foyer display will be managed by the Creative Arts and Design Departments as a showcase for their work and as an inspiration to others.

DISCUSSION POINT

• Does such a policy statement 'legislate for the impossible'?

Resources

Schools vary in the way in which they fund classroom activities. The current framework developed from provisions in the Education Reform Act 1988 requires LEAs to devolve increasing amounts (now up to 90 per cent or more) of the aggregate costs of running schools to the schools themselves in a locally developed scheme which must allocate at least 75 per cent of the total sum available according to a formula that relates to pupil numbers weighted according to age (McAleese 2000).

Whatever the method of allocation, those responsible for site-based management face a major problem because usually between 78 and 85 per cent of the organization's expenditure is on staffing costs. Add to this the necessary building costs and the maintenance of services and it is easy to recognize that the amount of money available for books, equipment and 'development' activities is a very small proportion of the total – for example, possibly only £80,000 in a £1.6 million budget in a school of, say, 950 pupils.

Approaches to decision-making within the school also affect the resourcing available at subject teaching level. Levačić (1995) has outlined approaches based upon rationality, that is where decisions are made in the light of the need to achieve the aims of the school most effectively through three inter-related stages:

• agreement and articulation of aims of the school and each subject area and of the priorities necessary to achieve the aims
• collecting and analysing data to inform choices based upon monitoring and evaluation of past experience
• selection of the best set of actions to achieve the aims and objectives.

Decision-making may follow procedures which vary from the formalized and autocratic to the less defined and collegial but the essential purpose is to achieve the stated aims of the school. The autocratic usually results in an allocation from senior management according to their view of subject need, and the collegial approach usually involves an annual round of discussions of need followed by allocation based on the agreed priority attaching to a particular need. Many schools meet competing pressures by using a system whereby a basic allocation per subject is made according to a formula, and this may then be supplemented by funds arising from bids to a centrally held fund (Bush 2000).

Simkins (1989) has contrasted this process with the political approach where the decisions are taken as the result of tensions between power groups – what Fullan (1992) calls the 'balkanization' of power. If political power is the most significant element in financial resource allocation there may be a continuation of allocations based on past power group relationships.

The likely effect of political tensions is that each department or year will get an allocation based upon a weighted formula – with the weighting based upon the strength of power rather than need. In the Framework for Ofsted (1995) inspections allocation according to the needs for achieving the aims of the school has been recognized as an essential criterion in judging the effectiveness and efficiency of the school. An example of good practice is given in the comment which follows from a 1996 Ofsted inspection report.

> The school development plan is very comprehensive and gives a very detailed picture of the school's priorities for development. Financial planning is becoming closely linked to the school's aims and priorities, with funding appropriately targeted. Governors are closely involved with the strategic management of resources and there are detailed policies for charging and pay. The school recognizes the importance of value for money and carefully assesses the benefits of expenditure on staffing, premises and learning resources.

DISCUSSION POINT

- How is resource allocation driven by the development plan in a department and school known to you?

Headteachers have commented that whatever system of allocation may be in use, it can be thwarted by local decision-making late in an academic year. Failure by central government to maintain funding initiatives, and changes by LEAs in the way in which funding is allocated, can lead to inconsistent resourcing year on year. Interviewees pointed out that the effect of this was to divert more money to contingency reserves to ensure that staffing costs could be met. The effect has been to reduce both the certainty and level of subject funding.

Within schools judgements are being made on four aspects of resource allocation in achieving overall school success and consideration of these may help teachers assess the allocation of funds being made to their subject. These are

- *effectiveness*: the link between resource allocation and educational outcomes
- *efficiency*: achieving effective resource allocation at minimum cost
- *economy*: achieving the cheapest possible resource allocation
- *equity*: achieving the fair use of resources for all involved in the learning process.

The desire to develop a system which reflects demand and which changes the public service sector into a marketplace in an attempt to increase efficiency and effectiveness brings with it attendant problems.

There are a number of important questions which recur in secondary school discussions. For example:

- If income is related to student numbers, how will schools continue to make provision for those with special learning needs who require a much higher staff–student ratio?
- What will be the effect on 'minority' subjects at all levels if the institution fails to recruit sufficient student numbers?

While there would seem to be general acclaim for a system which allows organizations to determine their own spending plans according to their governing body's interpretation of local need (in the case of schools, within the limits of the National Curriculum) there has been much discussion about the equity of such a system. Simkins (1995) explores this issue and asks whether, within the changed framework, schools should not explore the following more fully:

- the relationship between resource deployment and pupil outcomes
- the need for a foundation entitlement for all pupils
- the need for criteria for differential resourcing above the foundation level
- the concept of minimum attainment linked to entitlement
- the balance between efficiency and equity.

This brief account of the process of funding allocation helps to explain the great variation in resourcing between schools and between departments within a school. Before considering the next check point it is helpful to reflect on the allocation process within the school and its implications for the classroom experience. Three problems can arise and lead to further difficulties:

- the pace of technological change and the necessity for new equipment
- the standards of care of existing resources and the arrangements made for security
- the opportunity cost of funds spent on competing needs and the way in which these are prioritized.

Check point and possible action		
All the necessary equipment is available in the room	There is a central equipment and resource base	There is a lack of resources for all levels of teaching in this subject
Is this safely and securely stored and yet accessible to students?	Are arrangements for the use of the equipment consistent and pre-booked to fit lesson plans?	What steps have been taken to increase senior staff and governors' awareness of the problems?

A separate issue arises where the school may well be able to fund good resources for classroom use but then is restricted in what can be available for homework – reflecting the high cost of textbooks and the possible inadequacy of published material for the courses that are being followed. Many schools have attempted to overcome these difficulties by creating worksheets for homework activities but these can be costly in staff time, cumulatively expensive and of inferior quality (Glover et al. 1998).

Check point and possible action		
There are adequate and varied resources to support homework tasks	Arrangements for sharing mean that all students have access to homework resources	Homework has to be tailored to meet the availability of resources
How is the use and care of resources monitored?	Has the use of some non-shared resources produced by school been investigated?	Has the impact of this been detailed and made known to parents and governors?

In a glimpse into the schools of the future, Bowring-Carr and West-Burnham (1997) suggest that the school day will be longer and more flexible, that learning will be largely individualized and managed rather than taught, that the boundaries between the school and its community will be less well defined, and that traditional roles and responsibilities would need redefinition. Whatever may occur it is clear that the learning environment will have to meet the needs of a more technologically refined age. The resolution of problems of resourcing will be fundamental to student and teacher participation in new learning structures but the existence of a learning environment will remain fundamental.

Experience

At the start of this chapter we said that the teaching and learning environment has been variously defined. We have spoken of the external environment as the relationship between school and community, and the internal environment in physical terms. Interviews with groups of students have however, shown us that they interpret the environment in a third way as the total classroom experience. As it was expressed by a Year 11 boy for whom environment is holistic, 'it's all that goes on in the classroom. You know that in some lessons you will hate it because the room is always the same, the books tatty, and the furniture really awful . . . and somehow the teacher is also dull, but we do go into some lessons where everything is bright, and that includes the lessons and the teachers'.

Land and Hannafin (1996) suggest that there are five elements in the learning environment:

- *psychological*: awareness of learning processes
- *technological*: availability of learning resources
- *pedagogical*: matching processes and resources
- *cultural*: aspects of ethos, management and relationships
- *pragmatic*: the capacity to cope with a changing situation.

The environment thus described is broader than the elements we have considered in this chapter because aspects of ethos and relationships will be considered elsewhere. However, the framework they offer presents a useful structure for reflection on those aspects of the learning environment that get taken for granted. The psychological and cultural aspects are fundamental to attitudes within the classroom and form the basis of expectations – what is, and what is not acceptable within any classroom. The chapters that follow examine further these aspects of the total learning environment.

DISCUSSION POINT

- How far are schools of the present locked into structures and standards which will inhibit schools of the future?

Further reading

There is relatively little material directed solely at the internal physical environment of schools and classrooms but for those interested in this area materials produced by the DfES Architects Branch offers a good starting point.
Matters of finance and resource allocation are fully dealt with in
Coleman, M. and Anderson, L. (eds) (2000) *Managing Finance and Resources in Education*. London: Paul Chapman.
The teaching and learning environment is interpreted in different ways in
Bowring-Carr, C. and West-Burnham, J. (1997) *Effective Learning in Schools*. London: Pitman.
Tuohy, D. (1999) *The Inner World of Teaching*. London: Falmer.

And to start the internet trail we suggest you go to the DfES site and follow school buildings in the search facility – and that really will open up some lines of further investigation.

④ Expectations

● **Background**

Governmental pressure on schools and LEAs to set and achieve targets is a reflection of the view that much is to be gained in educational improvement if the expectations of all participants are enhanced. For Ofsted (1995, 1998) the effective school has high expectations of what students can achieve, and these are clearly communicated to all students through intellectually challenging lessons. This builds on the findings of Sammons et al. (1995) and the plethora of investigative and anecdotal work in the early 1990s. MacGilchrist et al. (1997) demonstrate that expectations can be raised only if there is an understanding of where schools and students are starting from, and that there should be some measurability about the process. Finnan and Levin (2000) set any analysis of expectations within a framework of schools' expectations for the students, the students' own expectations for their school experience and the expectations of, and for, the adults involved, both teachers and parents. Putting enhanced expectations into practice is not as easy as it may seem. Consider our starting point in the cameo.

Joe Pugh is the 43-year-old Head of Art at Ferndale Secondary School. He entered teaching after a period as a freelance artist and taught in a neighbouring school for four years before moving to Ferndale in 1989. Circumstances within the school were such that he was, as he freely admits, 'in the right place at the right time' and was appointed head of department in 1994, shortly before the appointment of the present headteacher. Joe still considers that the 'new' head is a climber and that he does not understand the culture of the school, which has served the neighbouring council estates since 1971. In Joe's view there is very little opportunity for improvement because the students are being expected to jump through hoops which are externally set without any reference to the real social conditions of the area – in short, 'they just aren't capable of being interested in art'.

After two abortive attempts to introduce an effective appraisal system the head decided that he would use the opportunity presented by the possible introduction of threshold payments for competent teachers to carry out thoroughgoing observation of the teaching staff at work. To this end he gave Joe a fortnight's notice that he would be coming to watch him teaching a Year 8 co-educational mixed ability group and asked Joe if the group presented any problems. Joe's response was only that they lacked interest and that Friday afternoon was not the best time to see them!

On the agreed afternoon the head arrived in the two-roomed Art Block about 10 minutes before the lesson was due to start. The head had to admit secretly to himself that he ought to have visited this remote area of the school more frequently than he had done in the past but even so there was little justification for the bareness of the walls and the lack of colour and inspiration in any displays. Perhaps the comments of the Ofsted inspectors about lack of visual stimulation had been right after all!

The bell for the start of the lesson sounded and over the next 10 minutes the 22 students arrived in groups of varying size and state of readiness. They were almost oblivious of Joe, who had started the lesson at the right time and who simply called to each group to settle down and then he would go through things again. As the first group moved off to get their materials the subsequent groups then said that they could not hear the renewed instructions and whether from habit or nervous tension, knowing that the head was in the adjoining store area, Joe became more inclined to shout and the voices of the students were raised to counter this. Eventually the lesson got underway and Joe circulated among the students.

He had a reputation as a clever artist and the students respected the work he had done in decorating the walls of the local sports club – occasional banter suggested that his interest in rugby league resonated with many of the boys in the group. The head noticed, though, that as he circulated, Joe was avoiding working with the small groups of girls and that he was happier following the interests and activities of the boys. Although not an artist, the head was aware that the students were all working on the same topic – impressions of a crowd at a football match – and that there was little attempt being made to extend those who had a natural ability, or to work with those who were facing problems even starting on their task. Within 10 minutes there were obvious signs of boredom, increasing noise at some tables, and then disruptive behaviour as an argument broke out between a group of girls.

Joe intervened by shouting at the class as a whole rather than by walking to the table concerned and once again, as his voice rose, so too did the response of the students. At this point the head emerged from the store area and in their surprise the class settled; 10 minutes later Joe called them together and spoke for a few minutes about the use of light and shade on people's faces and was applauded by many of the group because of his 'Rolf Harris' quick and bold brush example of a crowd scene. The class returned to the grouped activity at the tables until shortly before the end of the lesson when Joe called to them to clear away. As the bell went the class rapidly disappeared . . . and Joe and the head were left to talk against the retreating sound of a barely controlled gaggle.

This cameo introduces all the issues inherent in enhancing expectations within the school. Think of its implications for the head. Had he involved Joe in the process of establishing expectations within the school? If so, this could not have been a successful involvement because Joe takes refuge in the oft-stated view that 'you can't do much for children from this sort of background'. Was Joe aware of the meaning of raised expectations within the classroom? The lack of displays and the limited content and pace of the lesson suggest that he may not have internalized any messages from the comprehensive and ongoing programme of professional development within the school aimed at improving teaching and learning. Were the students aware that there were personal and group targets set for them, and did they know how they might improve? Certainly, Joe believed that the students should enjoy their work – but were they working, and what was being done to raise their sights? Did they, and Joe, know where they were coming from and where they were going to? Above all, how had this situation arisen and how symptomatic was it of a malaise within the school community?

DISCUSSION POINT

- Look back at the first paragraph and then apply the criteria for enhanced expectations either to Joe's situation, or to your own.
- What are the fundamental problems and what are the implications for the school as a whole?

The nature of challenge

While the need for maintaining high expectations is accepted and funda-mental to the school improvement movement (Teddlie and Reynolds 2000) the reality is that the social context of many schools militates against the possibility of enhancing the pupil experience (Cullingford 1999). There is now accepted evidence that schools *can* make a difference and the political will is that target setting and school support from the LEAs should enable schools to raise the expectations of all students whatever their socio-economic context (Barber 1996; Gray et al. 1999). The comments made above by Joe are no longer acceptable as an explanation of underachievement and it is no accident that 'planning and setting expectations' is placed at the heart of the model of professional characteristics for effective teachers (Hay McBer 2000). It is argued that teachers have always been aware that students learn in different ways and at a differing pace and that they know their students and their capabilities. The easy informality of the past is no longer acceptable and the effective teacher is one who

- cares for the pupil
- expresses positive expectations
- strives for the best possible provision
- challenges others in the pupil's best interests.

(Hay McBer 2000)

Such a teacher will also be able to recognize and measure progress, respond accordingly from a range of teaching and learning strategies and extend the learning process so that each student makes progress towards individual, group and whole school targets.

There are problems, however, in the interpretation of terms. Expectations may well imply a level of attainment that just meets the target set and this has underpinned action in some schools to target those students who are at the grade D–C borderline for GCSE, or at comparable levels in the Standard Assessment Tasks (SATs) tests. This brings us back to the criticism that current educational policies are leading to teaching and learning which is based upon 'jumping through hoops' with the associated arguments for and against competence-based assessment of students and teachers (Eraut 1994; Bennett 1997).

Challenge implies something more demanding. This may come about because a student is required or driven to achieve beyond the set expectations, or because self-motivation on the part of the student results in the unlocking of potential. Tuohy (1999) shows how expectations are related to the culture of the community as well as of the school and the classroom, and suggests that the development of student profiles which record and review motivation, as well as achievement, may offer a starting point for students and school improvement. Kaye (1995) demonstrates that underachievement is almost inevitable when a school is believed to be doing well – coping is sufficient and the pressure to extend student achievement is not of strategic importance.

Check point and possible action		
All the class cope all the time	Some of the class experience problems	All the class find difficulty with the work
Is more challenge needed?	Is there a need for different approaches or outcomes for some students?	Is a review of the lesson objectives and pace needed?

Differentiation

Differentiation involves meeting the needs of the individual and the group. Three questions need to be asked concerning the teaching approaches used for any group of students:

- Is grouping by ability sufficiently refined to allow teaching to the group as a whole?
- Is the basis of grouping sufficiently understood by those who will be teaching them?
- Is there a continuing assessment system and subsequent action to allow movement between groups in a flexible fashion?

For an improvement in the degree of individualization of learning to occur teachers have to develop strategies that enable them to meet individual and group needs in different ways. This differentiation has been the subject of a considerable programme of in-service training (INSET) operating in the UK between 1995 and the present. Differentiation may be directed at securing changes in gender responses to teaching and learning (Sukhnandan et al. 2000), at enhancing motivation and achievement in the work undertaken by individuals (Pollard and Triggs 1997) and in securing challenge for all levels of ability being taught within the same classroom at the same time (Jack et al. 1996). Much of this work has been developed from attempts to ensure that both the most and least able academically experience challenge in their work usually through the idea of differentiation by knowledge, task or outcomes.

Maker (1982) considers that differentiation can occur in four ways:

- by developing the learning environment – providing practice in group and independent activity leading to sharing, explanation and acceptance of ideas
- by content modification – providing materials which appropriately challenge the thinking and skills required of the student
- by process modification – providing opportunities for materials to be used in more challenging ways and at a differing pace
- by product modification – providing challenge through the outcomes of the activity.

To this list Stradling and Saunders (1993) add differentiation by dialogue thereby recognizing that teachers need to communicate with individuals in a way that reflects awareness of the student's ability level and socio-emotional needs.

The skill of the teacher may impact on the students without them knowing that differentiation is occurring. Work plans, activities and lines of investigation may all be subtly differentiated. Much depends upon the way in which the class groups are organized – the contention being that groups of similar ability require less differentiation than those of mixed ability.

DISCUSSION POINT

- Is there validity in the view that ability should be the basis of differentiation?

Further, some subjects are more open to differentiation than others. Where students are following individual programmes of work, as for example in design technology, differentiation can be achieved by the succession of tasks developed by the teacher to ensure the completion of a project within the limitation of skills already developed. The use of individualized plans for students with special educational needs is an attempt to ensure that the development of skills, knowledge and attitudes can be enhanced through a programme of work which can be totally differentiated from that used by others in a group or class.

Stradling and Saunders (1993) suggest that teachers need to recognize the differing learning needs of students and to develop a wide armoury of strategies to be used including regular review of the materials being used; building upon past achievements; organizing learning space to allow a variety of activities; ensuring coordination of information on progress being made by students and monitoring and review of progress made with the student as part of individualized discussion between teacher and taught. They stress the need for a whole school policy that recognizes the implementation of a philosophy of differentiation through curriculum planning to meet individual needs. This requires effective assessment and continuity of progression arrangements based on the earlier learning experiences of students. Learning needs, thus analysed, can then be met through the provision of the necessary support to remedy deficiencies, and the use of flexible approaches in responding to these needs.

Check point and possible action

Individual and group objectives differ within the class	Group objectives differ within the class	There is an homogeneous approach for the class
How is the variety of learning material, expected outcomes, and the learning process matched to individual needs?	How valid are the criteria by which learning groups are established?	How is this related to ability levels and outcome needs in the group?

At Elm High School students are made aware of the fact that they will be following differing programmes of work. At the start of each half-term the teachers issue a subject-based work programme for the coming six-week period. This outlines the main learning objectives and the skills to be developed as well as the areas of knowledge to be adopted. Where there is a relative degree of homogeneity in ability students then record progress made towards these objectives at the end of the last lesson in the subject each week. Because this is a small secondary school with only three forms of entry, students will be working at different levels the work programme additionally outlines what has to be achieved to attain intermediate and higher outcomes. Students are made aware of the level towards which they should be working. At the end of the six-week period a review of progress takes place during a lesson when all students are working as individuals. New targets are noted, for example, to work at the intermediate level in the coming module.

DISCUSSION POINT

- How does such a system meet the needs of differentiation by knowledge, task and outcome?
- What are the problems inherent in such an approach?

Maintaining momentum

Whether successful differentiation occurs or not, educational progress towards measurable individual, school and class attainment depends upon sustaining concentration – usually by varying activities. Challenge can be met only if motivation to learn occurs. Tuohy (1999) suggests a

> Contingency Model of Motivation: (i) motivation is based on the expectation that effort will produce a particular outcome, which in turn will bring a reward; (ii) recognizes that the promise of reward only motivates effort if the reward itself is something that is valued.
>
> (Tuohy 1999: 36)

This presupposes that the teacher is able to offer reward – hence the significance of commendation systems, but this has to be seen against the inhibiting factors of lack of willingness, especially on the part of boys, to be identified for their efforts (Sukhnandan 1999). Much depends upon the way in which student–teacher relationships, and the capacity for mutual respect, underpin activity in the classroom. The importance of student self-esteem, initially investigated by Coopersmith (1967) and Rosenberg (1965) has been recognized in many of the school attitude surveys currently in use (as demonstrated in Johnson 1998). For motivation to occur there is need to sustain pace and progress in classroom management and Pollard and Triggs (1997) suggest that this should follow a three-phase development pattern of

- introduction or motivation – introducing concepts and activities
- incubation and development – thinking, exploration and tasks
- review – reinforcement and reflection.

They recognize, however, that changes in the proposed pattern of a lesson or series of lessons may be needed as the progress of students is evaluated.

Differing problems require differing approaches either through a change of activity, the use of an alternative teaching strategy, the use of alternative materials, or the rearrangement of working groups within a class. Joyce et al. (1997) offer a wealth of alternative learning and teaching strategies, and we found evidence that some teachers are now using a process model of learning

(Dennison and Kirk 1990) by which students are required to follow the practice of undertaking an activity, reviewing their progress in the work, learning about the significance of the knowledge, skills or attitudes concerned and then applying the learning to changing situations.

The importance of assessment as a motivating force is clear when it supports rather than undermines student self-esteem. Regular testing offers the opportunity for consolidation of learning, its application in alternative situations, and the development of reasoning. Motivation can be maintained where this then provides for the identification of elements of learning that need reinforcement, an opportunity for student reflection on progress and attitudes, and the setting of targets for future achievement. Where the hurdles are too high or the review process too public, or embarrassing for the individual, motivation may give way to frustration. Once again, the use of pedagogic processes that recognize the needs of the individual as well as of the group is essential.

Check point and possible action		
A planned variety of approaches, style and objectives is used	There is a regular, but predictable, routine of changed activities	There is a standard teaching and learning routine
How is the effectiveness of approaches in attaining learning objectives monitored?	How do the changed activities meet the needs of students at any one time?	To what extent is predictability inhibiting enthusiasm for learning?

Checking understanding

The need for, and the processes of, monitoring individual and group progress is now explicit in the practice of every teacher as shown in standards for the career entrant (DfEE 1998) and those for the intending head (TTA 1998a). FitzGibbon (1996) offers three areas of monitoring:

- assessment of the acquisition of knowledge
- understanding the development of attitudes
- charting the processes by which learning in its broadest sense takes place.

Together these form the basis for a model of data collection offering both continuity and coherence. This is now developed in every school through consideration of a policy for assessment, recording and reporting on pupil achievement although Ofsted reports indicate that these policies may lack consistency both between subjects and in their application in the same subject area. There is, however, a difference between the formalized checking of understanding used on a termly or annual basis and the informal day-to-day and lesson-by-lesson practice by which teachers who know their students well use directed and appropriate questioning to ensure that progress is built upon understanding.

There is also concern that the process of checking understanding through testing may detract from the time needed to complete work programmes. The Task Group on Assessment and Testing (TGAT 1988) set out the criteria for an effective assessment system as one that is

- criterion-referenced – measuring what a student can do rather than his or her position with regard to the rest of the group
- formative – providing evidence for the teacher's plans to meet future learning needs of the individual and the group
- moderated – consistent and fair across groups and schools
- progression based – offering routes for student development and learning.

These criteria were fundamental to the national Key Stage assessments of learning but they are also of importance in securing consistent practice that is useful to teacher and taught within a subject department or across a school. Variation in practice between subject departments is confusing to the learner and can lead to misunderstandings by students and parents. TGAT stressed that attainment testing of any sort was a means to the end of learning.

At Elm High the Student Record is used as the basis of recording and assessment. At each review session in each subject a pro-forma is completed to record

Review date: Topics covered:
Attainment test results:
Agreed strengths in the work:
Agreed weaknesses to be overcome:
Agreed targets for coming review period:

Although staff have sought a greater degree of flexibility in the use of recording and are encouraged to adopt additional systems, this framework is used as the basis of links between subject teachers, form tutors and parents and has been praised for the consistency of approach that it has generated.

Check point and possible action

Formal testing supported by regular and recorded checking	Formal testing and informal checking	Testing only as required by school systems
How are students made aware of the objectives for each test?	How effective is the informal checking and what records are maintained?	Does the removal of frequent checking inhibit student achievement?

Reinforcing understanding

While continuous and often informal checking is part of the armoury of effective teachers (Reynolds 2000), it is not always easy to reinforce understanding when fundamental principles have been shown to be lacking. There is much to be gained from 'reinforcement practices' and Joyce et al. (1997) have developed these at length as the basis for structuring experiences aimed at helping students to learn:

- *inductively*: through data collection, analysis, hypothesis testing
- *conceptually*: through data presentation, conceptualization, analysis of thinking
- *metaphorically*: through description, analogy, revisited experience
- *mnemonically*: through classifying, connecting, recalling
- *disciplined inquiry*: through group inquiry, analysis and processing
- *studying values*: through enactment, discussion and evaluation
- *by counselling*: to help in developing insight, planning and integration
- *through simulations*: offering opportunities for orientation, activity, debriefing.

While the use of alternative strategies may be successful for reinforcement as well as original learning, there is a need for a positive classroom working environment with a high proportion of students 'on task' and evident motivation. Without these, 'it gets boring if the teacher just goes over the same thing for those who haven't got it' (Year 8, mathematics group). We would argue that it is not going over the same thing but going over it in the same way, which is unproductive. Egan et al. (1998) offers a view of understanding based upon the totality of cultural experience. While philosophical in nature this helps the classroom practitioner by suggesting that students draw upon their background of mythical (oral story based activity), literacy (reading and writing), philosophy (experience in classifying and making abstractions) and ironic (non-linguistic) ways of expressing ideas. The challenge for the teacher is to recognize that alternatives may be necessary and how they can be translated into real activity.

Check point and possible action		
Frequent whole group activity for the reinforcement of learning	Reinforcement to meet evident need	Individual support if required
How are individual and group needs met without detriment to overall progress?	How is this need made evident – hunch or evaluation?	What steps have been taken to ensure that students will seek help when required?

Moving forward

The reactions of students to features of their experience of teaching and learning indicate that, although most feel that they can cope with their work, challenge is inhibited by lack of differentiation, minimal variety in approach especially during preparations for external examinations, and limited obvious use of formal and informal monitoring. It is clear from the open comment made by students that this is a sweeping statement; in our survey 10 per cent draw attention to the variety of their learning experience in some way, and 18 per cent acknowledge the stimulation provided by specified subjects. There is a great range of responses between subjects in the same school and between differing schools. It is significant that schools with low scoring responses on aspects of the learning process are also those that have been subject to most criticism in their Ofsted reports. This suggests that the anxieties shown by the headteacher when considering Joe's contribution to teaching effectiveness are not misplaced. The evidence at Ferndale suggests that there is a need for greater consistency in practice so that the highest expectations can be maintained. This is not, however, possible unless the teaching staff as a whole accept the basic values and aims of the school.

In Chapter 1 we considered issues of leadership, management and a corporate culture in the schools with whom we have worked. We conclude this chapter with an example of good practice that addresses the fundamental premise that effective educational improvement can develop only if it is understood and implemented at all levels (Hopkins et al. 1994; MacGilchrist et al. 1997; Gray et al. 1999; Altricher and Elliott 2000). This requires the development of a vision of the way forward by the governors, head and senior managers but it also requires the communication of this vision to all involved in the core purposes of teaching and learning. This can occur only if the accountability of the head is directly related to what happens in the classroom. At Oak Grove School the use of an open and school-wide system of collecting evidence for headteacher appraisal has led to a clear understanding that the headteacher has a responsibility for what happens in each and every classroom. Despite the introduction of a revised national performance review assessment system in 2000 (DfEE 1999, 2000) the governors have determined to continue their own appraisal system in the way outlined in order to maintain the accountability of the headteacher for establishing, implementing and evaluating the values underpinning expectations in the school.

> The introduction of headteacher appraisal at this school predates all current developments and grew from the wish of the Personnel Committee to establish a system that combined annual assessment of the work of the head with measurable process and outcome targets that could drive school development. The requirement was for a system that linked whole school development and what happened in the classroom. The work of all staff was considered fundamental to any assessment of the headteacher's success.
>
> The appraiser was an independent educationist involved in educational policy research work. This association of appraiser and the school was

important in that relationships had already been established. The staff knew the appraiser and the appraiser knew the school – an essential feature for open discussion.

The head's appraisal had a threefold purpose:

- to establish progress made towards identified school process and outcome targets, and to revise these for the coming year in the light of progress made and developing school needs
- to ascertain the contribution of the two deputy heads, who were to be appraised by the head, in the development process, and to establish corporate targets as a joint senior management responsibility
- to review the progress made by the head towards the achievement of his personal development targets and to establish new areas for future personal development.

All staff were aware of both the purpose and the system of appraisal and agreed to a system which would involve up to one-third of their number in half-hour interviews with the appraiser. The agenda for these meetings was known in advance. In the earliest exercise the theme was established as ascertaining 'their views of the development of the school'. While this was implicitly used as the basis of the head's appraisal no direct link was made. The following year saw an extension of the theme to include staff views of the ways in which senior management was helping teachers to achieve the aims of the school. At this point no link had been made to performance achievement but the open discussion and readiness to share ideas resulted in more direct interviewing techniques with a clear idea that the head's contribution to development was under scrutiny.

As the scheme developed in 1998 and 1999, the appraiser spent about two hours with the head before meeting the staff. This enabled discussion of developments within the school and progress towards the main elements of the School Improvement Plan, a review of staffing changes and any perceived emerging problems, and consideration of the resource framework for development. This also provided an opportunity for the appraiser to check the progress being made towards objectives within each of the subject areas.

The appraiser spent two days each year in the late Summer term meeting with about 14 staff who happened to be free of teaching commitments at some stage during the day but who represented all sections of the staffroom. This included staff who had been at the school for many years and staff who had been appointed relatively recently; staff from the range of subject disciplines and non-teaching staff; staff from all stages of career progression, and those who had been in other schools for a considerable part of their career to date. The interviews were semi-structured. Staff were assured that anonymity would be respected; the interviewees were sufficiently confident to use the opportunity to reflect on the head's perceived contribution or otherwise to success in all aspects of school development. This imposed its own burdens on the appraiser, who was faced with transmitting the message but not identifying the messenger to the head. The interviews usually probed five basic questions:

- what progress had been made by the member of staff towards departmental or personal targets in the past year
- what was the role of the senior management in supporting these developments
- how had personal development needs been related to the development needs of the school and been supported by the head and senior managers
- what were seen as the inhibiting factors which prevented the achievement of the aims of the school
- what were their perceptions of the role of the head and the senior managers in carrying the school forward.

Such a structure was not directed solely at assessment of the role and performance of the head and senior managers but was intended to act as a spur to common room debate and to revisit previous developments to ascertain the extent to which they had become embedded into the practice of the school. A particular example was the development of a total quality management (TQM) philosophy. In 1995 comment was concerned with the pressures such a shift in thinking was creating but there was almost universal acknowledgement of its potential for whole school improvement. The problem was that in succeeding years 'initiative overload' had inhibited whole-school emphasis on TQM in practice.

Conceptual discussion became more evident as teaching staff were prompted to reflect on their own role in supporting the head and senior managers. A frequent topic across the years had been the tension between admiration felt for the head as the visionary and driving force, and personal irritation felt by the drive for ever higher standards seen in small matters such as the presentation of displays, and in major matters of competence and effective classroom management. The opportunity to reflect on such tensions often resulted in a greater understanding not only of the way in which the head worked but also of the personal philosophy and tremendous personal investment in the continuing development of the school. It also opened the way for discussion of what went on in the classroom and the way in which the teaching staff saw their efforts being driven by the head.

Such debates and the interview notes were fed back to the head in outline as the starting point for the appraisal meeting. This was usually held about one week after the interview. This had given time for reflection by the head and the appraiser but also had the advantage of being more distant in time from any staff opinion which needed to be seen in context. The agenda has been relatively constant:

- consideration of the established targets and the way in which interview evidence had shown them to be achieved or otherwise

- consideration of such data as could be then available summarizing progress towards targets
- consideration of those factors which had inhibited the achievement of targets
- consideration of the role of the senior managers in the achievement of maintenance and development work
- discussion of the impact of these on the development objectives for individual subject areas
- discussion of the impact of all these on the head's own personal development programme.

The impact of the system on whole school development has been challenged by several staff who have felt that this is probably a cosmetic exercise aimed at 'whitewashing a year on year rise for the boss', but other staff have expressed the view that such a system of headteacher appraisal has clear advantages:

- it links school improvement initiatives with the school and personal targets of head and deputy heads
- through line management systems any debate at senior management level and any subsequent policy decisions do filter through the school
- discsussion of staff responses to development intitiatives does permit something of a two way debate between head and staff through the appraiser
- any lack of consistency across departments or groups of staff emerges from interviews as well as from outcome data
- any serious staff concerns about aspects of leadership and management can be filtered and then developed in such a way that objective discussion of issues rather than personalities can be achieved
- the readiness of the head to be part of such a stark assessment procedure and the availability of a listening ear from outside the school contribute to an atmosphere of openness and demonstrate the accountability of head and senior managers.

DISCUSSION POINT

- In what ways could such a system have avoided the problems outlined in the opening cameo?
- Does the attitude of the headteacher really affect what occurs in the classroom?

However successful the headteacher may be seen to be in the evidence from such a system of appraisal which strengthens accountability, much depends upon his or her ability to ensure that all colleagues are aware of the provenance, variety and uses of learning styles. Expectations alone are insufficient, there is a need for staff awareness and use of a range of teaching and learning approaches.

Further reading

The importance of raising expectations is documented in differing environments by

Joyce, B., Calhoun, E. and Hopkins, D. (1999) *The New Structure of School Improvement: Inquiring Schools and Achieving Students*. Buckingham: Open University Press.

Gray, J., Hopkins, D., Reynolds, D. et al. (1999) *Improving Schools: Performance and Potential*. Buckingham: Open University Press set expectations into the context of school improvement.

Tuohy, D. (1999) *The Inner World of Teaching: Exploring Assumptions, Which Promote Charge and Development*. London: Falmer considers those barriers to improvement and the way in which expectations are related to typologies of schools.

And to start the internet trail we suggest you go to the DfES Standards site on http://www.standards.dfes.gov.uk. There is also a considerable amount of material on http://www.kented.org.uk/school-effectiveness but if you search on school effectiveness or school improvement there is much to choose from.

5 **Learning styles**

How do we learn?

So often it has been assumed that provided something is taught, it will be learnt. Such simplification ignores the way in which we learn. The concept of the 'learning cycle' is a useful shorthand to describe learning processes. It was developed by Kolb et al. (1971) and is based on a four-stage experiential learning cycle. This describes a series of discrete mental processes:

- concrete experience
- reflective observation
- abstract conceptualization
- active experimentation.

This can be applied to the learning process in a classroom or laboratory and leads to the view that learning is concentric and constantly being reassessed as we develop knowledge of subject matter, skills in handling that matter and attitudes towards what we have already learnt.

The idea has been subject to criticism. In applying an experiential learning cycle to a classroom scenario, Whitaker (1995) has argued that we should try to distinguish between 'incidental' and 'deliberate' learning. The former may not be recognized by the learner but is nevertheless important in defining values and attitudes. Brookfield (1987) stresses the importance of a greater element of critical evaluation in the learning process so that the learner develops skills in

- identifying and challenging assumptions
- identifying and assessing context
- imagining and developing alternatives that might explain, or expand thinking
- developing a 'reflective scepticism' in considering alternatives.

These elements are an encouragement for teachers to identify and work on learning issues rather than simply to spoon-feed their students. To this end it is necessary to enhance the depth of learning – from shallow fact to deeper understanding and application. Argyris and Schön (1981) have distinguished two levels of learning complexity as part of their exploration of the learning process: *single loop learning* (where simple changes are made when an activity does not work well) and *double loop learning* (where students actively question the underlying assumptions informing an activity). Much of the curricular development of the 1990s has been directed at enhancing standards by moving from the acquisition of knowledge and concentrating more on its sources, application and critical evaluation. Information retrieval is now more readily available but the way in which the information is used requires a deeper skill development. Students cannot achieve this without some training – developing their own learning styles.

There is a complementary view of the learning process grounded in our increasing understanding of the way in which the brain works. Caine and Caine (1997) describe the brain as a complex system that functions by searching for patterns in experience so that our lives have meaning. If this is accepted then it is possible to argue that learning is developmental and can be enhanced though appropriate thinking exercises. Feuerstein (1980) and Diaz et al. (1991) used this as the basis of exercises to develop the thinking capacities of those who might be socially disadvantaged in their home context and who have not experienced stimulating learning processes as they have developed. This approach has now been made more widely available and is exemplified in the work of the Cognitive Acceleration through Science Education (CASE) organization. Unlike the 'thinking skills' of Feuerstein that are not subject specific, CASE integrates these into subject learning with a focus not so much upon the content but on the thinking which students need to employ. The process is one of sequential activity involving

- *concrete preparation*: helping students to understand terminology and the practical context of their work
- *cognitive conflict*: examining assumptions through activities that challenge previously held ideas
- *metacognition*: basically the ability to think about the thinking process
- *bridging*: stimulating the application of findings and ideas by transfer.

While this suggests that a thoroughly practical approach should be used it is important to stress that thinking skills are applied in differing ways, for example, in mathematics there will be a tendency to use the language of numeracy, or in history the language of literacy. For the classroom teacher recognition of the various approaches to learning is fundamental to providing a breadth of teaching approaches catering for the range of learning needs in any class.

Preferred learning styles

We all have a preferred learning style. This is the way that we can most effectively process our experiences and perceptions to make sense of them, and to provide the basis for future activity. The rich variety of experience at pre-school, school and subsequently, have given us two abilities:

- the ability to reflect and act on the basis of our reflection (Schön 1983)
- the acquisition of a range of responses that enable us to repeat an action in similar contexts on a future occasion (Duignan 1989).

There have been many attempts to theorize about the way in which learning takes place. Pollard and Triggs (1997) classify these into three groups:

- *Behaviourist models*: these build on the concepts of training and are responsible for many of the hardships endured in the name of education in the first half of the twentieth century. The learner is passive, knowledge can be transmitted, retraining takes place, and subsequent learning assessed. The stress is on the second of the two abilities listed above.
- *Constructivist models*: these build on the link between experience and reflection so that we learn as a result of knowing how we coped previously. This springs from the work of Piaget (1950), who suggested a sequence of learning that moves from the experienced to the known and then to the abstract. The acquisition of reflection is enhanced at each stage of development.
- *Social constructivist models*: these extend the developmental theme of Piaget onto the social environment and concentrate on the way that we learn from each other. Vygotsky (1978) and Bruner (1966) have explained this as the development of our learning capacity through the interaction with those who have already made sense of the learning process and established their own understanding of their situation. There are two concepts involved in this – the Zone of Proximal Development (the potential to make sense of learning) and the culture of the organization within which the learning occurs.

DISCUSSION POINT

- Consider the plan of a lesson you intend to teach, or have taught, and see to what extent your inclination is towards one of the three types of theory of learning outlined above.

According to Gregorc (1982), our learning styles are determined largely through how we perceive and order information – ranging from the *concrete* (rooted in the physical senses, emphasizing the observable) to the *abstract* (rooted in emotion and intuition, emphasizing feelings and ideas), although most people prefer one particular mode. This is a reflection of the Piaget approach from the concrete to the abstract and from the known to the unknown. Gregorc also argues that our ability to order information is both *sequential* (storing information in a linear, logical, step-by-step way) and *random* (storing it in non-linear, holistic and kaleidoscopic ways), though again most people have a preference. This leads to

- concrete sequential
- concrete randomized
- abstract sequential
- abstract randomized ways of learning.

While individuals may use all four learning approaches to some degree it is clear that we may incline to some more than others.

If we use this framework to analyse the learning profile of a Year 7 student attempting to come to terms with a modern foreign language the following may be observed:

- new vocabulary of items on teacher's table = concrete learning
- mental picture of a baker's shop = abstract
- vocabulary recall of list in text book = sequential
- recall of taped conversation in which the word is mentioned several times = random.

In effect these very rarely occur alone. Melba (1997) has listed the possible combinations of preferred style and outlines ways in which, for example somebody who has a concrete sequential way of learning would be happiest with problem-solving followed by recording results in a structured way, while a student with an abstract random style would prefer individualized research using a variety of resources and freedom to present findings in the way that best reflects understanding. The importance of this for improving teaching and learning is that the teacher needs to be aware of the preferred learning styles of each individual so that information and argument can be offered in varying ways. Later writers have moved from the theoretical learning styles models to the more practical.

Like Gregorc (1982), Honey and Mumford (1986) also emphasize that learning is as much about developing personal competence as about accumulating knowledge. They stress that learning effectiveness requires the ability to identify and build upon four ways of learning. Building on Kolb et al.'s (1971) work, they identify four ways of learning all of which must be present in some part if learning is to occur

- *activist*: linked to activity and experimentation, for example, role-play
- *pragmatist*: linked to concrete experience and problem-solving, for example, fieldwork
- *reflector*: linked to reflective observation, for example, recording logs and journals
- *theorist*: linked to observation and conceptualization, for example, classifying findings.

A similar but possibly more readily understood analysis that can run alongside other models of learning is that outlined, among others, by Jester and Miller (2000) based on the way in which our senses are used in the learning process. Once again these may be seen as supplementary to the models we have outlined briefly above. For them the four styles of learning are:

- *visual/verbal*: relying on what is seen and in a written language format
- *visual/non-verbal*: relying on what is seen but presented via pictorial or graphic media
- *tactile/kinaesthetic*: relying on physical involvement, for example, experimentation, hands-on
- *auditory/verbal*: relying on the presentation of material in oral language format.

Comparison of the models shows that the whole process of learning is much more complex than simple presentation suggests. Consider the following variety of learning needs taken from evidence gathered at Ivy High School.

The Special Needs Department at Ivy High School has become a beacon to other schools within its LEA because of its ability to provide for the needs of a diversity of young people, including learning handicapped and physically handicapped individuals and those with behaviour disorders. There is praise from the local LEA inspector for the care provided, the use of individual education plans and the generally happy integration of students within the mainstream school. There is concern, however, on the part of some parents with children in the same class who feel that the needs of their children are not being understood by some of the school staff.

Mrs Ranjit Singhar is the mother of a boy with attention deficit disorder, and although the 13-year-old is happy while working within the special needs unit he attends for four mornings a week he encounters problems in some of the mainstream classes he attends. Particular problems occur in two subject areas:

- In history where there is a tendency for the teacher to use a didactic approach and lessons follow a common pattern of exposition, reading and then answering questions which are intended to reinforce learning but which, in the eyes of the pupils, are seen to be 'the same thing every lesson'.
- In maths where the teacher has organized the class into seven subgroups, one of which includes the 'naughty boys' who are not allowed to participate in experiential activities until the completion of a 'daily dozen' arithmetic calculations. This means that they move forward only when all the table has answered the daily dozen and slow progress has inhibited involvement in those activities which are seen to be 'fun' by the others in the class.

Mr John McBride is concerned that his son, also a 13-year-old with learning difficulties stemming from undetected dyslexia in his primary school, complains that he cannot make progress in maths where so many of the questions are verbal in nature and where the presence of a boy 'who is always making problems to attract the attention of the teacher undermines behaviour for which the whole table is being blamed'. Mr McBride had spoken previously to the maths teacher but had been told that there was little that could be done to affect the working arrangements because of the decision that pupils of similar ability should work within the same group.

Mrs Meg Fairweather has a daughter of the same age. The daughter has hearing problems and despite the efforts being made to secure a seat at the front of the class, frequently complains that she cannot hear what the history teacher says and then she misses out on instructions. In order to compensate for this she asks her friend to help her and is 'constantly in trouble for talking to her friend'.

The three parents met up at the class parent liaison meeting and after realizing that they had some common ground they decided to ask to see the form tutor. Miss Carstairs attempted to defuse the situation by arguing that the children concerned were a cause of difficulty for the teachers of history and maths and that it was a matter for the teachers to organize their activities in a way which best met the needs of the class as a whole. The parents also met up with Noel Christmas, the head of the Special Needs Unit, who spoke of the individual education plans put in place for the children and the efforts that he was making to ensure that the targets were being achieved. Unguardedly, though, he asked them not to be too outspoken in their criticism of the school or of the teachers concerned because he felt that this could rebound on the pupils. His final comment was: 'You have to realize that some staff feel that many of the parents of those with learning and behaviour problems were incapable middle-class climbers wanting the school to achieve progress in meeting problems that parents have been unable to face'.

Before they left the school the three parents looked back over the evening. Mrs Singhar suggested that they had to be ready to praise those areas of teaching where they knew that their children, all with very different problems, were happy and making progress. English was mentioned because the teacher seems able to give her pupils work which 'is interesting and which uses a lot of different ways of teaching during each lesson', 'PE [physical education] because there is no distinction made between any members of the group and they are encouraged in the things they can do' and art because 'the teacher treats him like a person and gives him things to do which help him to feel wanted'.

A fortnight later the parents asked to see the head to outline their anxieties but to do so, as Mrs Fairweather had said in her letter asking for an appointment, 'knowing how much good the bulk of the teachers do for our children'. John McBride, however, as their spokesman began by repeating the unguarded comments of the head of special needs . . . and the head listened . . .

This debate is a reflection of the many influences that affect teaching and learning. Teachers come to their work with their own background and preferences. The history teacher had probably been brought up in a behaviourist tradition and thought in a concrete and linear way. The mathematician had clearly moved towards a more active form of learning but by putting in the 'daily dozen' had created a hurdle that was too great for some students. Other staff had clearly developed ways of stimulating learning through interest and variety and the use of personalized challenges. The problem for the parents appears to be that they had become caught in the crossfire between behaviourist and constructivist attitudes among the staff. The problem for the headteacher was the reconciliation of these views and the need to balance individual student requirements and those of class management as a whole. The starting point has to be an explanation of the varying ways in which learning takes place but how ready would Mr McBride be to listen?

DISCUSSION POINT

- To what extent could knowledge of the background to learning styles have helped with the development of a more effective learning strategy for these students?
- Is this knowledge available to most teaching staff?

While we might pinpoint many of the key ingredients which support or frustrate effective learning, the process itself still remains messy, unpredictable and hard to pin down, even by researchers. Postman and Weingartner (1971) suggested that 'good learners'

- enjoy problem-solving
- know what is relevant for their survival
- rely on their own judgements
- are not afraid to be wrong and are able to change their minds when necessary
- think first – rather than appear to be fast answerers
- are flexible and adaptable to situations and challenges
- have a high degree of respect for facts
- are skilled in inquiry
- do not need to have absolute and final solutions to every problem
- do not get depressed by the prospect of saying 'I don't know'.

It is a useful exercise to relate their views to the various typologies of learning styles outlined above.

We may hope that students show all of these qualities but consideration of the assessment profiles of most students reveals areas of strength and weakness. This leads to the view that the learning experience ought to promote all these overall through the so-called key skills. However, conventional teaching and learning methodologies are increasingly attacked as incompatible with concepts like the 'learning age' and are criticized for their rigidity. At the same time employers are quick to suggest that while effective experiential learning and 'learning-on-the-job' is seen as a better match for postmodernist demands, these approaches lack clear objectives and coherent structures. There are potential advantages in both the active and the reflective modes of learning: the management of these imposes considerable demands on the class teacher. The current vogue for consideration of learning style has led to a considerable amount of material on the internet that could be of great value to the practitioner. Some references are given at the end of this chapter. Amongst the resources are some excellent diagnostic questionnaires that can be used briefly at the start of each year to assess the preferred learning styles of students. The problem is that once such information is available practices within the classroom should build upon them rather than simply use them as an explanation of learning problems.

Learning in action

The individual

The students detailed in the case study were all known to have special educational needs and, in accordance with the legal requirements, individual education plans had been provided both as a guidance to staff and as a framework for learning known by the student and parents. Knowledge of preferred learning styles can be of great value as the basis of this planning. Stradling and Saunders (1993) consider this for lower attaining students. They note the difficulties that arise because students who are in mainstream schooling may fall victim to organizational arrangements whereby the special educational needs may be known but specialist subject teachers lack awareness of strategies to meet the needs within their own subject area. Similar problems arise with students at the higher attaining end of the spectrum who are frustrated by the slow progress being made as a result of whole-class teaching. The use of individualized learning as opposed to whole-class teaching can offer a way forward for all students.

Joyce et al. (1999) extend the argument by noting the difference in the impact of central and peripheral strategies for improvement. They argue that where targets are set at the teacher–student level (proximal) they are more likely to be successful than where they are set as a result of national systems (distal). In the classroom the teacher can know the learning needs of each individual and offer appropriate remediation or extension activities but nationally devised systems may seem too remote to be real to the student. This may well explain the limited success of some aspects of the extension of the national literacy strategy into secondary schools in England and Wales.

Check point and possible action		
Individual activity is a regular element in lesson planning	There are occasional opportunities for students to work on their own	Pressures are such that individual work is left for homework
Is this recognized by students as a response to specific needs?	Are they sufficiently well trained to work alone – what additional key skills are needed?	How are necessary skills for success in individual work at home being developed?

While the theory of individualized learning is accepted as an ideal the reality is that individual programmes are difficult to construct, very time consuming, and in need of frequent revision.

At Oak Grove School the following system has been developed within the humanities faculty comprising history, geography and religious education subject areas. All students complete a learning styles inventory at the start of each academic year and are aware of the ways in which they learn best – active, reflective or theorist are used as descriptors. Students are taught in three classes in each half year and these are broadly setted by ability. The pattern of lesson planning is one of the introduction of the topic to the full class followed by group activities to research and develop the knowledge base for the topic. On completion of the group report students move on to individualized learning. This consists of compulsory work with some alternative activities, for example, analysis of trade data for a nineteenth-century town, or reflection on a contemporaneous account of life in the same town. Extension work offers yet more choice with activities colour coded according to learning preferences. In this way the essential learning is supported by the use of key skills and activities based upon learning preferences. Staff report that it is successful because all students have an opportunity to succeed – the downside is the time taken to prepare each topic!

The group

One way in which awareness of learning styles can be used to advantage is in the use of group work activities. If the groups are based on teacher awareness of individual strengths, and the tasks matched to the use of these abilities in a cooperative way, it is assumed that the sum of learning as a result of group participation is likely to be greater than that achieved by each individual. Tuohy (1999) develops the 'Biggs' model. This brings together three aspects of learning – the product or aim of the learning activity, the process of motivation to learn, and the presage, or values context of learning. The application of this model offers the following insights for group work. When the teacher has determined the learning product for the activity there is a need to plan for the group to work in such a way that they deduce the necessary facts and then move on to see how these contribute to an overall structure – as for example when a group has sources of information about the physical geography, climate, and land use in an Alpine valley and is then asked to suggest what daily life is like in the area. The process of learning will be at one of three levels

- superficial and concerned with just completing the task
- achieving with a higher level of engagement with the material
- deep with an interest beyond the materials that have been made available.

The presage or context for the activity has to be managed by the teacher so that all members of the group are prompted to move towards the deeper process level and so develop their own capacity to organize their learning. The danger is that in a group situation superficial learners may give the minimum to the activity and bask in the achievements of others who have been thinking at a deeper level. The skill is to maximize the interaction of members of the group so that all are prompted to move to a deeper level as shown by Hartman (1995). Monitoring is, therefore, an essential for success.

Check point and possible action		
Group work is a known and often used learning technique	Group work is used from time to time in the classroom	Group work inhibits the attainment of teaching objectives
Is the time taken and the learning achieved monitored to ensure effectiveness?	Is the novelty such that students have to be re-trained each time?	Has there been consideration of the merits of joint investigation and learning from each other?

Information and communications technology

We have referred earlier to the effectiveness of activity structured to meet the personal needs of the student in facilitating learning. Joyce et al. (1999) explain that the limited progress towards the use of ICT may be related in part to the fact that most students have perhaps an hour or two of access to computers each week but fail to develop facility in their use because they are remote from normal practice. It is also possible that some students are un-happy with the learning styles needed to develop skills in the use of ICT.

DISCUSSION POINT

- Consider the relationship between learning style and the use of computers in learning.

Simpson et al. (1998) have shown that ICT can underpin a learner-centred approach but that this requires the development of teaching skills so that the work for the class can be both individualized and appropriate. Efforts have been made to ensure that ICT is not seen as a male-dominated active pursuit but as a means of accessing and developing learning for all (Gardner and McMullan 1990). Colley et al. (1998) describe work towards this end in music as a subject area but their evidence is that many students have developed negative attitudes by the time that they reach the secondary school. Our research shows that there is a very low level of use of computer technology overall in the ten schools in the sample. Where it has been used successfully it appears to be:

- accessible – available readily and without complex procedures
- appropriate – with a clear learning purpose
- normal – used as part of the learning process in the same way as a text-book or a video clip
- reliable – used with support from staff who are trained in use
- supported by technicians who can ensure minimalization of time loss as a result of inadequate maintenance by untrained staff.

It is possible to argue that ICT is too dependent on the practical and the concrete and that this may exclude the reflectors and those who are interested in the abstract from their use. While this may be so where use is limited to word-processing or the preparation and use of spreadsheets, the opportunity to access sites via the net, and to use paint programs as an adjunct to the basic text can do much to enhance emotion and values. Pressure from many groups seeking access to the equipment may be a disadvantage but where readily available technology enables small groups with complementary learning skills to function this could enhance outcomes. One subject teacher at Oak Grove expressed this as 'having the computer to go alongside the library materials, the coloured pens and the modelling materials, so that it aids rather than dominates the learning'. Once again the starting point has to be awareness of differing learning styles.

Check point and possible action		
Computers and software are readily available in the classroom	Computers and software can be used with prior booking	Problems in resourcing are such that ICT interferes with teaching
How is their effectiveness in teaching and learning monitored?	How is their use integrated with the sequential flow of teaching?	Are these fundamental or a reflection of the need for further staff development?

DISCUSSION POINT

- In what ways can the use of information and communications technology be monitored so that it supports individual progress?

Back to basics

Whatever the preferred learning style students do need to maintain a record of the work they have been following. The example from Ivy High shows how difficult the use of routine teaching, recording and testing can be for students with problems in some areas of learning. Behaviourist theories lean towards recording through notemaking. At its worst this is achieved by copying from the board, or an overhead projector transparency; at best by offering a skeleton structure for use by the students. One teacher in our research argued that it was possible for this type of notemaking to involve all types of learners 'if it includes writing, sketching and the use of material searched out from the textbook'. When challenged on this his reply was that the use of auditory senses in listening to what was being said, visual in copying down the notes, and the verbal in setting down facts and ideas in a structured way met all needs. For those with a constructivist or social constructivist viewpoint such an apologia must call into question the nature of the learning that has taken place. For them the creation of opportunities to learn by reflection, possibly supported by minimal aide-memoire notes, and discussion, building towards a summary that could be retained either as a handout or as a spider diagram would be more successful.

There has to be a balance between the need for a record of lessons to help with the knowledge or skills based learning required for subsequent examinations, and the opportunity for creativity and learning by experience. While pre-prepared duplicated notes can be just so many words they can be used as the basis of other reinforcing activities that enhance both the record and the understanding of completed work.

Check point and possible action		
Notemaking is sparingly but systematically used to help students to keep a record of each lesson	Notemaking is left to the individual students and records of each lesson develop from learning tasks	Notemaking is regularly used to ensure that all students have got a full record of factual content
What techniques are used to maintain interest?	How is this record monitored?	Is this to the detriment of student interest and the development of key skills?

Bowring-Carr and West-Burnham (1997) suggest that the diagnosis of preferred learning style can help students because it identifies optimum learning circumstances, prompts the use of appropriate learning strategies, and relates learning needs to learning styles. It is also important to relate learning needs to teaching styles and mismatch can be the basis of behaviour problems in the classroom. Those with limited powers of concentration may become bored by overuse of a notemaking approach; those who are theorists may be similarly bored because the transmission of facts does nothing to stimulate their need for understanding relationships. Tuohy (1999) also suggests that failure to recognize the depth at which students are functioning may cause problems of frustration. Superficiality and factual retention offer no challenge to the deep thinker. This leads to consideration of the concept of intelligence.

Maintaining the challenge

It was formerly thought that intelligence was a single innate ability to handle knowledge and understanding. This was the basis of selective schooling for over a century. However, Gardner (1983, 1993, 1999) offers a convincing argument that intelligence is much more multifaceted, much more complex and much more open to development, than had previously been considered. He defines an intelligence as an aspect of activity which has the potential to be isolated, is capable of psychometric analysis, is evolutionary and has recognizable core requirements. Using this as the basis of his work he identified originally seven, and now possibly eight or nine intelligences. These are

- *linguistic*: use and appreciation of words and music
- *logical-mathematical*: abstractions and their relationships
- *musical*: competence in composing, performing, and listening
- *spatial*: appreciation of the visual world
- *bodily/kinaesthetic*: ability to control and use bodily movement
- *naturalist*: appreciation of the natural world
- *personal intelligence*: the ability to recognize feelings in self (and possibly separately in others)
- *existential*: the ability to cope with fundamental questions such as existence.

Gardner (1993) argues that awareness of the complexity of intelligence is important to teachers because it offers 'entry points' for learning. These bring together aspects of intelligence as

- *narrational*: the descriptive background
- *logical-quantitative*: ability to understand the concepts involved
- *foundational*: setting the topic in context by asking questions
- *aesthetic*: relating the topic to sensory experience
- *experiential*: applying and developing the ideas underpinning the topic.

This analysis offers at least two typologies of learning to the teacher. Identification of the preferred learning style may show one set of needs but this must be matched to known intelligences so that learners can be provided with an armoury of learning opportunities. We have suggested earlier in this chapter that it is possible to devise activities that meet the learning needs of the individual. It is questionable whether teachers can know the precise level of development of each of the intelligences required in any element of learning. However, it can be argued that the provision of a range of learning experiences with a range of resources rather than routine processing of information, does offer opportunities for intelligences to be developed. This can be audited by recording the resources used for learning over a period of time.

Check point and possible action		
A variety of resources are used in the course of lessons	Sometimes there is a change in the use of resources to encourage interest	The importance of a regular discipline in the subject inhibits variety of approach
How are the varied resources evaluated to secure effective learning?	Is this for change's sake or is there a rationale for different techniques?	Is this masking problems with resourcing, class management or the need for professional development?

Teachers are aware of the background to the learning process. Problems develop when they lack confidence in using a variety of approaches. This requires considerable professional development and the sharing of ideas. The improvement strategy at Ivy High School offers an example of such a programme.

The impetus for initiatives aimed at improving teaching and learning comes from the deputy head responsible for curriculum issues. He has oversight of all aspects of teaching and learning and drives most of the school's development in these areas. Based on his interests and expertise, the school has a number of initiatives in place at the moment that have both a precise focus on teaching and learning and also on areas of the curriculum that will have a direct impact on improving learning particularly, for example literacy.

The context for much of the work has sprung from the performance league tables and in particular what would on the surface appear to be very low levels of attainment, mainly at Key Stage 4. There was also originally some push from the LEA to participate in a county-wide scheme involving many schools. Due to cuts in funding this participation has ceased but it did offer the 'pump priming' to get improvement work underway. The school wants to keep teaching and learning as a constant focus and ultimately wants the various initiatives in place to become established practice.

The aims and objectives are primarily to raise attainment. Initiatives include:

INSET 'Inductive teaching'
Following in-service sessions directed at understanding the learning processes these were applied to lesson planning. It was agreed that if everyone on the staff planned one lesson each week using new approaches and learning styles then in a short period of time all students would encounter an enhanced learning experience. Monitoring and evaluation of these lessons would then lead to further changes.

Setting learning objectives out on the board

This was developed as a single method of improvement to be adopted by all staff. In so doing both the content and the process of learning objectives would be known to students. Further, staff would be more likely to change their patterns of work once the objectives overtly drove the lesson planning.

Curriculum statement

It was agreed that all subject areas would be involved in a review of the curriculum which classified elements into three groups of subject topics and approaches: positive, and worthy of further development; promising, but needing further planning work, and negative, to be either lost or redeveloped. The advantage of this was that staff thinking moved from a topic based viewpoint to one that balanced content and method.

Modelling timetable on six-week cycles

The timetable was reviewed so that all teaching could be accommodated in six week blocks culminating in assessments. These short-term blocks are seen to support the progress of students by delivering the curriculum in short manageable chunks and offering opportunity for review and re-planning in order to cope with identified learning difficulties.

Consistent observation practice

One of the developments has been an increase in the number of staff willing to share their experiences and offer their lessons for observation by others. To this end there has been agreement on a common structure for all lesson observations recorded in the school. This is according to learning context, challenge, pace, variety, involvement, planning and structure, knowledge, skills and understanding.

The school staff are aware that they are still developing these approaches. Staff are growing into some of the changed methodology and the deputy feels that it is an ongoing responsibility of his to keep it high profile and support staff continually in keeping it there. Only by repetition can initiatives like the skills teaching model become second nature. There has been an increase in individualized learning and the more able students are now following work programmes with 'accelerated learning' techniques.

This account of efforts being made in one school is by no means comprehensive but a reflection of a dynamic situation in which the process of learning is constantly being revisited. As our understanding of learning processes increases, so too does our ability to meet learning needs. This means that the standard classroom practice of exposition, recording, practice and repetition is no longer acceptable as a way of teaching. We have to be concerned with the approaches to teaching which can best meet learners' needs. Atkinson (1998) has stressed the importance of this in research into design technology teaching. His observations in eight schools demonstrate how failure on the part of the teacher to recognize an overall 'cognitive style' in each student, can lead to lower attainments. The problem is that the cognitive style has also to be understood within the context of the available teaching approaches for the subject being taught and learnt.

Further reading

We have already mentioned Tuohy (1999) and Bowring-Carr and West-Burnham (1997), who outline approaches based upon the recognition of varying learning styles.

Further case studies showing how learning can be matched to individual need are given in

Cooper, P. and McIntyre, D. (1996) *Effective Teaching and Learning: Teachers' and Students' Perspectives*. Buckingham: Open University Press.

Many of the issues outlined in this chapter, although with a primary school perspective, are also considered by

Collins, J. and Cook, D. (2000) *Understanding Learning: Influences and Outcomes*. London: Paul Chapman.

McGuiness, C. (2001) *Core Concepts for Teaching Thinking*. London: Paul Chapman offers some evaluation of methods used to meet learning needs.

For those seeking a more conceptual approach

Olson, D.R. and Torrance, N. (eds) (1998) *The Handbook of Education and Human Development*. Oxford: Blackwell brings together a number of chapters by the 'real experts' and offers some really detailed bibliographies.

And to start the internet trail we suggest you go once again to the DfES Standards site on:

http://www.standards.dfes.gov.uk

Among other sites offering considerable help on learning issues are:

http://howtolearn.com/personal.html

http://www2.ncsu.edu/unity/lockers/users/f/folder and

http://www.ldpride.net/learningstyles

A fair degree of caution is needed because much of the material is being commercially offered for the industrial and commercial human resource market and will need adaptation.

6 Approaches to teaching

Matching teaching and learning

In Chapter 5 we suggested that we all have preferred learning styles and that effective teachers attempt to match their teaching approaches to the learning styles of the students. But how do we classify teaching approaches? Broadly they can be either transmissive – based upon a behaviourist view of the educational process – or experiential – based upon the constructivist and social-constructivist viewpoint.

Transmissive approaches have tended to dominate in secondary education for several reasons. They are a reflection of the teaching experienced by most teachers. They offer much to those who seek to judge educational outcomes by the transmission of what Bennett (1976) called 'known knowledge'. The current concern with assessment based upon factual knowledge and under-standing has led to a preference for 'chalk and talk' approaches that underpin teacher accountability and promote pedagogic tidiness with learners cover-ing the same material at the same pace. Habermas (1972) considered that such approaches enhance the opportunity for social control and this may be seen in some heavily formalized classroom management strategies. These approaches also simplify relationships between teacher and taught because the teacher controls the learning process and students become passive recipi-ents (Bernstein 1977). For Hargreaves (1982) this is exacerbated because secondary school teachers tend to use the authority of their subject as maths teacher or a history teacher – 'they know and they are not satisfied until they have told their pupils what they know'.

By contrast experiential learning implies a seamless, unending process that goes on both within and outside formal education structures, yet the ubiquit-ous nature of learning by 'experiencing' or 'doing' belies its complexity. The term is used for a range of activity-based learning approaches including experimentation, role-play, discussion, fieldwork, observation of others and so-called 'discovery' methods. Problems with the organization of activities and the assessment of outcomes from experiential learning; inadequate know-ledge of the way in which the learning process works, and the difficulty of securing student improvement with such pedagogy suggests that teachers may be under pressure to use the tried and tested didactic approaches. Lofthouse (1994) has suggested that bureaucratic demands placed on schools have actively discouraged the development of experiential learning techniques.

Although transmissive approaches have been readily attacked, learning through experience has also been criticized for lacking in objectives and a coherent structure. A common complaint when learning through experience fails is that there is too much activity and not enough learning. It is important, therefore, to identify objectives, establish a coherent structure and undertake a review process within an experiential framework where this is used as a teaching and learning strategy. To be effective, as with any other learning approach, experiential learning needs to be well organized and purposeful. A basic objective in any experiential situation is to help learners construct and control their own 'learning cycle' within a framework that establishes purpose, explores possibilities for learning, and promotes reflection. Although the level of teacher control and direction may vary with any given situation, teachers – as with the transmissive approach – need to provide a structure for learning. This should recognize the learning needs of the groups and individuals concerned.

There is, however, another dimension: this is the depth of learning. Bowring-Carr and West-Burnham (1997) explore this as a progression from an increase in knowledge, reinforced by memorizing and the acquisition of facts. From these gains students are led to abstract meaning, and to use this in the interpretation of reality that might in the course of time lead to a change in the attitudes of the learner. The desired depth of learning has considerable implications for the nature of teaching. Transmissive approaches may well cope with the first stages of the progression – the learning of tables of verbs is an example, but the appreciation of the culture of another country is dependent upon the use of those verbs in communication and then in enhanced understanding of the culture. It is not simply the way in which we teach but also the depth of understanding that we are able to promote that needs to be recognized and managed.

The headteacher at Ash Grove had recently undertaken an audit of teaching approaches evident within the school. This had been carried out by the use of a structured observation sheet that had been agreed by the heads of department at one of their termly meetings. In the use of this format the headteacher had classified types of teaching and then recorded the time taken in what she defined as

- 'didactic' teaching including teacher talking, board exposition, reading of texts and notemaking
- 'experiential' teaching including discussion, experimental activity, creative activity and role-play.

The staff had not objected to her presence in their rooms but they were dismissive of her conclusion in a paper for the staff meeting that there was 'need for greater awareness of staff of the learning needs of students and use of a wider range of teaching strategies and techniques'. They were also critical of her suggestion that a programme of peer observation of lessons could be beneficial to teaching and learning overall. They argued that not all subjects would provide evidence of similar teaching approaches, and that the lessons being observed were but one in a continuing programme being developed by the teacher. The headteacher countered these arguments by attempting to persuade all staff to undertake a classification of activities in their own lessons for, say, three days over the course of a year. She argued that this would put the ownership of the investigation into the hands of the staff themselves and thus meet the problems they envisaged. This had not been well received and any decision on the proposal was postponed.

At the ensuing staff meeting it was clear that the staff were divided into three camps. Paddy Waterfall led a group of traditionalists who were critical of any attempt on the part of the head 'to judge what are essentially subject-based approaches and techniques'. The evidence he used to support his argument was that some subjects were more likely to involve experimental or creative activities and overall students would get a pretty wide range of ways of doing things in the course of a week when all subject areas were taken into account. When the head argued that all teaching and learning embraced certain generic qualities such as pace, appropriateness and interest, Paddy countered by saying that there were some aspects of teaching that required a discipline which students had to learn and while that may not necessarily be interesting it was part of the educational process.

A second group were less critical of the head but their spokesperson, Jill Fowler, argued that there were twin pressures at work that constrained the willingness of staff to become more adventurous in their approach. 'On the one hand we are encouraged to offer a variety of ways of doing things but we are under pressure to deliver results for school targets and we daren't do anything that might not enable the students to score the highest possible grades; on the other hand we would like to be more adventurous but we are inhibited by the time it takes to develop new approaches and the cost of additional resources'.

Lucy Miller spoke for a third group and suggested that there was 'something in what the head was saying'. She said that the problem for many staff was that they needed more opportunity to investigate the points which the head had raised in the report. She wanted to know whether there could be some curriculum-wide investigation of what the learning experience of students was according to age and stage in the school. The emphasis in the head's survey had been too teaching oriented and may have been judgemental in that it had been concerned with delivery rather than with the learning process.

After some discussion there was a consensus that the six staff currently undertaking a postgraduate course would use this as the focus of the investigation in the coming term. Their outline plan was to find out what students thought of the way in which they learnt in each of the main subject areas. In the meantime it was agreed that the coming in-service session would focus on the ways in which variety could be achieved and the production of an 'aide memoire for lively teaching' within subject areas. The head asked each department initially to quantify what the costs in time and resources would be for changing the approaches used in Year 9. She agreed to approach the governors with an argument for variation of the School Improvement Plan to accommodate this work.

DISCUSSION POINT

- What would be the basis of such a submission to governors within a school known to you?
- How would you counter the probable view that 'looking for variety is pandering to the students too much'?

It is likely that your consideration of the issues would have identified the problems of organizational 'stasis'. This is the problem resulting from a long period of stability during which ideas had passed unchallenged. Teachers have heretofore enjoyed a relative autonomy and isolation (Dale 1997; Garrett and Bowles 1997) and have been able to work in their own way in their own classrooms. The development of Ofsted inspections and mutually supportive continuing professional development has opened the doors of classrooms to other professionals. At Ash Grove it appears that the fundamental change needed for any move forward is to consider the extent to which the members of staff are prepared to share their experiences. The completion of an audit would be the first stage in determining the actual repertoire of teaching approaches used within the school but it will also require a much greater expansion of mutual observation as a continuing force for improvement in the school. Fullan (1991) has argued that participants in change need to feel that they are gaining from the process. The headteacher had recognized this in attempting to provide some resourcing to make development possible.

Even when the audit has been undertaken there will still be gaps in the headteacher's awareness of all that the school is achieving. This is because the audit has been used to record the techniques of teaching being used but it has not been used to ascertain the depth and the transformational quality of the knowledge, skills and attitudes gained by students. This requires an awareness of curriculum design, a topic that we return to in Chapter 8.

The basis of changed approaches to teaching and learning is that educational thinkers in the last quarter of the twentieth century were concerned that students should be able to cope in a new learning context. Handy (1989) offered a theory of active learning that was

- not just knowing the answers
- not the same as study
- not measured by examinations
- not automatic

- not only for intellectuals
- not finding out what other people already know.

(Handy 1989: 50)

Ferguson (1982) has also offered an 'emergent paradigm for learning' that is concerned with the nature rather than the substance of learning and which differs from mere schooling. New learning assumptions will require a greater concentration on ways of developing learner-autonomy and meeting the requirements for 'lifelong-learning'. Nisbet and Shucksmith (1986) see this 'learning how to learn' as a vital skill. However, they go beyond this to suggest that there is a seventh sense – that of metacognition – which encapsulates our ability to recognize, organize and develop the learning process. If teachers accept that the context of learning has moved in the directions forecast in the late 1970s then teaching approaches must be directed at enhancing metacognition as a new learning when so much more information is available to students.

Reference has already been made to thinking skills in Chapter 5. There is evidence that these can be incorporated into all teaching styles as part of the vocabulary of strategies used to enhance learning by developing the brain. Cordellichio and Field (1997) suggest the following as a means of exercising the brain:

- *hypothetical thinking*: challenging standard responses with 'but why do you think that is so?'
- *reversal*: developing hypothetical thinking by questioning the role of previously unnoticed elements of events or situations
- *changing symbol systems*: developing the capacity to represent numerical ideas verbally, and vice versa
- *analogy*: stimulating the ability to think through one set of ideas by reference to a similar set, but extending beyond example to consider implication
- *point of view analysis*: developing the rationale for alternative viewpoint
- *completion*: exercising the ability to handle multiple responses through the use of logic
- *web analysis*: linking ideas in diagrammatic form.

Returning to our starting point West-Burnham (1992) identifies the polarities between transmissive and experiential approaches. He offers descriptors of the range of teachers from 'masters' to 'facilitators', and of students from 'servants' to 'active learners'. The ability to facilitate active learners is reflected in the approaches being made to teaching and in the use of supportive thinking skills as the basis of lesson planning.

DISCUSSION POINT

- How can current assessment through external tests meet the needs of the experiential learner?
- Should they do so?

The spoken word

Instructions

One of the recurrent comments of students who are asked why they are not making progress in a given subject was that they 'couldn't understand what the teacher wanted'. Communication is fundamental to the learning process and there is a need for balance in the use of language so that it meets the perception levels of each individual in the group, and yet still extends and challenges. This suggests that there is a great need for teachers to consider the level of vocabulary they are using and the assumptions of prior knowledge and learning upon which the spoken communication is built.

At Sycamore High School this has been recognized and staff have agreed that a member of the special educational needs staff should analyse taped recordings of occasional lessons to determine the vocabulary level being used and to compare this with the known cognitive assessment data for the students in the group. The match or mismatch is then fed back to the teachers concerned so that some attempt can be made to adjust the language being used. One of the findings has been that while language is appropriate to student needs in the course of subject teaching there are problems when teachers rush the homework instructions at the end of the lesson. As a result students are either misrecording instructions or relying on copying from faster colleagues who may themselves have made errors in setting down what was said by the teacher. To prevent this it has been agreed that teachers would either ensure that the instructions were written in the students planners as part of the work in class or duplicated and circulated.

DISCUSSION POINT

- Do you consider that the circulation of instructions does meet the requirement to provide an efficient and effective support for the use of homework?

Check point and possible action		
Instructions are given in different ways to ensure understanding	Instructions are dictated at an appropriate point in the lesson	Instructions are included in written material used by students
Is the variety used matched to the learning style of the students?	Is there time for students to check their understanding?	What opportunities are there to develop understanding of what is written?

Although our concern has been with the perceptions of the use of instructions it is also a reminder that homework is an important element in teaching. The way in which it is developed, completed, assessed and used in subsequent learning varies. Parental comment surveyed in Ofsted reports indicates that it is a frequent source of tension between parents and schools arising from perceived failure on the part of teachers to set adequate and challenging learning tasks. The conventional uses of homework are to

- provide an opportunity for continued research using specified or non-specified sources
- apply principles, skills or knowledge developed in the lesson
- practise skills and/or concepts
- develop material begun in the lesson either through extension work or the 'fair copy' of work already drafted
- extend reading or practice
- learn text, principles or argument.

Hallam and Cowan (1999) have shown that homework that prepares for future work or revises previous work is apparently more beneficial than work related to concurrent classroom activity, and that ready and full feedback is an essential if homework standards are to be maintained. Perhaps most significant for improvements in teaching and learning is the finding that teacher expectations appear to be most decisive in motivation of students. Experience shows that challenging work within the ability level and learning capacity of students which will be collected promptly, marked and used in subsequent learning is more effective than drilling, completing or unchecked exploration activity. At Oak Grove students have been invited to submit homework by email in some subjects. The novelty value of this led to an initial improvement in the quality of submission but the teaching staff concerned are now dealing with the usual problems of incompleteness, carelessness and late submission.

Teacher–student interaction

Cullen (1998) has examined the nature of teacher talk and the classification of teacher–student interaction as 'communicative' when the nature of exposition, questioning and leading discussion promotes learning, and 'uncommunicative' where the teacher talk and subsequent understanding is inappropriate. He argues that this is simplistic but the ability of teachers to reflect on whether they have enhanced or confused the learners is not inappropriate as part of the armoury of a successful teacher. The use of questioning that has purpose, enhances understanding and leads to the sharing of responses is an art. Tabberer (1995) comments that only about 2 per cent of classroom time is spent on asking questions with challenge. Pollard and Triggs (1997) suggest that if a framework for asking questions is understood by the teacher more effective learning follows. They distinguish between

- psycho-social questions which are designed to encourage responses, develop interest and develop respect for the attitude of others, as well to assert control, and
- pedagogical questions to check understanding, to promote recall, consolidate learning, develop discussion, reinforce application and broaden attitudes.

They offer a classification of questions based upon Brown and Edmondson (1984) that includes

- *extension*: asking a string of questions on the same topic
- *funnelling*: using open questions to prompt interest and then moving to a more focused deduction or problem-solving
- *random walk*: where questions are used with no discernible pattern.

At Oak Grove lesson observation has become an integral part of monitoring and evaluation with one hour each week allocated to heads of subject for this purpose. It was realized at a comparatively early stage in the development of monitoring processes that questioning was being used in a random fashion by all except four teachers. It was, the headteacher felt, no coincidence that these four also had consistently high external examination results. Following discussions with the four staff a schedule for question analysis was drawn up for use by all subject and peer observers. In the course of a lesson the observer using the schedule would note on a 'quick tick' grid:

- nature of the question – recall, development, application, observation, reflection
- structure of the question – open or closed or indeterminate
- direction of the question – awareness of gender, ability level
- appropriateness – vocabulary, learning challenge
- pacing – time for response, maintained interest, prompting.

The staff have commented that the construction and use of the schedule presented a good development opportunity and had led to 'questioning the use of questions' but that monitoring is more difficult especially where questioning is used intensively during a lesson.

One argument encountered by the headteacher at Ash Grove was that some subjects did not lend themselves to varied activities to meet learning needs. While this is true, for example, when contrasting a practical art lesson with a structured science lesson, all lessons to a greater or lesser extent make use of the spoken word. This has been the subject of several pieces of research. Wilson and Haugh (1995) have shown how 'collaborative modelling' by which students, working in pairs, read and then re-present a section of text in a different medium can be successfully used in a range of subjects including science and geography. In this way the preferred learning style of the pairs can be complementary and knowledge developed in one way can be strengthened in another. Meyer (1997) point to the possibility that students may react differently when faced with differing teaching approaches. They have classified students as:

- 'risk takers' – those who are prepared to make an attempt to produce an answer
- 'risk avoiders' – those who play safe, fail to answer or only do so in a secure relationship with the teacher.

For our purposes the range of activities provided in the course of a lesson or a series of lessons should recognize this difference by creating situations where the risk avoiders are able to develop confidence.

Check point and possible action		
Talking to students is followed by a range of activity to reinforce learning	There is a predictable pattern to the lesson which relies on alternation of talk and written activity	The importance of completing the syllabus is such that most lessons have to rely on teacher talking and homework to follow
Does the balance between talking and activity recognize attention span and learning style?	How is the impact of this assessed to ensure that all students are given a learning opportunity?	How is homework structured so that the students can learn by using different approaches?

Cooper and McIntyre (1994) investigated the relationship between the way in which the teacher thought that the lesson was being taught and the way that the students perceived it. Two conclusions emerged. The relationship was much more transactional than had been thought hitherto providing evidence that even where didactic approaches were being used they were being 'sold' rather than 'delivered'. This is evidence of the use of language to interest and persuade. Further, despite the identification of models of teacher-centred and student-centred teaching approaches most teachers use a range of techniques at different times in the lesson in order to meet the learning needs of individuals and the group. Teachers are much more flexible in their use of techniques than is sometimes thought. The important conclusion from this is that teachers need to know what approaches meet specific needs within their subject area. Our evidence shows that where the students know the intention of the activity they are more ready to progress towards the stated outcomes because they develop confidence in both coping with the work requirements and communicating with others.

Check point and possible action		
Students are given an outline of elements and outcomes at the start of a topic	Students are given a copy of the syllabus for the subject in the coming year	Students are given an overall programme but without detail so that anxiety can be minimized
Are opportunities provided for this to be reviewed and for learning difficulties to be identified?	Is this used as a check list for topics or as a review of learning?	What steps can be taken to ensure that they see each element in teaching as part of a whole?

Discussion with the staff responsible for ICT in some of the schools in the research sample indicates that this sort of review is essential because of the individualized nature of much computer based work. To this end provision at Hazel School has been subject to a development plan rather than to an offer of the resources to all staff at the same time. As a preliminary measure all staff have been offered a basic competence training session over the course of a year. All subject leaders have spent time with the ICT coordinator identifying the ways in which ICT could be of help in subject-specific areas. This builds upon the teaching of computer key skills undertaken by the ICT staff over the first three years of secondary schooling. The subject-based discussion also identified the ways in which computers could be most successfully used either as stand-alone machines in individual classrooms or as a suite for class use, or both.

In the event the school used technology college grants to allow the development of two suites, six stations with four machines each, and a stand-alone machine in every teaching room. After the initial discussion the subject leaders then completed a form showing when and how it was intended to make full group use of computers 'in an ideal world' in the coming year. This allowed the development of a timetable to meet departmental needs for enhanced access at certain times, coaching of staff at an appropriate time to support computer-based activities, and the staged purchase of necessary software and applications. Two years into the revised way of using ICT, support staff have been ready to make greater use of electronic whiteboards, and there has been a much enhanced use of computer-based learning for extension, enrichment and development work on an individual basis.

Maintaining variety

We have considered the nature of talk and computer-based activities in effective teaching but considerable use is made of written activities. The early Ofsted secondary school reports record evidence of poor teaching where students were involved in copying notes from the board, in writing dictated notes, and in unchallenging tasks such as copying and colouring in material from textbooks – all of which our readers will have experienced in their own education. While their work was in infants schools, Bennett et al. (1984) identified five types of tasks – incremental, restructuring, enrichment, practice and revision – and these are no less applicable to the secondary situation. They are frequently evident in lesson planning as a learning cycle is used as the basis for teaching a new topic. Much of the new material introduced in the course of a lesson is incremental in that it builds on what has gone before. Usually this is an oral activity but the opportunities for restructuring to advance this learning, developing ideas through enrichment, and practice through the application of ideas in written work. Revision often appears either written as homework, or spoken as a result of questioning and the cycle then recommences. Problems emerge when students recognize that the cycle is about to begin again and that 'it is the same learning, just different topics' (Year 10 boy, Ash Grove).

There is considerable evidence that the most effective learning is that which is higher up another teaching progression. This is from the comparative ineffectiveness of a lecture as a means of teaching, through increasingly more learning-efficient reading, visual presentation, demonstration, discussion and practice to involvement in teaching others. This offers a framework that can also be tied into enhancing the level of cognitive understanding. Bloom (1956) identified six thought processes, again of a hierarchical nature:

- knowledge
- comprehension
- application
- analysis
- synthesis
- evaluation.

The first three are comparatively low level in their demands. The latter are higher level because of the challenge they provide.

DISCUSSION POINT

- How can cognitive level awareness be integrated into lesson planning?

Our evidence shows that students do benefit from a variety of activities in their learning. Effective teaching is that which matches the level attained by the student to three features. These are

- the stage in the learning cycle
- the hierarchy of challenge in activities
- the cognitive demands being made.

In the day-to-day life of a school much of this appears to happen by default rather than design – it may be a skill learned by the teacher but not always recognized. It is only through recognizing that such analysis of teaching approaches is possible and that activities can then be matched to student needs, that more effective teaching can occur. Maker (1982) offers three levels of awareness of teaching activity to promote this:

- *Learning environment*: this should be student centred, encourage independent learning, open to new ideas, complex in the pedagogic diet available, and offer high mobility in and out of a learning situation.
- *Content modification*: this is aimed at removing artificial barriers to learning through variety, complexity, increasing abstractness and the development of methods of inquiry.
- *Process modification*: this should allow for freedom of choice, a variety of learning processes, variable pacing, group interaction, open-endedness, creative thinking and the transformation of learnt material, and then through debriefing lead to the identification of higher levels of thinking.

Joyce et al. (1997) stress the importance of the teacher providing the opportunity for the student to learn through providing those conditions that are most likely to promote connections on the part of the learner. This involves the teacher in establishing the objectives of the activity with the learner; presenting stimuli for learning and enhancing student attention; developing recall; providing the right conditions for subsequent performance; offering sequences of learning and then prompting and guiding that learning. Variety of activity can go far to meet these needs. For Joyce et al. (1997) this can be achieved through the use of a variety of 'models of learning'. These include:

- *inductive learning*: concerned with data collection, examination, classification and creating hypotheses
- *exploring concepts*: developing concepts, testing concepts, analysing thinking processes
- *metaphoric learning (synectics)*: consideration of analogy, exploration, re-examination
- *mnemonic learning*: making connections, expanding sensory images, recall
- *group investigation*: problem-solving, role assignments, review and recyling activity
- *simulation learning*: orientation, participation and debriefing.

The staff at Oak Grove School have explored the philosophy behind such thinking in a series of staff development activities. Again they have argued that the theory is fine when time permits its use but they have worked at the production of guidance for meeting individual needs that draws upon environment, content and process descriptors as a review framework for lessons. They have also used the learning models classification as the basis of further analysis of the processes used in teaching. This has led them to be 'much more active in the way that we plan lessons' and 'more ready to see whether the same material can be effectively taught in a different way – teaching mnemonically is not the only way to cope with the acquisition of historical facts, group investigations have shown that there can be more fun in learning' (teacher of history).

Check point and possible action		
Varied activities are used in the course of the lesson to match teaching to learning style	Varied activities are used to maintain interest in the lesson	Pressures on time inhibit the use of a variety of approaches
How has the learning style been identified, and how is progress monitored?	How can this be further developed to meet individual learning needs?	How can this be overcome? Have alternatives been tried?

Much depends upon the structure of the lesson. Often despite all planning, there is a certain unpredictability that is in itself a journey and a source of interest to the students. Potter and Duenkel (1996), looking at active learning in outdoor education, give a useful checklist of the essential elements of a successful lesson. These are likely to include:

- a clear purpose
- a defined student focus
- active learning
- exposition
- emotional investment and risk-taking
- a mixture of content and process
- varying work relationships
- reflection and evaluation
- reciprocal teacher–student learning.

DISCUSSION POINT

- Can these desiderata be applied to all subject areas?
- What inhibits lesson planning based upon such criteria?

The student has, however, a part to play in this – it requires them to be able to reflect on their own progress as a result of the teaching they have experienced.

Reflective learning

There is always a great temptation for students to follow a topic, make their notes, complete tasks to develop understanding and application and then move on to something new. One of the problems of modular teaching is that completion of a theme may mean that students do not revisit prior learning. There is considerable evidence that an ability to develop reflective learning ensures that cyclic learning takes place and that this underpins conceptual development and understanding. Schön (1983) has set out the ways in which reflection occurs through experiential learning. In simple terms as we ask why one course of action works and another fails and generally, we learn not to repeat the unsuccessful strategy. As basic knowledge and skills are developed, for example in problem-solving mathematics, the student should develop the capacity to modify future practice in the light of past experience. This characterizes much sixth form work. Schön refers to 'reflection in action' characterized by three elements:

- the spontaneous, intuitive performance of tasks
- actions, recognitions and judgements which we may be unaware that we have developed
- internalized understandings which have grown from our daily practice.

Schön argues that if the innate processes which he has outlined can be identified then we will be in a position to develop and articulate reflection in action. If students are able to reflect on their achievements then prior learning may offer the key to both enhanced self-confidence and cognitive development. In the classroom this means training students to ask three fundamental questions:

- How does the work I have completed add to what I knew previously?
- How does it relate to what I am doing in my subject now?
- What difficulties does it present and how can I find the answers I need?

Brookfield (1987) regards these questions as the basis of critical thinking. In terms of secondary school teaching reflective learning requires that students develop this critical faculty. At Ash Grove the students have been in the habit of attempting a review of their work with subject staff on a termly basis. Students use a structured form which they complete before their subject interviews. This involves an assessment of the topic recently completed under the headings of interest, new learning, learning problems. Subject staff then considered the form and completed the matching 'action' boxes. These are then used as the basis of targets for the coming term.

Check point and possible future action		
Students keep and review a record of their work and assessments with criteria for future success	Students have a record of work topics	It is for the teacher rather than the students to maintain the work record
How is this organized so that the student can recognize future learning needs?	Is this a missed opportunity to develop student self-assessment?	How could this be developed so that students feel some sense of responsibility for their learning?

Moving towards focused teaching

Awareness of the learning needs of students and the availability of a vocabulary of teaching responses requires an increasing individualization of work programmes. At Oak Grove the staff have developed a variety of materials coded by ability level and teaching style as a starting point for this and following whole class introductions to a topic students have a prescribed set of tasks that develop their understanding and application of ideas. The key to the successful use of this approach has been that time has been taken each term to allow for individual target setting in each subject area and then to revisit this at the end of the following term. One teacher said 'the initial work was horrific – there was so much to do and we had to prepare for every learning eventuality but having gradually introduced change from Year 7 through to Year 11, and having developed the use of computer technology as an aid in the production of materials we can now revise what doesn't work on a year by year basis' (science teacher). The school is using materials that have been developed in accordance with our knowledge of the way in which the brain works. This is a complex area bringing together neuroscience and pedagogy. It requires awareness of the way in which the brain functions and how each functional area can be stimulated – known as mind mapping. We give you further leads in this area at the end of this chapter but the following material shows how new thinking is being applied to teaching processes.

The staff of Poplar School have made determined efforts to focus their teaching on learning need through the adaptation of the principles of accelerated learning. This has been of particular importance in a school which, although continually improving, is still in the lower quartile of the national league tables for GCSE A–C grade results. The implementation of changed teaching practices was undertaken in a way that corresponds with the desiderata for successful change management characterized by a carefully structured programme, owned by the participating staff and directed at securing measurable outcomes. In this case the pilot group was a small sixth form and the purpose was the enhancement of learning strategies for a group needing considerable support if they were to meet the expectations consequent upon their GCSE results. Our exemplar has been prepared by one of the participating staff.

Most of the ideas were taken from Alistair Smith's (1996) book, *Accelerated Learning in the Classroom*. A range of material was 'unpicked' from the book and a working party of 15 interested teachers agreed to use a range of them with their Year 12 teaching groups. The rationale behind the involvement of these teaching groups was twofold: there was a 'valued-added' dip in exam performance post-16. This has meant greater scrutiny is being placed on teaching and learning in the sixth form. Further, given the experimental nature of some of the activities, for example, physical exercises at the start of lessons to generate oxygen supplies to the brain, it was felt that it would be relatively easy to pull back these groups of older students should things get out of hand!

The method chosen by the working party was that an agreed 'diet' of strategies was to be adopted by the group for a five-week period. At the end of this time, the teachers would report back and then offer feedback on the efficacy of the strategies. The second five-week block would allow the group to experiment with any of the strategies that they felt most comfortable with. The end game to this was that the INSET day devoted to implementing accelerated learning techniques in the classroom would have not only some groundswell of support among colleagues but also some evidence of how it might work in our school's situation.

In choosing the strategies, we broke down the lesson into four parts:

Getting the environment right
- Visual dimension – checking displays, seating, layout, lighting, heating appropriate to activity
- Mood – creating supportive relationships that are non threatening and build on high esteem and developing self-confidence.

The start
- Physical activity – stimulating blood flow to the brain and invigorate the group
- Connecting the learning – providing a rationale for learning by reference to previous learning and showing how it supports the present lesson. Give the students the opportunity to predict where the learning will go. Provide the learners with the learning outcomes, the key words and the questions they will be able to answer by the end of the lesson
- Big Picture – setting the aims for the lesson and provide an overview of the whole lesson and its component parts. Important to explain what they are going to cover and why (content and process)
- 'WOW' start – using a stimulating or challenging learning device
- Visualizing the outcomes – target setting so all know where the lesson is going by using a mental approach learnt from sport. Students are encouraged to visualize what they are hoping to have learnt and how that learning will be expressed (differentiate by must, should and could).

The doing bit
- Connecting the hemispheres (visual, auditory, kinaesthetic) – using varying approaches give out the new knowledge. The brain will start to put it into long-term memory if sufficiently distinctive (visual, auditory and kinaesthetic); use active listening with rich language to develop and conceptualize learning. Keep this bit short!
- Movement – to avoid boredom and to stimulate learning use a balance of activities, use individual, pair and group activities
- Encourage learners to measure their own performance against success criteria as the lesson progresses
- Demonstrating – applying learning. Learners *have* to demonstrate their understanding of the new knowledge through demonstrations, tests,

quizzes, talks, mock lessons or quick mini-displays. Teacher must provide feedback that is immediate, relates to criteria set and is educative.

The end of the lesson
- Review for recall and retention. Review is vital to long-term recall and retention. Use a variety of review techniques that apply the six times rule (by the end of the lesson, the students will have received the key information in at least six different ways).
- Teach the best ways to memorize – matched to the individual needs of the students.

Part of the rationale behind improving learning is to consistently use a structure matched to hour and a quarter long lessons that follows this accelerated learning in the classroom cycle.

The meetings at the end of the two five-week blocks took the form of an evaluation. The general consensus was that all the strategies had made the teaching staff concentrate more on pedagogy in general and they felt that key learning goals were achieved particularly with the bits on connecting the learning, pupils having to demonstrate their learning and the review at the end. (A distinct 15 minute plenary at the end of the National Literacy Hour has arguably been one of the most vital elements in the programme which has helped contribute to the improved Key Stage 2 English SAT scores across England and Wales.) The most difficult bit has been to sustain the initial variety of learning activities (audio, visual and kinaesthetic) created at the start. This element was felt to be something that would be achieved in the longer term. It is recommended that schools see this transformation as a three-year cycle and not something that can be achieved overnight. The quest for change continues!

The development of accelerated learning for other years of Poplar School is not yet policy but staff, once trained in the approach, are inevitably making use of strategies that have been successful elsewhere. Strangely, the inhibiting factor to further change appears to be concern that the very short physical element at the start of each lesson may be an opportunity for misbehaviour. This leads us to consider the importance of relationships between students and staff in school and classroom situations.

Further reading

The sources mentioned at the end of Chapter 5 are also relevant in this context but considerable detail of teaching strategies is given in
Pollard, A. and Triggs, P. (1997) *Reflective Teaching in Secondary Education*. London: Cassell.
Fuller consideration of possible patterns of teaching is given in
Joyce, B., Calhoun, E. and Hopkins, D. (1997) *Models of Learning – Tools for Teaching*. Buckingham: Open University Press.

The text used by staff at Poplar School is

Smith, A. (1996) *Accelerated Learning in the Classroom*. Stafford: Network Educational Press.

And to start the internet trail we suggest you go to http://web.indstate.edu/tstyles3.html which gives an inventory. Although this is applicable to college situations the scoring gives a good overview of teaching preferences. These are then used in the classroom with detail from http://www.kcl.ac.uk/kis/schools/education/Courses/modules/teacstyl.html or from http://integratedlessonplans.com/newteacher1.html. The latter is material for 'new' teachers but there are times when we can all benefit from beginning again.

7 Relationships

Motivation

The importance of the management of relationships has been identified by Hay McBer (2000) as fundamental to the development of 'classroom climate' in their model of teacher effectiveness. This can be summed up as 'a measure of the collective perceptions of pupils regarding those dimensions of the classroom environment that have a direct impact on their capacity and motivation to learn' (Hay McBer 2000: 1.1.5).

The relationship between teacher and taught is variously one of inspiring, cajoling or coercing the student to undertake a programme of work in a way that will enhance learning for both the individual and the group. This is a matter of motivation. It is generally accepted that much human behaviour is driven towards achieving goals in order to satisfy particular need. Handy and Aitken (1987) divide motivation theories into three categories:

- *Need theories*: these maintain that an individual acts in order to meet a need or set of needs; for the student this may be seen as working as a means to the end of securing a good job so that there is some chance of meeting the basic needs for food, shelter and warmth and then moving on to enjoy a better life.
- *Goal theories*: these argue that we direct our actions in order to achieve particular goals. These may not be the means to an end but simply the achievement of something for its own sake; for the student this may be through reaching a particular academic level or reaching particular standards in fitness or creative activity.
- *Self theories*: these hold that we act to maintain or improve our image of ourselves and therefore our sense of self-respect. Three subsidiary theories have developed out of this focus on self-concept. They are:
  - reinforcement theory – for the student the achievement of the positive is in itself a support to self-esteem
  - attribution theory – for the student this is a reflection of labelling where the sins of a sibling are unfairly used as pressure

– expectancy theory – for the student this may mean that he or she behaves because of implied messages about capacity to undertake the work being offered.

Handy (1993) points out that elements of all three types of motivation theory may be evident in a person, and that they may vary over time. He offers a list of assumptions the understanding of which may help teachers to recognize and respond to varying classroom behaviour problems.

● Rational-economic assumption that people can be driven to complete tasks because they know that they need to achieve their economic needs – 'complete the work or you won't get to university'.
● Social assumption that people gain their sense of identity through relationships with other people and that the effective teacher can mobilize and use these social relationships – hence the importance of peer counselling in overcoming bullying behaviours.
● Self-actualizing assumption that people are primarily self-motivated and self-controlled, making them able to integrate their own goals with those of the organization if given the opportunity – the basic thinking behind rewards systems.
● Complex assumption that at any one time many motives will be at work but they may not all need to be satisfied at the same time since much depends on a personal assessment of the appropriateness of the situation for need satisfaction – the problem of what 'turns' students on.
● Psychological assumption that people are complex and maturing organisms, passing through psychological and physiological stages of development. People evolve an 'ego ideal' towards which they strive: over and above their basic drives – the importance of self-esteem in behaviour management.

Importantly, in the classroom the bigger the difference between the 'ego ideal' of the students and their self-perception the more angry they become with themselves and the more guilty they feel when they cannot attain their objectives. Because work is part of our identity (our ego ideal), it is important that opportunities are provided for students to work towards this goal and thus become motivated. The assumptions we have about the way in which people are motivated will obviously lead us to adopt different approaches to motivating people in organizations. Thus, assumptions that humans are 'rational-economic' leads to a bargaining approach and to a concern with the benefits that education will bring. The adoption of 'self-actualizing' or 'psychological' assumptions is likely to show itself in a greater concern with creating development opportunities in teaching and learning.

Handy's (1993) model – the motivation calculus – focuses on the way 'the individual deals with individual decisions' and he outlines the notion of the 'psychological contract' that each individual develops with the group that they become involved with. He categorizes organizations according to the type of psychological contract which predominates and points out that the contract is usually 'calculative'. It can, however, be 'cooperative' or, where the contract is not freely entered into, coercive. In looking at relationships at Holly Lodge School it is possible to determine a recurrent thread of failure occasioned, in part, by a lack of understanding of what motivates students and by the presumption that coercion works.

Holly Lodge School, a boys' denominational comprehensive voluntary school in a declining manufacturing area in the north-west of England, has been judged to be failing following an Ofsted inspection. The possibility that it might be failing had been brought to the attention of head and governors by the local LEA pre-inspection team two years previously but there was a stubborn resistance to this idea from all sections of the staff. The results at GCSE, although only 22 per cent A–C grades, had doubled between 1998 and 2000; there had been a concerted attempt to reduce absentee rates and attendance had improved from 78 per cent to 88 per cent in the same period, and considerable efforts had been made to create a more welcoming set of buildings by using local volunteer help to decorate and upgrade the circulation areas.

The view of governors and staff was that the school was being judged unfairly. 'It is no good them coming in from outside when they don't know our problems,' said Father McSweeney, chairman of Governors, and the head had stated to the local paper that 'our staff face an impossible task, traditional values such as respect have been undermined and we can no longer run things in a way that was previously successful'. He was particularly annoyed following a visit from the local LEA 'inclusion officer' and resented the assertion that the school was making too much use of temporary exclusions because 'these are the only way in which we can get the parents we want to see into school'.

The LEA had referred to the 'prevailing macho culture' of the school. This had been shown in the relationship between staff and boys with 'continuing use of surnames, a lack of courtesies such as please and thank you, and in the prevailing untidiness of the buildings'. The headteacher was aware of these comments but felt that those who were looking at the school had failed to understand that boys were 'used to the rough and tumble of the male-dominated society which is all around them on the estate'. The headteacher, in an attempt to disprove much of the criticism, then invited a researcher from a nearby college of higher education to interview students throughout the school. The interviewer worked with a group of boys from each of the years and reported as follows.

The boys say that you have to be tough to survive in this school. They mention the intimidation that often occurs when older boys want younger boys to be part of their gang outside school, and to ensure that they will conform to prevailing attitudes to staff, work and social activities. They speak of the need to be hard, especially if you are to survive for example, in physical education lessons, and in those lessons where personal opinion has to conform to the norm for the local area. Staff may be told of problems, and there is evidence of the existence of policies, but the boys say that little action is taken and that they suffer in the long term if they make a fuss. It was, said the report, regrettable that 78 per cent of those interviewed stated that school life was unhappy, and only 30 per cent felt that they stood any chance of examination success.

The conclusion to the report included references to 'softening the culture, enhancing the relationships between staff and boys, developing an encouraging rather than an intimidating atmosphere, and insisting on basic courtesies in relationships, language and behaviour'.

This was a severe shock to both the chairman of governors and the head, who recalled that the school had turned out many people who, as pillars of the local community, had done much to show that the values and training provided by the school in the past had been to their advantage. The comment of the chairman of governors was that 'the school will have to change to meet new expectations, but we are being asked to do the impossible – once we drop our defences the boys will have the upper hand'.

It is likely that many readers will feel that this is a stereotypical description of a male-dominated organization. It does, however, raise many issues. Do males use differing modes of address when females are not present? Are male staff harder and more dismissive of sensitive students and is a bullying culture more likely to develop in a male-oriented society? That said the problems outlined above are not limited to single-sex schools. It is possible for staff to behave in such a way that they develop a counter-culture in opposition to that pervading in the school as a whole and their defence is often that this is their way of classroom management and, unless it is proved to be unsuccessful for the students involved, it should be tolerated. Problems arise when changed policies are required but cannot be easily developed by all the staff. This is especially so where the so-called male leadership characteristics of imposed order, and arrogance, are at variance with the softer feminine characteristics of reason and respect. The chairman of governors at Holly Lodge School and the headteacher were facing problems not only within the school, but also because of the traditionally 'hard' nature of the local context. This tension can manifest itself in the classroom of any school where the values of teacher and taught are at variance.

DISCUSSION POINT

• What are the manifestations of the culture of relationships within your school or organization?
• Although extreme, Holly Lodge School raises problems that occur in many schools: what strategies for change might be used?

The learning culture

In Chapter 1 we outlined the notions of culture within the school. This was conditioned in part by the organizational structure but the attitudes shown by both students and teachers and the behavioural patterns that develop are also of considerable importance. Dimmock and Walker (2000) show how the organizational culture is a reflection of, and is reflected in the interpersonal relationships and fundamental values of the school or college. They demonstrate this by comparing the following dimensions of collegial and hierarchical school cultures:

- *power*: equality and teamwork versus top leadership and status
- *group*: harmony and networks versus creative conflict and self
- *consideration*: meditative and student centred versus edict and staff centred
- *proactivism*: 'can change' and individualized care and support versus change resistance and conformity
- *generative capacity*: problem-solving and experimentation versus referral and traditionalism
- *relationships*: relationships dominate versus task more important

These are evident in the classroom where a teacher may see their role as fostering collaborative or coercive approaches to teaching. James (1998) has investigated the relationship between the culture of cooperative and hierarchical approaches and suggests that improvement can be fostered through awareness of the advantages of the former genre of teaching and learning. Hierarchical attitudes lead to disrespect, arrogance and perceived unfairness with consequent poor listening, inconsistency and abrasiveness in relationships. She calls the cooperative approach 'democratic' because unless the skills of working in a team are developed neither students nor teaching staff will be able to use the learning situation to advantage. For her the key democratic skills are a progression from

- broad team skills such as discussion, problem-solving and decision-making
- functional skills such as initiating, informing and planning
- collaborative interpersonal skills such as listening, non-judgemental tolerance, to
- collaborative interpersonal attitudes such as respect, trust and empathy.

Where the progression has been completed during previous learning experiences it is likely that students will be able to move more rapidly towards genuine learning of knowledge, skills and attitudes.

Tuohy (1999) builds upon the work of Schein (1985) to suggest that there are five 'cultural assumptions' that affect the way in which school and classroom function. In summary, and applied to the classroom situation these are as follows:

- *The school's relationship to the environment*: this goes far to determine the ethos of the school and arises from expectations of what the school can achieve and how it functions as a society and within its community. In the context of 'quasi-market competition' where schools may be competing for students recruitment is dependent upon community perceptions of the ethos of the school. Tension may develop between a liberal progressive classroom culture sustained by one member of staff and a conservative atmosphere in other classrooms.

- *Human activity*: the aspirations of a school are summed up in its mission and values. There can be a marked difference between the reality and the rhetoric in such statements. Where there is a predominantly fatalistic view that little can be done to change the lives and achievements of students there is a greater likelihood that students will be judged on passive conformity. Where the leadership at all levels believes that the school and its teachers can make a difference there will be a greater emphasis on creativity and adventure in learning.
- *Truth and time*: truth can be objective and rooted in a rational approach to the world, or more subjective and growing from the opinions of the individual, or the group. This can affect the view of time. For those for whom the values of the past are highly significant much of the teaching process is about passing on the values of the past. For those with a more subjective view the emphasis may be on relevance or future need – an altogether more speculative approach. In the learning situation the placing of the teacher at a point on this continuum can affect the way in which learning takes place. The greater the objectivity the more likely that lessons will be predictable and grounded in the past; the greater the subjectivity the greater chance there is of flexibility and adaptability.
- *Human nature*: McGregor (1960) analysed viewpoints of human behaviour as either Theory X with an assertion that humans are basically lazy and untrustworthy unless made to conform to the ideals of the organization, or Theory Y which offers a more positive view of people who are motivated by attainment and responsibility. This disparity of views underpins and explains many of the problems seen by students who feel that teachers do not trust them and those who resent the fact that they are not allowed an opportunity to develop self-reliance in learning.
- *Human relationships*: basic assumptions about human nature can lead to differences in the way in which human beings act and interreact. Matters of status, modes of address and classroom conventions reflect these assumptions. These can also be manifest in the use of competition as a spur to achievement or of cooperation to bring out the best in learner relationships.

DISCUSSION POINT

- How does your own teaching style relate to the assumptions proposed by Tuohy (1999)?
- Attempt to match these to the needs of one of the groups of learners with whom you work.

Responding to self-perception

So many of the problems of relationships both between students and between students and teachers arise from aspects of self-perception on the part of the students. Parker (2000) details how this may be worsened by negative feedback that triggers yet lower self-esteem, and consequential unwillingness to participate in learning activities leading to disruptive behaviour, poor classroom relationships and eventually truancy. There is a difference between driving students to work and developing their self motivation. Williams (1997) reports that where students have been given the opportunity to establish effective communication with staff about the way in which they prefer to learn, and have identified the inhibitors and the enablers of learning they have shown that teachers should

- demonstrate that they value each student's work
- demonstrate that they value all students as learners in a positive way
- actively help and provide opportunities for those experiencing difficulties
- respect the individual 'intellectual space' of the student by allowing learning in the most personally effective way.

The actual culture of a learning situation has been described by Tuohy (1999) as analogous either to that of a garden where the emphasis is on nurture and development, a factory with an emphasis is on order and quality, or an orchestra where harmony and cooperation predominate. In reality there are times when something of each of these are evident in the classroom according to context, expectations and the approach of some form of assessment.

Check point and possible action		
Students think that they are made to work hard	Students think that they sometimes work hard	Students do not feel under any pressure with their work
How can this be achieved with willing cooperation?	Is this only directed at the need to secure examination success?	Why is there a perception gap between teacher and taught?

Diagnosis and support

Whatever the nature of relationships within the school the process of monitoring and evaluation of learning is fundamental to the establishment and attainment of future targets for students. This requires awareness of monitoring procedures and the use of the data so obtained to support and stimulate learning. At the simplest level teachers ensure that all work is marked fully and promptly returned to the student. Our evidence is that some schools are developing much more sophisticated marking policies and maintaining student records that provide the basis for individual and group evaluation.

At Elm High School the staff have agreed the following set of marking conventions.

Elm High School marking policy
To ensure that all work can be marked quickly and used as a source of information for both student and teacher we have agreed to use letters that indicate how the student can improve on his or her work. We have also agreed that there will be a final comment based on a target for learning – words such as good, fair or satisfactory are too subjective to be of value.

S = spelling error (correct spelling alongside for three key words in each piece of work)
G = grammar error (corrected for three key points in the piece of work)
D = missing data or material (with T for textbook as source, W for worksheet and O for observation)
A = faulty argument (brief indication)
R = inadequate reasons (with T for textbook as source, W for worksheet and O for observation)
H = handwriting needs to be improved (indicate size, form of letters)
P = presentation needs to be improved (indicate detail, tidiness or conventions, for example, science, geography)

The learning target can be stated as 'you need to revise the section in the text on osmosis', or 'in your next piece of work try to use the "fairground" vocabulary'
   This will not solve all our problems but when we are used to the system we should be able to be more effective in marking all the work and more constructive in what is offered to students. This marking will also ensure that problems have been identified for all those students who have special learning needs.

Teachers need to be aware that they may have their own prejudices in the way in which they work with students. Lee (1996) has shown that basic ideas held by teachers of the way in which intelligence can be developed may underpin their attitudes and pedagogy. He distinguishes between

- entity theorists – those who think that intelligence is a fixed and innate quality, and
- incremental theorists – those who think that they may be able to affect learning by developing intellectual skills.

Research shows that the former tend to be more judgemental and to use more transmissive teaching and as a result students appear to develop 'according to their labels'. The incrementalists are more likely to develop teaching strategies that enable students to build on prior attainment and develop towards constantly moving targets.
   Brookhart (1997) suggest that there is a definable 'classroom assessment climate'. This results from the way that students perceive the efficacy of each assignment event such as the marking of homework, response to activity and

discussion, and the feedback on work in progress. Where these are positive, supportive and structured rather than negative, critical and random, there is likely to be a consistently positive classroom view of development through assessment.

Check point and possible action		
The teacher uses ongoing subject assessment to develop the next stage of learning	The teacher refers to the subject assessments in establishing targets	No use is made of subject assessments between formal report stages
How can this be integrated as a regular element in the learning process?	How can this be developed to offer specific learning hurdles?	What alternative diagnostic assessment is used?

Monitoring learning

Classroom management requires a watchful eye at all times and successful teachers appear to be able to keep the maximum number of students on task and productively engaged throughout the lesson. Cameron (1998) suggests that where individual students are less than cooperative supportive rather than coercive management can be successful. Learning can be encouraged through the development of

- an individualized curriculum
- the teaching of self-regulatory techniques as basic 'rules of engagement' in the classroom
- the use of mentoring and peer support to meet individual needs
- the development of an intrinsic 'can do' motivation built upon the achievement of 'bite-size' targets.

Jack et al. (1996) stress that monitoring of behaviour and progress is more successful where exchanges are based upon positive rather than negative interactions – words of praise for what can be praised is more effective than condemnation of what has not been achieved.

Students in our research have shown that they dislike those teachers who appear to favour either individuals or groups within the class. Hurrell (1995) has considered the extent to which teachers discriminate while undertaking classroom management. He identified two important relationship variables – the variation in student conduct from teacher to teacher, and the extent to which some teachers favour students of particular social class or positive behaviour pattern. He showed that although discrimination based on social class or ethnicity is minimal, there is extensive evidence that girls were significantly less likely to be punished than boys. We shall consider this gender-related issue in Chapter 9.

Check point and possible action		
Students are aware that they are being 'watched' in all activities	Students are assessed in some activities	Group activities are seen as a relaxation in the course of the lesson
How is the balance maintained between freedom to develop skills and necessary assessment?	How does monitoring take place to ensure all activity is productive?	Has the frequency, organization and perceived outcome of activities been investigated by teachers?

Monitoring can be incorporated into the lesson in such a way that it is a routine activity. Hultgren and Stephens (1999) use the phrase 'indulgent persuaders' to convey the idea of the effective role of the teacher monitoring work, rather than 'sergeant majors' when dealing with secondary students. This meets the view of many students that they 'want to know where they are going wrong but don't like the way that we get bawled at in public' (Year 10 boy). However, there is a difference between the actual and the perceived communication between staff and students. There has been considerable research into 'teacher–pupil discourse' and the language of instruction, control and encouragement can affect the likelihood of success in building relationships in the classroom (Rismark 1996). It is however, important that teachers should do more than 'watch their language' but should move forward with students to establish ways of working that lead to a successful completion of tasks.

At Rowan High School where there is frequent use of peer observation of class teaching to provide opportunities for sharing good practice, it was decided that staff–student exchanges would be taped and then subsequently analysed to see whether there was 'a gap or a gulf' between the professed values of the staff and the way in which these were manifest under the pressure of classroom teaching. The ethos of the school is one of 'open relationships, honest expression of views and equality of opportunity'. One of the senior staff, a mathematician, was surprised to find that in the analysis of a 35-minute lesson he taught there were only seven significant teacher–student exchanges, all related to answering 'how do I do it' questions; that four sets of instructions were given to different individuals without the use of the word 'please', and that one student was told to 'get on without making so much fuss' and another 'to use what bit of brain the good Lord gave you'. He considered the data and replied that the students knew him well, and that they expected him to 'egg them on a bit'.

By contrast, a home economist was observed to have twenty three student exchanges within the same length of lesson. All were noted to have had some form of respect either through appreciation or constructive criticism with 'thank you' and 'please' used at some point in each exchange. Seven of the exchanges noted were concerned with the rationale for student activity, four were evaluative, and six were concerned with 'doing this better on the next occasion'. The teacher concerned was surprised that the analysis had been so positive and referred to 'getting the most if you give them respect'.

At a subsequent staff meeting when the exercise was discussed without outlining details, the deputy headteacher spoke of 'the value of being seen as students see you' and it was agreed that the standard lesson observation schedule would be amended to include a count of students' exchanges classified as 'instruction, exhortation, questioning, discussion' and an open-comment section on 'language and manner' in exchanges.

DISCUSSION POINT

• What are the necessary features of the 'culture of relationships' for such an exercise to be successful?

The nature of the exchanges that promote successful learning has been investigated by Stefani (1999). He has also shown that assessment procedures have a profound impact on the attitudes students develop towards their work. The greater the level of interaction between teacher and taught, the more successful is assessment as a developmental tool. He argues that in order to become effective and autonomous learners students have to be able to understand the criteria by which their work is being judged and then 'empowered through meaningful feedback' in a working partnership. Fisher et al. (1998) have considered the way in which the relationships that promote effective learning partnerships are a mirror of teacher personality. Effective teachers are open in their encouragement and discourse and trusted for their confidence and capacity to enthuse.

Check point and possible action		
Students know how they are making progress as an integral part of the lesson	From time to time the teacher assesses and develops specified skills and knowledge	There are stages in the school year when students are made aware of their progress
How does the assessment provide rolling targets?	How can this process become integrated into normal routine?	Does this process provide sufficient opportunities for developing work strategies?

Encouragement

Student perception of the learning process often demonstrates the importance of teacher encouragement (Johnson 1998). This has been demonstrated in the open comments from our own research. For example, 'I like the lessons where the teacher is interested in what we are doing and then tells us when we are doing well' (Year 8 boy) and 'It makes a difference when the teacher smiles at you, it gives a bit of warmth to things' (Year 10 girl). Moss (1999) has considered the view of American researchers who commend the idea of the 'transcendental teacher' who overcomes all the contextual and organizational inhibitors to teach in an energetic and enriching manner with 'calm presence and a sense of humour'. He argues that skilled leadership can promote cultural and attitudinal changes in school and classroom, but does not underestimate the effort involved. Canter and Canter (1999) argue that for this to be successful teachers need to

- define the mission – the principles that underpin the purpose and practice of teaching
- turn round negative assumptions – rephrasing the negative in a way that fits the mission
- reframe problems – going beyond the negative statement to find the real problem, and
- build trust – minimizing stress and welcoming contact reduces the possibility of misunderstanding.

Steve Simmonds was the newest recruit to the Design Technology Department at Sycamore High School. When he was introduced to the department one of his colleagues suggested that he was in the wrong job. 'Why does a fellow like you want to come into a dead end job?' was the greeting. Steve replied that he had hoped that he would be able to make a difference to the lives of some students – and that he intended to do so. At this point the head of department commented that Steve should take no notice of the cynicism of his colleague – it was 'just the way he was'.

During the course of the term Steve felt increasingly under pressure from the cynic, especially when they were jointly teaching two groups of lower ability 13-year-old students. His head of department suggested that 'he keep his head down' and that there was much to be learnt from the experienced colleague. For Steve this was not a sufficient answer. He argued that the way in which the boys were addressed by surname, referred to as 'thick', and drilled rather than taught was demeaning for the students and was contributing to the lack of progress. The head of department suggested that it would be better to put Steve's view to the test by reverting to single group teaching at the end of the term. This was not acceptable to the cynical colleague, who argued that it was more important for the boys to work flexibly in two media rather than to have to follow a course with either a woodwork or metalwork basis.

The head of department persisted and the groups were split. This left Steve with his group and the opportunity to 'treat them as human beings and to show them that they mattered'. Problems arose in the early days of the new arrangement because two of the boys were determined to show that they were 'top dogs' but overall the group made good progress and respected Steve's ability to interest them and as time went on the workshop had a purposeful and challenging work atmosphere. When asked to explain why this was, Steve said that his approach was 'to show them my respect and to expect their respect in return'. At the end of the term students were required to make their subject choices for the coming year. The fact that all in Steve's group had chosen his option prompted the response from the cynical colleague that 'they are just going with him because he's a soft touch'.

DISCUSSION POINT

• It has been suggested that every school needs a cynic to challenge opinion – is this valid?
• How should cynicism be managed within a subject department?

Check point and possible action

Encouragement is a regular feature of assessment of activities	Students feel encouraged as individuals but less so when working in groups	Students complete their work but do not feel that they are actively encouraged
How is encouragement used as a formative process?	How is group work managed, monitored and commented upon?	Have the core values of all teachers been worked through and developed?

The elements of relationship outlined so far do require teachers to reflect on their own attitudes, language and value systems. Problems arise when there are marked differences in the way in which some teachers behave in their relationships with students within the same school. When asked about this, one headteacher replied that

although we have a set of values that we all hold to be right for the school, there are some staff who work in their own way, and some for whom any request to behave in a particular way can only mean diminished effectiveness. I think it possible that too much attention is given to what some see as political correctness. Providing that teachers are consistent and support learning in their own way I don't see that we have a right to ask for any change from fellow professionals.

(Headteacher, Hazel School)

These comments do raise problems where staff are being required to work in a different way from that which they feel is most likely to be successful for them. Knowledge of teaching style is fundamental to this – whether transmissive or transactional depends on personality traits and pedagogic skills. Examples abound of effective teachers who fall into both camps or use something of both approaches according to need. So far regard for teaching as a profession has enabled teachers to work in their own ways to ensure that effective learning can be experienced. Anxieties are evident, however, where Ofsted lesson schedules are interpreted too prescriptively, or where the extension of the national literacy and numeracy projects into secondary schools will challenge the established practice of some teachers. We return to this 'competence' issue in Chapter 10.

DISCUSSION POINT

- How can the practice versus professionalism dilemma be overcome?
- Should it?

In an attempt to secure a way of working with students that built upon the best features of relationships, offered opportunities for students to reflect on their work and used objective data as the basis for the establishment of individualized targets, Maple School instituted a Dialogue Day.

Following considerable interest in the use of data to improve student performance Maple School decided to close for one day each year in order to enable quality student performance dialogues driven by data about prior and potential achievement to take place.

Aims and objectives
- To improve student performance by informing and clarifying for each student past, present and potential levels of attainment.
- To do so by holding a quality Performance Review Dialogue for every student with a tutor at a specified time allowing 15 minutes per student.
- The outcome of the dialogue to be individualized Learning Objectives for each student.
- To contribute to the overall ethos of high expectations and shared responsibility for learning.
- To make the Learning Objective the focus for future reporting, discussion, monitoring and target setting.

Organizational principles

- All staff were involved to allow 1100 interviews to be held.
- Form tutors decided who they wished to interview from their own forms and who they felt would be more effectively passed to others – some chose to pass on their more difficult students, others passed on those who presented fewer problems.
- It was agreed that the dialogues would be more effective if they were confidential and without parents present. This allowed a more open and honest approach and reflected student opinion.

Inputs to the dialogue

- A personal information sheet – students' self-perception
- Current performance sheet – completed by all staff who taught the student
- Student data sheet – including reading ages, Cognitive Ability Tests (CATs) and predictive data based upon these and staff forecasts.

The dialogue process

- Each tutor had a structured format for discussion based upon the three input sheets.
- The tutor negotiated up to five Learning Objectives, the achievement of which would move the student further along the path to realizing potential.
- The basis of the discussion was to consider a comparison of the student's own view of themselves with those of the teachers and the objective data.
- One of the difficulties was the need to be open and honest with students to enable them to develop a realistic view – and, in many instances, to help them to set appropriately high targets.
- Evaluation of the process was undertaken by PGCE (Postgraduate Certificate in Education) teachers in training and the use of evaluation sheets, to be revisited at the end of the year, to a 25 per cent sample of students.
- The tone of the school was purposeful and positive. Both staff and students were casually dressed to add to the relaxed and non-threatening atmosphere.

Outcomes

- Despite previous in-service training many staff felt insecure with the principles of developing Learning Objectives that were measurable, specific and achievable within a specified timeline and capable of being monitored.
- The pattern of Learning Outcomes included end of course or Key Stage assessments, some specific subject targets, general behavioural targets and some suggestions about more positive participation in school life.
- The interpretation of data relied heavily upon the background material and national comparators provided by the senior management team.

- Following the dialogue a report was prepared by the tutor for each student. Copies were kept in the student file, the Record of Achievement file and the student's personal planner.
- Arrangements were made by each dialogue tutor to meet with students from time to time to check progress towards stated targets. The material is to be used as the basis of the Dialogue in the following year.
- The Learning Outcomes were also discussed with parents at the subsequent parents' evening.

Conclusion
All subsequent efforts were made to ensure that the experience on the Dialogue Day, no matter how positive or otherwise, became a starting point for reinvigorating staff and student relationships and the shared process of lifting attainment. It has to become integrated into the annual cycle of life in the school so that it does not become merely a reflective activity – it has to be a driving force.

It could be argued that the strategy used at Maple School was directed solely at the achievement of enhanced examination grades and that improved student–teacher relationships were of secondary concern. However, leadership of the learning activity within the classroom requires four features that occur in many of the lists of characteristics of successful schools. Hay McBer (2000) define these as:

- *managing students*: with stated objectives, clear tasks, recapitulation and a sustained and positive atmosphere
- *passion for learning*: teaching, supporting learning and deepening understanding
- *flexibility*: recognizing that approaches have to be changed fluently and according to need
- *holding people accountable*: both students and the providers of the resources for learning so that high expectations can be sustained and necessary remediation put in place.

All four are evident in the programme offered at Maple School but to these we would add, arising from our research, an awareness and application of the cross-curricular nature of so many learning opportunities. For this reason we also investigated the perceptions of students about the nature of the education they were gaining – the curriculum as a whole.

Further reading

Having introduced the concepts of culture at an earlier stage in this book we suggest that
MacGilchrist, B., Myers, K. and Reed, J. (1997) *The Intelligent School*. London: Paul Chapman, and
Prosser, J. (ed.) (1999) *School Culture*. London: Paul Chapman both reconcile culture and relationships in classroom practice.

For those seeking the 'how to do it' approach to classroom management:

Pollard, A. and Triggs, P. (1997) *Reflective Teaching in Secondary Education*. London: Cassell.

Stoll, L. and Fink, D. (1996) *Changing our Schools*. Buckingham: Open University Press both offer ideas in several different contexts.

Although written for the early and middle years there are many helpful lines of thought in

Merry, R. (1997) *Successful Children, Successful Teaching*. Buckingham: Open University Press.

Muijs, D. and Reynolds, D. (2001) *Effective Teaching, Evidence and Practice*. London: Paul Chapman builds on the theory outlined in our chapter to outline principles and practice in classroom management skills.

And to start the Internet trail we suggest that you go to http://www.lbro.ac.uk/idater/database/horne99.html for an exploration of the contribution of relationships to the total teaching environment. There is a great deal of 'how to do it' material emanating from the USA with some ideas for application at http://www.pacificnet.net/~mandel.html

You might also be interested in the concepts of relationships at work at http://www.nwrel.org/spcd/sirs/5.html and the collaborative classroom at http://ncrel.org/sdrs/areas.htm

Once again there is a lot of material on the DfES research briefs web site and the National Foundation for Educational Research (NFER) offers a way into recent research material.

8 The total curriculum

The curriculum debate

It is significant that much of the literature that has guided our thinking on the curriculum – the total learning experience – was developed between 1960 and 1990. This was a period during which schools exercised maximum autonomy over what was taught. It is also significant that much of that literature came from outside the world of education and arose from a growing concern that schools in the UK at that time were too concerned with a liberal student-centred exploration of ideas and values, and insufficiently aware of the needs of students setting out into the real world. Shipman (1990) saw the Education Act 1988 as a watershed because the freedom to determine the curriculum on a school-by-school basis was replaced by a National Curriculum which was to be centrally determined and nationally assessed. This could indicate that schools have lost their ability to lead curriculum development but it is argued by politicians that it is only the determination of basic content rather than approaches to teaching and learning which has been taken from the schools. Schools are, however, more aware of the need for responsiveness to prepare students for life in a period of continuous social, economic and cultural change. This has accentuated awareness of the need for more flexible and responsive learning strategies. Tensions have therefore developed between those who favour the retention of centralist decision-making on matters of curriculum content, delivery and assessment, and those who are fighting for schools to be able to develop curriculum policies appropriate to the local level.

Three writers from the 1980s helped to set the agenda for our current curricular debates. In so doing they have moved the emphasis from curriculum as the preserve of the headteacher who, by virtue of the allocation of time to subjects, was able to offer a 'package' for the school, to the individual teacher who is much more concerned with the development of skills and attitudes within the knowledge framework.

- Ferguson (1982) points to what she called 'the emergent paradigm for learning', which is more concerned with an active learning 'kindled in the mind of the individual'. She distinguished between learning and mere schooling. The difference in approaches can be shown in old and new paradigms of learning. The old paradigm is concerned with content, rigid learning structures, rationality, and the imparting of knowledge. The new paradigm is characterized by learning as a shared journey with flexibility, intuitive approaches and concern for wholeness. As society changes, Ferguson argues, so the needs of learners change. New learning assumptions will require a greater concentration on ways of developing learner autonomy and meeting the requirements for 'lifelong learning'.

- Peters (1987) stressed the need for a dynamic view of change such that it became something that was catered for by the educational experience rather than resisted. The idea of the learning institution underpins the successful management of change and enhanced continuing professional development within our schools.
- Handy (1989) also argued for continuous learning, and learning organizations but his approach is through some 'upside-down thinking' about our approach to learning so that people can 'grow while they work'.

We have already noted that the ability to see learning as greater than the pursuit of knowledge and as a basis for living in a period of change has been summed up by Nisbet and Shucksmith (1986) as a 'seventh sense . . . metacognition [reflection], the awareness of one's mental processes, the capacity to reflect on how one learns, how to strengthen memory, how to tackle problems systematically – reflection, awareness, understanding, and perhaps, ultimately, control' (Nisbet and Shucksmith 1986: 8).

The development of metacognition requires breadth and diversity in learning. The National Commission on Education (1993) considered that the curriculum for the future will be dependent on a framework of values which

- motivates and challenges students through a variety of learning experiences
- challenges low expectations
- develops the range of intelligences or abilities in all students
- provides for progression whatever the ability level
- measures attainment.

This suggests that there is a need for balance between the traditional view of learning as knowledge and the development of a curriculum meeting the needs of every student and developing their capacity to learn. Hargreaves (1994) believes that differentiation is the key to achieving the framework set out by the National Commission. This still poses a problem if it is assumed that the National Curriculum is the 'ration' for all students.

DISCUSSION POINT

- How is the need for learning for the twenty-first century recognized in a school known to you?
- What effect does this have on the attitudes of the individual class teacher?

Rowan High School is a five form entry secondary comprehensive
school which serves a clearly defined rural town. It has enjoyed
good relationships with the local community and has benefited from
considerable local financial help in preparing and then undertaking the
development of a joint use school and community arts and leisure
centre. The management committee of the centre has been in place for
nearly three years and is chaired by John Gray, the managing director of
a local manufacturing company employing about 80 full-time staff. Julie
Ferris, the headteacher, knows that he has been outspoken at a local
meeting about the quality of applicants for vacancies at 16+ under the
Modern Apprenticeships scheme. However, she asked him to be one of
three speakers talking to parents and students as part of a symposium
on 'preparing for the future – our way through the careers minefield'.
The other two speakers invited were Dr Golightly, a representative of
the university college in a neighbouring shire city, and Mrs James, the
local representative of the Community Health Trust.

On the evening the views expressed by the speakers could be
summarized as follows.

John Gray
Great concern about the way in which education is going. Students
seem to be spending longer at school with no obvious return to either
themselves, parents or employers. Students are now being prepared for
examinations which are so easy because all the course work is done first
and the amount of retained and applied knowledge is reduced. The
National Curriculum has undermined what you always learnt at school
and there will be enormous problems because the able students are
staying on at school and the least able are incapable of coping with the
numeracy and literacy skills required by the working world – especially
when they can't cope with imperial measures.

Dr Golightly
Not terribly worried about the issues raised by the first speaker because
industry is now getting considerable financial support to put reorganized
apprenticeship schemes into place. In his view we should be aiming to
provide all students with the key skills that will enable them – and the
UK – to survive. Would not press for any return to the computational
basics of a bygone age but do regret that so much of the time when a
youngster first goes to college is spent in socialization skills, preparation
for individual learning and helping the youngster to settle into new
routines and regimes. Wants more general education for most students
and later decision-making to avoid good material going into local
unchallenging employment at too early a stage.

Mrs James
Considered that the earlier speakers were commenting from their own
narrow needs. She believed in school as a preparation for life in the

community and was much more concerned that students understood what the world was about. This could then lead to a reduction in teenage parenting, to less inappropriate and unhappy placing in jobs, and to some enhancement of personal self-esteem. Students should be being groomed for success and not spend their formative years jumping through hoops.

These divergent views set Julie Ferris thinking about the rationale, processes and purposes of the curriculum as offered by her school. Conversations with the senior management team were not totally successful because they seemed incapable of separating the messages from the messengers. Julie was not prepared to accept this as a viewpoint because she wanted the staff to look at what was being done to move away from the subject based view of the curriculum to a 'curriculum for life'.

DISCUSSION POINT

- Assess the evidence for the existence of a 'curriculum for life' in your own, or an institution, known to you.
- How are community expectations recognized and acted upon?

The outlines of the issues raised at Rowan High School reflect the tensions evident in many governing bodies of secondary schools. At one extreme are those who remember with nostalgia the days of rote learning, limited problem-solving and didactic teaching assessed by frequent testing. At the other are those who feel that students are rather more concerned with acquiring the ability to learn rather than with the content of their learning. Current political pressure appears to favour the former in order that students may achieve set personal and institutional targets. Teachers fear that concentration on test and examination performance will inhibit both love of learning and the capacity to reflect on and use what has been learnt. The 'curriculum for life' cannot be easily defined although most teachers are able to outline the changing context for their work. Perhaps the most significant way forward for Rowan High is to develop further the principles outlined by Nias et al. (1992) to secure curriculum planning based upon

- supported professional development for teachers as learners
- within a context providing time for change to be assimilated
- against a background of agreement on fundamental values
- with understanding of the dynamic nature of external issues that can affect outcomes.

Knowledge, skills and attitudes

So much of the curriculum management debate is concerned with the development of a balanced view of the content of the curriculum. This can be seen as a package of knowledge, skills and the development of attitudes as a result of the application of knowledge and skills. Despite considerable efforts by the Qualifications and Curriculum Authority (QCA) there is a predominating public view that factual knowledge is still the only material that can be reliably assessed by external examination. This tension is a reflection of another of the great curriculum debates, that of our approach to the planning of what is being taught.

Lawton (1983, 1990) outlined five levels of curriculum decision-making – at national, regional (for example, LEA), institutional, departmental and individual levels. Interaction between pressures exerted by the five elements determines what occurs in classrooms and so we can argue that there is a certain residual discretion left to the teacher. The way in which this is exercised is determined in part by the curriculum planning model favoured by the teacher either as a result of previous experience, or of a preferred teaching style. In brief there are four types of curriculum models.

- *Linear*: developing from the thinking of Tyler (1949). He argued that curricular planning has four key dimensions. These are the specification of objectives, the planning of content to meet those objectives, the development of methods and learning experiences to support the content, and the evaluation of the learning that has taken place. This linear model offers a great deal to the classroom teacher but there are limitations. Kelly (1989) argues that this is too simple particularly because continuous evaluation may be used to modify future planning before the intended process comes to its end. Indeed this leads him to stress the interaction between all four elements in the Tyler model.
- *Behavioural*: developing from work undertaken by Bloom (1956). His focus was on behavioural objectives suggesting that the curriculum can and should be defined in terms of pre-specified and measurable changes in learner/student/pupil behaviour as a result of the learning experience. His taxonomy has been criticized for presenting a very narrow view of the teaching and learning process and its failure to do other than prescribe a series of hurdles to be trained for.
- *Cultural*: developing from the work of Skillbeck (1989) and concentrating on matching the curriculum to the needs of the social context of the school. This leads to an extended planning sequence including:

  - situational analysis – determining the context of the curriculum
  - goal formulation – setting objectives to meet the contextual needs
  - programme building – with an awareness of the learning capacity of the school community
  - interpretation and implementation – through the development of the learning experience,
  - monitoring, feedback, assessment and reconstruction.

Our observation of teachers at work has demonstrated that while the National Curriculum may be prescriptive, the cultural context is regarded as a fundamental element in 'knowing the needs of the students and the limited background for which we have to compensate' (Year 11 tutor, Sycamore).

- *Process*: developing from the work of Bruner (1966), and fundamental to the approaches developed by Stenhouse (1975). This aims to set learning within the needs of the whole curriculum but by recognizing the methodology of each subject area should offer real experience of a diversity of first-hand learning. The student thus becomes involved in experiences that are both relevant and extending from the acquisition of knowledge and skills to the development of attitudes. The process approach also considers 'learning outcomes' and 'objectives', but focuses on the development of intelligence rather than quantifiable knowledge. It thus links with participative teaching and learning methodologies. Process approaches are then, in effect, guidelines which may prove appropriate to specific contexts and learning needs. In essence they are concerned with the 'how' rather than the 'what' of people's learning. This presents a dilemma for those who feel that the process is more important than the measurable outcomes.

Check point and possible action		
The teaching shows a heavy use of factual material for all work	There is some need to learn factual material as the basis of other work	There is little factual learning because students know where to look for sources
Is this factual overload inhibiting understanding and reflection by students?	Is there a balance between learning facts and knowing where to find them?	How can this be compensated for when sources are not available?

The acquisition of factual knowledge is not necessarily wrong. One of the arguments of the traditionalists is that students lack the ability to recall important factual data without recourse to reference books or other sources, to work out arithmetical problems without the use of calculators, and to use scientific data such as the periodic table without reference to wall posters. The counter-argument is that our bank of knowledge is now so vast that it is better for students to know where to look for the detail they require rather than to be able to recall all but the frameworks of their learning.

The staff at Elm High School, serving a widespread community on the rural fringe of a prestigious university city, had become disillusioned by the 'constant sniping' from two of the governors, who argued that students were being disadvantaged because of the failure of the National Curriculum to provide 'a broad and balanced background with understanding of their classical heritage'. The evidence for this sprang from the annual administration of a General Knowledge Prize by these two academic worthies. The prize had been developed 30 years earlier from a bequest directed at the promotion of general knowledge in all pupils, and the terms of the bequest were such that it had to be designed for all students grouped according to age as junior, middle and senior school. The bank of questions had been developed by successive governors and was heavily biased towards theoretical science, classical mythology, English literature, art history and classical music.

Change was achieved following the resignation of one of the two governors on the grounds that he 'found it intolerable that he should be associated with the decline in standards in what was once a creditable school'. The headteacher persuaded the governors that the terms of the prize endowment prescribed only the organization and not the content of the annual competition. He suggested that the question-setting group should consist of one governor, one member of staff and the three students who had won the prize in the previous year. As a result the areas of knowledge were extended to include contemporary culture, sport and leisure, information technology and 'living in the locality'. The quiz papers were set into a new format by the ICT coordinator. It was also agreed that following the use of the elimination paper and the quiz final with four finalists in each age group conducted in a *University Challenge* style, the winners would take on a governors' team as part of the Annual Parents' Meeting.

The scores overall were at a higher level in 1999 than they had been in the previous decade; the interest in the competition was such that it has been proposed to make it a constructive part of the end of term arrangements in the Autumn term, and in the first meeting between students and governors the latter were defeated.

DISCUSSION POINT

- What does this tell us about the standard of education, the capacity of students, and the effectiveness of the school curriculum?

One of the arguments likely to emerge from this type of discussion is that there is a certain basic curriculum of knowledge and skills that should be available to all. The concept of the entitlement curriculum was developed alongside the organizational device of comprehensive schooling in order to minimize the disparity of educational experience that was emerging in a tripartite system where some were educated, some schooled and some contained. The debate continued as the National Curriculum evolved and, although seen originally as some cross-curricular themes to be developed whatever the subject, we have now moved from concepts of entitlement to the notion of key skills.

● Key skills

Key skills development was initially evident in the post-compulsory sector of education where there had been a concern from the 1960s onwards that there should be a general education element in all vocational education as shown by writers such as Dore (1976) and Hall (1981). In the years which followed there was further consideration of the transferability of skills in a reassessment of the aims and objectives of higher education as outlined by Coldstream (1994) and Scott (1995). The debate has affected all sectors of education following the report of the National Committee of Inquiry into Higher Education for the Twenty-First Century (Dearing 1997) with its emphasis on flexibility of learning arrangements and lifelong learning. The imperatives for considering the inclusion of key skills at all levels of lifelong learning had their origin in the vocational education arena. Since the mid-1990s the pressures for labour market competitiveness in a global economy (Keep and Mayhew 1996) have led to the view that they should be part of the curriculum for all. Together with the political view that enhanced educational achievement is a basic requirement for the improvement of school and society showed in both the National Curriculum and official expectations reflected in target setting, key skills is now firmly on the education policy agenda (Halpin and Troyna 1995; Esland 1996; DfEE 1997).

Key, basic or core skills have been variously defined (among others, for example, Moore and Hickox 1994; Tobin 1998) but definitions usually include basic skills such as literacy and numeracy; coping skills such as team working, problem-solving and technological awareness with particular emphasis on information technology. The pressure for these cross-curricular skills to develop alongside subject-specific National Curriculum objectives in schools has caused tensions evident in the history of curriculum development in the UK during the 1990s (Nuttall and Stobart 1994). The early years of National Curriculum implementation were characterized by concern for subject definition, content and delivery but with reference to cross-curricular themes which facilitated generic skills development, as explored by Gardner and McMullan (1990). This was subsequently reflected in the criteria by which the success of schools would be judged in terms of raising levels of pupil achievement in inspections carried out by Ofsted. By 1997 the DfEE stressed that 'key skills are the skills needed in a wide range of employment settings and for lifetime learning'. Although these skills are related to the National Curriculum the DfEE urged that they should reflect the application of skills in a realistic work setting. Defined to specific levels, they are structured into six categories:

- Communication (including oral and graphical communication)
- Application of number
- Information technology
- Improving one's own learning and performance
- Problem-solving
- Working with others.

Check point and possible action		
Opportunities have been developed so that skills are used in applied learning	Skills, once taught, cannot be revisited because of the pressure of the timetable	The incremental nature of learning in the subject precludes the need for much skills revision
How is this skill development progressively built on?	What opportunities exist to help those who might have experienced problems?	How can such skills development be monitored?

While annual Ofsted summary reports indicate that there is a growing awareness of the need for key skills development in schools (Ofsted 1998), evidence from individual school reports suggest that this is a slow and variable development. Where it has been developed four common elements emerge:

• There has been the use of forms of curriculum audit to ascertain how far subject departments are already contributing towards key skills coverage.
• There has been extensive use of materials such as those provided by the QCA as the basis for staff training.
• Strategies have been developed to involve an increased number of staff through pastoral activities and in individual assessment.
• There has been experimentation with some form of accreditation to give activities enhanced credibility with students and parents.

Consider the messages to staff and students emerging from the approaches being made to developing key skills in two schools. Your reflection might be helped by a framework based on the issues of equity and effectiveness explored in Chapter 3.

In Ferndale School there was a general staff perception that the use of key skills could be instrumental in raising the quality of pupil performance. The school was already working on this and it sought additional funding from the local Enterprise Council to allow a more extensive development within the school, and a more intensive engagement with departmental subject heads. This was intended to identify key skills opportunities across the curriculum, to embed these opportunities in teaching and learning, and thus to raise pupil performance. To this end there was sharing of interdepartmental good practice, departmental development planning to include the development and mapping of key skills, and an improved dialogue with the primary schools enhanced by INSET activities.

In Holly Lodge School the approach had been through a target group that has been selected in Year 11 from those underachieving, those with poor attendance, those whose general attitude seems poor and those who have not succeeded in the system. The focus of the curriculum for the group is to extend the delivery of key skills and their accreditation. The timetable for the group is run by the literacy coordinator and includes two days at school, one day at the college of further education, one day of work experience and one day of youth and community work. The aim is for accreditation at GCSE in English and maths and level 2 in IT GCSE/key skills which involves communication, problem-solving, literacy, numeracy and information technology.

Relevance and learning

It is possible that you will have considered that the first school is offering key skills to all as an entitlement and that the second school is using the approach in order to ensure involvement from a group of disaffected students with little impact on curricular development in the school as a whole. Kinder et al. (1995) have detailed strategies that have been successfully developed for work with disaffected students but there are messages in this work for the learning of all. Their analysis shows that the irrelevance of school to students, the prescriptive nature of much of the National Curriculum, and the consequent sense of failure arising from lack of success in assessment combine to promote what is often perceived as an inappropriate pedagogy. Positive response has been seen in six of our sample of secondary schools where three strategies have emerged to underpin relevance in teaching and learning.

- The completion of an audit of subject content and the potential for the integration of key skills and cross-curricular themes. This is illustrated in the development of an agreed curriculum for information and communications technology at Ash Grove School. This identifies the use of ICT in Year 9 to provide data logging in science, the use of databases in history, the use of computer aided design in design technology, and the development of spreadsheets for comparative work in geography. It has also been agreed that access to the internet will be used in English and religious education as a starting point for consideration of the issues of prejudicial writing and tolerance in society.
- The use of a relevance check as part of the annual review of the curriculum. This is shown at Holly Lodge School where the staff teaching each subject list those topics being taught in the coming term that could be enlivened by time spent in 'relevance discussion'. This is an opportunity for teacher and learner to 'indulge in a spell of reflective or reactive discussion to ensure that the students are aware of the importance of the principles emerging from their subject work for their future life'.

This has had the effect of enhancing teacher awareness of the pedagogic advantage especially in mathematics and science where 'the staff knew the significance of ideas but they had failed to cash in on them for the students' (professional development coordinator).

- The development of opportunities for the use of work from several subject areas into an occasional integrative activity highlighting cross-curricular themes. This is illustrated in the use of 'enrichment activities' at Oak Grove School. This arrangement, despite the strictures of the National Curriculum, allows for two hours each week to be spent in additional cross-curricular activities undertaken across age groups. Every member of staff is required to offer an enrichment activity for two of the three terms of the year. This provides an opportunity for staff to be released for professional development work in one of the three terms. Logistical arrangements are complex and demanding although the use of outside assistance and help from the local technical college relieves some of the pressure. The enrichment offer ranges from supported use of the 'Success maker' basic skills programme, through creative arts activities, practical environmental science, social awareness, and integrated classical studies, 'science for life', and local studies to accelerated learning in languages, science and mathematics. At the end of each term students complete an evaluation sheet. Besides reflecting on the activity undertaken and its quality, the students are required to note how the activity has helped their subject-based work. Because of the range of opportunities this may be specific, for example, 'I have now used my German to translate a business letter received at the factory' (Year 10 girl) or it may be more general. This is shown in the analysis offered by one Year 9 boy who wrote: 'although the work has helped my understanding of electrical impulses I have applied the theory to develop a piece of equipment for a handicapped person (technology), researched the market need for this (business studies) and prepared the necessary handbook for its use (English)'.

Check point and possible action		
Teaching is enlivened by efforts to relate learning to everyday life	There is occasional consideration of the everyday relevance of learning	Little of the subject material can be related to outside issues
How is this related to cross-curricular themes to ensure that there is not overlap with other subject areas?	Is this seen as a teaching variant rather than as an integrated way of thinking?	Has an audit been undertaken comparing the syllabus with key skills and cross-curricular opportunities?

● **Issues**

Whatever the strategies that may be adopted to enhance relevance students seem more ready than their teachers to recognize that there can be times when the link to real life issues needs to be made. This is by extension from the subject-linked work to a consideration of the greater issues in society. The opportunity for pedagogic change to promote this is limited by national constraints. If learning is to be effective it is necessary to provide a coherent curriculum experience for pupils and students. However, it has been argued by Her Majesty's Inspectorate (HMI) and others that a wholly subject-based curriculum is not necessarily the best way of ensuring coherence.

The Education Reform Act 1988 takes up this focus, requiring all (maintained) schools to provide 'a balanced and broadly based curriculum', which

- 'promotes the spiritual, moral, cultural, mental and physical development of pupils at the school and of society' and
- 'prepares such pupils for opportunities, responsibilities and experiences of adult life'.

(DES 1988: 2)

This led to 'two essential and complementary perspectives'. First, that achieved through areas of learning and experience, and second, through the elements underpinning the learning process. The nine areas of learning are concerned with the aesthetic and creative; the human and social; linguistic and literary; mathematical; moral; physical; scientific; spiritual; and technological. The four elements of learning are focused on knowledge; concepts; skills; and attitudes. In addition, HMI pointed to seven 'essential issues' which need to be included in the curriculum, but not necessarily contained within subject confines: cross-curricular issues such as environmental education, health education, information technology, political education, and education in economic understanding. These aspects of the entitlement curriculum were subsequently largely incorporated into the National Curriculum through two dimensions (equal opportunities, multiculturalism); six skills (communication, numeracy, study, problem-solving, personal/social issues and information technology); and five themes (economic and industrial understanding, careers education/guidance, health education, education for citizenship, and environmental education). While this is translated into the detail of the National Curriculum and the five themes appear as part of the personal, health and social education (PHSE) programme in schools it is clear that students have varying perceptions of the value of this work. These perceptual differences are related both to the organization of cross-curricular teaching and to the attitudes of those who are undertaking the work.

DISCUSSION POINT

- What is the relationship, if any, between the entitlement curriculum and the theory of multiple intelligences?
- How can the entitlement curriculum be differentiated?

Check point and possible action		
'Real world' issues are used to illustrate and develop learning points	Some reference is made to the world beyond school	The syllabus is such that subject matter rarely relates to issues in the wider world
Is there opportunity for discussion of alternative viewpoints?	Is there any way in which this can underpin the development of attitudes?	Are there missed opportunities for active learning?

It is possible that most teachers use the opportunities presented in subject teaching to extend the thinking of the students and to enhance awareness of those issues that affect society. In doing so they may be influenced by their own views on the purposes of education. More complex typologies exist (for example, Preedy 1989) but the basic distinction is that offered by Davis (1976), who offers three approaches to the curriculum:

- The *Classical* perspective is autocratic in nature, with an emphasis on teacher-dominated, subject-based, class teaching characterized by discipline, certainty and competition.
- The *Romantic* perspective is laissez-faire in its relationship between teacher and learner with an emphasis on individualized learning, holistic and method based approaches leading to discovery, cooperation and a self-directed freedom.
- The *Liberal* perspective takes this further and is marked by participative learning within flexible learning groups, offering process and experience and directed at self-fulfilment in an unstructured way.

There are many voices urging that their particular interest be included within an already overloaded curriculum and some degree of selectivity is essential. The importance of awareness of issues that will affect the future lives of students is but part of the curriculum – there is also need for opportunities for the exercise of skills that are fundamental to life in a democratic society (Ranson 1994; Avis et al. 1996). Where a teacher favours one curricular perspective rather than another the opportunities for consideration of the broader issues and the pedagogy of cross-curricular teaching differs. This can be seen in the reaction of students to the PHSE at Hazel School.

The PHSE programme at Hazel School has been developed by Jane Carter, one of the senior teachers with responsibility for careers education in the school. She was concerned at the way in which her own programme was being squeezed into three lessons per year for the students of Years 9, 11 and 13 and at the reaction of students who saw the work as 'add-on' to subject work. The school had had a programme of PHSE education taught by three colleagues drawn from history, religious education and mathematics working with a colleague teaching home economics, who had been given a responsibility post to organize the PHSE programme. Every teaching group had one hour of PHSE per week but this also included time for religious education taught by that member of staff on a cyclic basis. This was far from satisfactory because the staff concerned saw their commitments as minimal and the limited time allocation and non-examination nature of the course offered little in the way of challenge to the students. Most of the teaching was transmissive with widespread use of worksheets, and it was clear that the work was having little impact.

This had been highlighted in the report of the Ofsted inspection that had noted the inadequacy and lack of challenge in both the programme and the teaching for PHSE. Jane Carter realized that the fundamental problem was one of an overly factual programme presented with few opportunities for interpersonal interaction – discussion was minimal and the development of attitudes was low on the list of priorities for those undertaking the teaching. She asked for an opportunity to make a presentation to the senior management group and proposed:

- that the mode of delivery of the PHSE programme should be changed to involve all staff
- that the poorly used tutorial period each day should be lengthened, incorporated into the assembly programme, and used as the teaching and learning opportunity for PHSE
- that there should be one day of in-service time in each of two preparatory terms to establish the principles and content framework for the new PHSE course
- that the course should be managed by herself and the seven year heads.

This was received with some apprehension because of the apparent erosion of time from the main curriculum and the protestations of lack of expertise from staff in all subject areas. However, after persuasive negotiation and the promise of sufficient resources it was agreed that the scheme would be introduced in a staged way over three years. The agreed scheme was based on a PHSE syllabus for all years, the use of a weekly assembly period to introduce or conclude a topic, the development of an extensive library of source books, teaching materials, and audio-visual aids, and the offer of ICT facilities on a pre-booked basis.

After three years of operation an independent observer undertook an evaluation. He concluded that the scheme had been successful for three main reasons:

- The staff felt that they had gained from a new purpose in the tutorial periods and the year heads had reported less misbehaviour in both tutorial periods and assemblies.
- The students generally felt that they were given a better opportunity to discuss issues with staff who knew them as people rather than students.
- The staff also felt that they had gained from the sharing of the PHSE curriculum and that there had been some carry-over of discussion into regular subject teaching.

DISCUSSION POINT

- Is there scope for the use of different curriculum perspectives according to the Davis (1976) model based on the purpose and content of intended learning?

Recapitulation

Approaches to teaching also impact upon the whole curriculum in so far as students do need opportunities to revise their work and to consolidate their learning. The same topic can be taught in two different ways to ensure that learning is complete and that the teacher has recognized the variation in preferred learning styles. In the open comment of the audit used as the basis of this research some 20 per cent of those noting their likes in their learning experience noted that teachers were prepared to go over work to ensure that it was understood. Some of the sample schools have recognized the need for re-capitulation as part of their teaching and learning policy. This may be achieved:

- by revisiting the topic on a planned basis
- by returning to a topic as the basis of building higher level learning in a cyclic fashion, or
- by providing 'learning clinics' to cater for individualized learning needs.

Check point and possible action		
There are frequent opportunities for recapitulation of work	Recapitulation is used when it is clear that detail and principles have not been understood	Once the topic has been covered there is very little time for revision
Is this developed in different ways to ensure that learning needs are matched?	How can this be routinely developed as part of the cycle of work?	Could this be overcome by the use of concentric approaches to learning?

There is evidence that this is now being seriously managed as schools develop strategies to enable them to achieve higher attainment levels especially for students who are at a borderline level in some or all subject areas. Practice varies from school to school but the following extract from the student planner at Oak Grove School shows recognition of the diversity of learning needs.

You will have spent some time with your tutor establishing the way in which you think that you learn most satisfactorily. These are not either/ or: there is some need for all learning styles but it might help you to apply your favoured style to your revision.

Visual learners
Use charts, maps and diagrams to summarize the facts you need to remember
Use highlighting for the subject notes you are using
Illustrate your ideas as a pictorial bubble before you write them into an essay
Put the main points onto a computer file and then précis this in successive revisions
Turn information into mind pictures to help you memorize material

Auditory learners
Discuss the materials with a colleague of similar learning style
Use a tape recorder as an aid and then play back to listen to the material
Develop mnemonics to help with lists of data
Dictate your thinking to a colleague or an adult
Develop verbal descriptions of ideas

Tactile learners
Have two or three topics under revision at the same time and switch from one to another so that ideas are kept fresh
Use bright colours to highlight material
Develop the use of posters or models to illustrate the main points of your work
Use differing ICT approaches to summarize your work, for example, spreadsheets, diagrams
Skim read material to get an idea of the drift before you settle down to thorough reading.

This does not mean that you will automatically learn. Some detail is more complex than other, and not all ideas can be expressed in other than verbal forms but you will find that if you try to use approaches that suit your style you may make more progress.

Remember that each subject department has developed support materials for each major topic – these include visual, auditory and tactile resources that can be used at Homework Club. One good hour with the learning style that suits you best may be worth three hours of rote learning for many people.

So far we have not made any distinction between boys and girls in the approach that they show to learning. In Chapter 9 we shall consider research that indicates that it is important to reconcile curriculum and learning needs with the differing capacities to learn.

Further reading

You will have realized that much of the curriculum debate took place before the passing of the Education Act 1988. Our references lead you to these sources. You might like to follow through the arguments about the impact of new technologies on what is learnt and how it should be learnt in

Paechter, C., Preedy, M., Scott, D. and Soler, J. (eds) (2000) *Knowledge, Power and Learning.* London: Paul Chapman.
Crombie-White, R. (1997) *Curriculum Innovation: A Celebration of Classroom Practice.* Buckingham: Open University Press offers more examples of good practice.

And to start the internet trail we suggest that you use curriculum as a keyword with the BIDS or ERIC search machines. There is a good investigative material with a thoroughly practical slant at http://www.qca.org.uk/menu.htm and helpful ideas on the use and development of key skills, although often with a higher education slant, are available at http:// www.namss.org.uk/studysk.htm and http://www.keyskills net.org.uk.

9 Gender awareness

Attainment

There has been much media concern at the apparent disparity of achievement between boys and girls at the end of secondary education in the UK. Sukhnandan (1999) stresses, however, that boys are not attaining less than in the past but that they have been outstripped by the gains made by girls. There is, though, some danger in the use of generalized statistics and our research showed that while there was little difference between boy and girl perceptions of effective teaching and learning overall, in five of the ten schools we surveyed there were markedly more disillusioned boy students. This points to the possibility that there might be social and cultural differences that affect attitude to learning. Arnot et al. (1998) demonstrate that while white girls are surpassing white boys from similar professional and intermediate social groups, Asian and African Caribbean boys consistently outperform girls. It seems therefore, that the gender question has to be seen within the social context of the school and strategies for enhanced student performance should be addressing cultural attitudes as well as gender issues.

Nevertheless, research by Cohen (1997) suggests that boys may have been underperforming for a very long period. She suggests that this is because of failures by the teaching profession. Her analysis is based upon consideration of the interplay of internal factors, for example, innate intelligence, and external factors such as the teaching methods being used at any one time. In the past boys' achievement has been attributed to elements of their make-up, and their failure to respond has been linked to the learning situation. By contrast girls' achievement has been attributed to their response to elements of the learning situation or other external factors, rather than to the internal factors that constitute individual make-up. If this is so it can, and has been, argued that the boys' failure is attributable to defects in teaching method, and girls' failure to lack of innate ability. The current emphasis on securing better results for boys is thus directed at teaching method and this could be directing resources at changing methods rather than at considering whether internal features of the male persona need re-examination.

DISCUSSION POINT

- Think back over your own educational experience. Did the attitude of teaching staff reflect an unconscious difference in treating boys and girls?
- How far do your own attitudes fit with Cohen's hypothesis?

Sukhnandan (1999) suggests that there are a number of factors to be considered in explaining gender differences in attainment. These include the following.

- The development of the National Curriculum as a framework directing all students to follow the same subjects rather than allowing for individual choice which for many boys had given a curriculum with a heavier practical content.
- The assessment of the learning process through assignments rather than straightforward acquisition of knowledge tested by terminal exams generally requires the more sequential learning patterns favoured by girls.
- Teacher attitudes appear to militate against boys because they tend to be more hostile but favour girls in that they generally have higher expectations of what can be achieved.
- There is evidence that there is an 'anti-intellectual, anti-educational and anti-learning culture among boys' (Sukhnandan 1999: 11). This may be attributable to early home and school experiences in a female-dominated environment but could also be related to the development of masculine identity.
- The attitude of boys and girls to school work and school life differ. Boys favour active learning, have lower standards of behaviour and offer more disciplinary challenge than girls. By contrast girls have higher self-expectation and work harder to compensate for what they believe are personal inadequacies.
- The process of socialization differs. Girls tend to be more conditioned to sit still and to listen or play quietly as infants while boys are encouraged to be active and many find that the first few months of primary schooling challenge developed behaviours. This leads to disillusionment with the school experience: many adverse attitudes appear to develop from this stage of education and undermine self-confidence and self-esteem.

The respondents to our research were asked to state what they liked and disliked about learning and their school experiences (Table 9.1). The differences between the boys and the girls are not as great as recent media reports suggest. Boys are more ready than the girls to list features of their favourite subjects and clearly have some preferred subject areas (mathematics, science, ICT); girls are slightly more positive about relationships with students and teachers. We considered the figures for the five schools where there was a marked discrepancy between positive scoring for girls and boys. Of these two were in areas where social and cultural factors played a large part in determining attitudes – a strong macho culture in the world beyond school clearly

Table 9.1 Gender and the learning experience (percentage responses n = 2256)

Criteria	Boys like	Girls like	Boys dislike	Girls dislike
Subject specific work	42	20	25	18
Verbal work	5	7	22	10
Group work	9	13	1	3
Homework	3	3	6	12
Teacher relationships	5	7	14	11
Student relationships	22	26	4	3

led to an anti-school male peer pressure. In the other three schools, gender issues are being considered as part of a strategic drive to secure enhanced achievement overall. Three of the remaining schools, all with a GCSE pass rate at A–C grade of over 60 per cent, showed very little male–female attainment difference and of these only one was applying specific measures to support boys' learning.

● Awareness

One of the most significant features of all successful teaching is that the teacher is aware of the learner's needs. These may emerge from continuous assessment of progress but our research shows that there is an enormous disparity in the figures of positive boy and girl responses in some schools with boys clearly less happy with their learning experiences. This suggests that in these schools teachers have not yet examined the impact of gender differences on the learning process. At Poplar School where boys' performance levels had been the subject of monitoring and positive intervention over the previous four years it was felt that student teachers would gain from this awareness and the development of monitoring techniques.

As part of a programme of understanding whole school issues, all PGCE students who train at Poplar School, as part of an initial teacher training programme, undertake a unit on Gender Issues. Specifically these examine how gender as an issue needs to be understood, positively acted upon and in some instances used as a tool to motivate and develop pupils.

Mapping teacher interaction within a mixed gender class
A useful starting point in getting students to recognize gender awareness as an issue is through an exercise that seeks to map the interaction between teacher and students within the course of a lesson. The observer draws a layout of the class with all the pupils noted as simply a 'B' (boy) or 'G' (girl) in the places where they are sitting. Every time the teacher interacts with any of the students during the course of a lesson, one of three marks is noted against that pupil. It will be either '+', indicating

that some positive interaction has taken place, for example, verbal praise or other positive recognition such as 'how are you?' If it is a neutral, such as 'have you got your book?' then the mark would be '0'. Any negative interaction, such as a verbal telling off, would be noted by the mark '–'.

Frequently traditional stereotypes emerge with minorities of 'naughty' boys dominating negative interaction and large clusters of girls, often having remained focused and on task through much of the lesson, with little or no interaction having taken place at all with the teacher. The point of this exercise is to demonstrate the range and type of interaction between teacher and taught. The usual outcome is for teachers to try to interact more positively with the motivated but largely forgotten girls. They often still find themselves persisting with the negative interaction with boys. The real challenge with this type of exercise is for student teachers to recognize that motivating boys can best be achieved through very positive 'stroking' and genuine and consistent use of praise. Once this is achieved, more sophisticated strategies for motivating boys such as, for example, greater use of visual stimuli and strict boundaries to written work can be put in place.

Gender learning preferences
When teachers in training have been made aware of the nature of teacher interactions they then consider the way in which an understanding of the preferred learning styles of boys and girls is increasingly influencing decisions made in the classroom by teachers. The methodology employed has to now take much greater note of the relative strengths and weaknesses of how girls and boys learn. As a generalization, teachers have to provide learning opportunities for boys that require short time-spans, have fixed parameters in terms of words written and time spent and utilize visual and diagrammatic stimulus. For girls, teachers need to provide opportunities for multi-tasking, more sustained study and more opened-ended assignments. The challenge facing all teachers is to meet the combined emotional, social and personal needs of both sexes and yet provide a diet of learning that directly meets specific strengths. To this end, the teacher in training then develops lesson plans that cater for the two learning styles simultaneously.

Gender and learning style

The traditional pattern of behaviour and attitudes presents boys as having less positive views of schoolwork and homework, low attention spans, poor behaviour and limited ability to respond to challenge. By contrast girls are more committed and better prepared for their work and show a realistic view of their capacity to cope with examination requirements (Warrington and Younger 1996). Such generalizations may lead to teacher attitudes that could be detrimental, for example, to boys who have a sense of pride in their work, or to girls who are responsive to challenge in practical activities and problem-solving in science. Murphy and Gipps (1999) stress that awareness of gender differences in learning should underpin the use of all teaching and learning strategies rather than lead to a separate pedagogy for each gender.

It may be that the specific subject curriculum has a determining effect on eventual achievement. Clark and Trafford (1995) examined the attitudes of boys and girls to learning modern languages and found that while the personality of the teacher was important for success, so too was the availability of gender appropriate learning materials. This accords with the view of Wragg (1997) and Bray et al. (1997), who note that boys prefer factual accounts while girls prefer fiction – but Ofsted (1996) notes that few teachers actually monitor the differences in boys' and girls' reading experiences. A further factor in modern languages and oral English work is connected with the ability of boys to handle risk in such lessons, fearing that they will suffer the embarrassment of failure.

Other subject areas do, however, encourage risk-taking in a different way. Boys are more ready to hazard an answer in mathematics, science and design technology situations. Whether this is because they view such areas as their rightful gender domain or because of different teacher relationships is not yet clear (Howe 1997; Pickering 1997). Rismark (1996) argues that success in any subject is the result of productive discourse between teacher and taught and it is possible that the attitude of the student reflects what they perceive to be the attitude of the teacher. A strong male role model prepared to suggest risk-taking as a feature of mathematics problem-solving is more likely to encourage boys and their consequent dominance of classroom discourse is likely to inhibit responses by girls.

MacDonald et al. (1999) stress that while there are a large number of classroom strategies based upon perceptions of the way in which boys learn there is, as yet, only limited evidence of gender-related preferences. They argue that there are often greater differences in attainment within a group of boys or a group of girls, than between boys overall and girls overall. However, there does seem to be support for the view that boys need to be more active, structured and short tasked in successful work strategies than girls who prefer a more verbal, open-ended and reflective approach to their work. It is not possible to offer a panacea for all gender-related learning ills but research shows that it is possible to cater for the learning preferences of most boys and most girls by developing lesson planning on the following premise:

Boys prefer:	Girls prefer:
Highly structured lessons	Opportunities to develop ideas
Teacher-led work	Self-developed learning
Clear objectives	Open-ended activities
Detailed instructions	Guidance but with freedom
Firm presentational requirements	Individuality in presentation
Clear and firm deadlines	Emotional literacy
Practical literacy	

Single-sex education

It has been argued that if boys and girls learn in different ways the most effective way of meeting these needs is through single-sex education, either in separate schools, or in separate teaching groups. Sukhnandan et al. (2000) present considerable evidence that boys prefer to work in such situations while girls are less happy to do so. Advantages accrued to boys and girls:

For the boys:	For the girls:
Subject content could be matched to their interests Competition increased motivation Male subject teachers became role models Boys felt that they were more valued Contributions were more readily made and less gender oriented Some improved behaviour and less distraction	Teachers were less involved in discipline matters Confidence and readiness to contribute were boosted

Single-sex classes or grouping have been used as a means of improvement in about 40 per cent of the LEAs investigated by Sukhnandan (1999) but there are ideological concerns that such arrangements may create an unreal learning experience. Just as the move to co-educational schooling was argued on the grounds that men and women would need to understand each other in adult life, it seems illogical to attempt to separate them in their adolescent one. The matching of boys with male staff in mixed schools was seen to exacerbate macho behaviour in social activities and the failure to gain the perspective of the views of the opposite sex was considered educationally unsound especially in those subjects where emotion and empathy are involved including English and history. Although there is evidence of high success rates in specific subject areas as a result of such strategies there are counter claims that low-attaining boys become even more disheartened and difficult when they see themselves established as a 'sink' group (Kinder et al. 1995).

The staff at Ivy High School have considered the balance of professed advantages and disadvantages. Their solution to perceived gender-related learning problems has been to create flexible arrangements so that staff can use different organizational arrangements as appropriate. Ivy High is a five form entry co-educational school working to a timetable constructed for half-year groups. As a result there are three or four groups from the same half-year in each faculty area at any one time. This allows maximum flexibility for departmental organization. Arrangements vary from subject to subject and from year to year.

Mathematics is taught in co-educational and mixed ability groups in Year 7 while students are following a totally individualized course. In Year 8 the three groups in each half-year are sorted by ability with a gender mixed 'top' group and separate boys and girls in two 'main' groups. At GCSE level the groups are again co-educational throughout but setted according to ability – the basis of this is the view that boys and girls have overcome gender-related problems by this stage.

In English teaching is in mixed ability co-educational groups for Years 7 and 8 although in each year students are given two opportunities to select literature that may be seen to be more attractive to boys than to girls and for these six-week periods the classes tend to be dominated by one gender. In Year 9 ability groups operate with the lowest group split into two for literacy support work. This is generally co-educational but from time to time this group is also split into boys and girls to develop themes of interest.

The development of ICT skills is seen as fundamental to all work. Experience has shown that boys come from primary school with superior attitudes to the use of computers and associated technology and so for Year 7 boys and girls are separated for teaching. This overcomes problems of lack of confidence expressed by many of the girls and offers opportunities for challenge to many of the boys. In Years 8 and 9, although the classes are co-educational the students work on personal portfolios in same-sex pairs and are thus able to complete work without overt competition between boys and girls.

The importance of personal work portfolios also underpins much of the work in science. There are four groups in each half-year with teachers drawn from biology, environmental science, chemistry and physics backgrounds. The work is organized as six half-term modules. These are taught in a totally flexible way – traditional class groups, separate boys' and girls' groups, and increasing elements of choice allowing for the needs of the individual, the group and the topic at any one time.

Student support systems

The variety of strategies seen in use here demonstrates that there is no one answer to gender-related teaching and learning issues. We have argued throughout that there is a need for differentiation according to the capacities and preferences of the individual – and these vary from boy to boy and girl to girl. Schools that have been successful in developing differentiation rely heavily upon pastoral support for academic progress. In the schools with which we have worked three strategies have been evident.

Individual tutorial work

This offers opportunities for all students to reflect on the work they have done. Macdonald et al. (1999) stress the importance of regular personal interviews for setting targets. These may be results related to, for example, the achievement of over half marks in the work in all subjects in the following review period, or skills related, for example, through developing the ability to use particular computer competencies within a set period. Targets alone are of little value unless assessment and monitoring systems are used to spot weaknesses and to ascertain both the cause and possible remediation. It is possible that these weaknesses are not sufficiently serious to warrant special educational help but simply some deficiency in a key skill that needs to be challenged by restructuring an approach such as to problem-solving, or a learning technique such as spellings involving 'gh'.

Mentoring

This offers help by providing an opportunity for students to share their learning experiences with somebody who is outside the immediate learning situation. The pattern varies from school to school. Within the research group we have seen paired mentoring with a more senior student of the same sex, voluntary adult help, and mentoring by a teacher who is not a subject teacher or tutor to the student. Sukhnandan et al. (2000) see the advantages arising from improved relationships including enhanced self-confidence, self-esteem and motivation, and note the encouragement that such a system gives to self-responsibility for learning and career development. Disadvantages arise when the mentor has not been fully and appropriately trained, when there may be insufficient time for what is essentially a counselling role, and where there is instability, for example, as a result of an adult volunteer failing to attend meetings regularly. Initially schools have been concerned that student–student mentoring may show all these problems but successful schemes are in place.

> At Ivy High School senior pastoral staff have embarked on the process of using positive role models from higher up the school to work with students who might be underperforming and beginning a downward spiral of demotivation. These are identified in Year 8 by using CAT scores that indicate a potential for borderline achievement in future GCSE examinations. Too often, though, this particular strategy has been dominated by male mentoring of younger boys, as a response to addressing the national underachievement of boys, and there is now a feeling that the scheme should be available to all students who would benefit from help. Much more could be done with underachieving but compliant girls who do not surface in staff thinking as needing support.
>   The format of the mentoring programme takes the form of arranging a series of meetings between the students during PSHE time. The older students have attended a series of training sessions with a member of

the senior management team previously. This has involved knowing
how to steer a meeting towards looking at the strengths and weaknesses
of the younger students' school experience and then moving towards
setting targets that are SMART (specific, measurable, achievable, realistic
and time-bound). These meetings take place every four weeks over a
period of two terms and while formal mentoring may cease at this stage,
informal contacts have continued.

Evaluation takes the form of a questionnaire sent to the teachers of the
Year 8 students. Specifically it asked if the subject teachers had noticed
any significant improvement in attitude and motivation. The results from
this were mixed. The quality of the dialogue and commitment from both
parties in the meetings is absolutely critical. However, there were several
cases where the right combination was found when an articulate and
dedicated mentor was paired with a Year 8 student and subject teachers
noted some significant improvement. Further development of the scheme
hinges upon refining the training of mentors and building bridges
between the mentors who can establish the needs of the younger
students but who lack the ability to alert staff to potential problems.

Additional literacy support

We are aware that boys are generally less attracted to verbal learning and
that the development of reading and the use of language is fundamental to
securing overall improvement (for example, School Curriculum and Assessment Authority (SCAA) 1996; Arnold 1977). This may, in part, be explained
by external social factors. Powney (1996) shows how the 'cultural capital of
the home' enhances achievement in both boys and girls because of the
nature and content of language use but this may be countered by the tendency of boys to develop ICT capabilities from a very early age and their
involvement in video- or computer-based activities rather than absorption in
reading for pleasure (Bray et al. 1997). If this is so, then it is likely that
additional literacy support can be a compensatory provision within schools.
Sukhnandan et al. (2000) show that this is effective where resources are
directed at enhancing self-confidence in literacy rather than working directly
on the mechanics of reading. Under these circumstances, and providing a
contact that is not seen to be authoritarian in the way that a teacher is,
volunteer adult help has been successfully used and contacts have been
developed into a general mentoring role. This has been especially productive
where male mentors have supported boys but there is evidence of similarly
successful work with girls. Recruitment and training of suitable reading
volunteers is imperative. Topping (1986) points out that this is more likely to
be a problem in disadvantaged schools thus exacerbating a problem for the
boys. Reading alone is insufficient for success. Those who come from culturally deprived backgrounds, whether boys or girls, need opportunities to talk
about what they have read, to assess the implications of new expressions and
vocabulary, and to develop a reflective stance to new knowledge and ideas.
At Holly Lodge School a mentoring system for younger students aged 11–13

has been built around the need to hear reading and it is seen by the deputy headteacher as 'an opportunity to give some structure to the mentoring process so that the students don't feel that they are having to talk about generalities – there is something for them to focus on, and a measurable output'.

DISCUSSION POINT

- Is the consideration of techniques for the improvement of gender-related learning problems any different from that for students with behavioural, specific learning or physical disabilities?

School organization

Although we have concentrated on the application of enhancement strategies for individual students it is evident that schools that have been successful in developing the learning abilities of both boys and girls have done so as the result of whole school policies. These usually include three elements.

Staff professional development

This has been most successful where an evolutionary process of problem-stating, problem-solving and implementation has been followed. The starting point has been action research into differences in gender achievement. The material for this has emerged from senior staff consideration of student achievement and the use of CAT results on entry, and GCSE results at age 16 to determine the potential and actual results. The identification of discrepancies then leads to consideration of the ways in which attitudes to boys and girls differs.

At Ash Grove School this was an uncomfortable process because it touched many staff on a raw nerve. The school, formerly a traditional grammar school, had developed its ethos from that origin. There was high respect for learning; strong competitive sport for the boys, and musical activities for the girls; ability grouping arrangements for all years, and a curriculum that favoured the more academic students.

When the staff met to consider the emerging disparity between boys' and girls' examination achievements the immediate observation from a group of male staff was that 'the boys need to be kicked into action . . . the school has got too soft'. This was challenged by two of the younger female staff who urged that 'not all boys are the same and some need more gentle encouragement' and 'there are some for whom the macho image creates considerable unhappiness'. When the battle lines had thus been drawn it was clear that there were underlying problems. These included resentment by the women staff that most of the men took part in inter-school staff football or cricket matches on Friday evenings and then adjourned to a local bar with the male deputy headteacher; a feeling that the girls were always put into the situation of 'doing the housekeeping bit for any school function', and that 'there is more to life than academic success and some boys need to get their encouragement on the rugby field'.

The headteacher was aware that some constructive way forward had to be found and gained the agreement of the staff to the use of an attitudinal survey that had been developed to test opinion on the way in which boys and girls were treated within a community. On the basis of the report the head proposed that the values of the school should be re-examined and that only when that had been satisfactorily achieved could strategies for improvement for all students be suggested. The report showed that the girls perceived that they were fulfilling gender stereotypes and that the attitudes of male staff were such that the girls felt embarrassed by the way in which the boys were treated. It was a surprise to a hard core of male staff when the boys' results showed that they felt that they were treated in a rough way by many male staff and indulged by some female staff. Possibly more likely to affect long-term results was the fact that both boys and girls objected to the way in which they were streamed into classes at the beginning of Year 7 and moved from these groups only in most extreme cases. In the words of one boy 'once labelled you are there for good so what's the use of trying', and of one girl 'there just is no way you can be yourself – girls don't do some subjects and that is that!'

It was subsequently agreed that the common values of the staff of the school would be restated as:

- We value all students irrespective of ability, gender and individual personality.
- We recognize that the staff are the biggest influence on student attitude and determine to offer role models that are non-threatening and do not reinforce traditional stereotypes.
- We recognize that students change over time and agree to consider how we can provide greater flexibility in learning approaches and arrangements.
- We recognize that there is an entitlement curriculum for all students and that this should be experienced, as far as ability allows, irrespective of gender or handicap.

DISCUSSION POINT

- The conclusions may have taken the school some way along a road to improvement but there are still potential problems. What do you consider these to be?

Translating philosophies into action

Your discussion of the issues arising at Ash Grove School may have led you back to the tension between reality and rhetoric. How can a statement from the staff really change the way in which they act over a period of time? The generation of policies was the next move undertaken at Ash Grove School. The provision of a clearly stated and consistently applied policy for behavioural management was regarded as a starting point. Glover and Cartwright (1998) showed that this requires all staff to abide by the rules and that the fundamental issues need to be revisited by both staff and students from time to time, for example, frequent reminders about anti-bullying procedures appear essential if the fundamental value is not to be lost. The staff at Ash Grove School also reconsidered the way in which ability grouping 'had become a God' and after some consideration favoured an alternative that allowed subject setting within half-year groups thus allowing all students in Years 7, 8 and 9 to be in different ability based sets for each subject (see also Warrington and Younger 1996). There was also considerable support for a recasting of the PHSE programme and the use of a tutorial group system which in the view of the headteacher 'forced the reactionary staff to consider some of the issues that we wanted the students to face'.

Involving other stakeholders

Ofsted (1996) note the importance of developing boys' perceptions of themselves and their attitudes to their future life if they are to achieve any success. It is possible that schools are taking too much of the blame and that other stakeholders need to be involved in changing stereotypical attitudes. Randall (1996) deals with the hold that local cultures can have upon school-based attitudes – in this case demonstrating how boys are encouraged to retaliate when faced with aggression. Pickering (1997) shows how both role model compliance and peer pressure impact upon boys and inhibit any determination to move out of their perceived ability or cultural grouping. Unfortunately, some schools report that the involvement of members of the local community as governors and voluntary helpers has not always been successful especially when they bring with them prejudices that reinforce traditional attitudes. One of the pastoral staff at Oak Grove School commented: 'we hoped that having the managing director of a local firm as a mentor would give something of an uplift to Tim Lazenby – unfortunately the views he put forward just convinced Tim of his own inadequacies and he retreated further into his shell'. The school was so concerned with prevailing attitudes within a relatively isolated decaying industrial area that it decided to challenge prejudice by meeting it head-on and organizing a series of work-based visits for students but asking the senior managers of the local firms to allow the students to make a presentation on 'Why sex doesn't matter'. The preparation of the presentation allowed the students to explore issues that were then discussed in a wider arena.

In the final analysis though it is the attitude of the student that needs to be changed. MacDonald et al. (1999) urge that this should be achieved

- by taking note of the views of students so that they feel genuinely empowered within their educational setting
- by reviewing curriculum, pedagogy and ethos from the student perspective to facilitate their empowerment and provide a stimulating educational diet and context.

These are required for all students and the underlying message is that all students want to be valued, individually supported and appropriately taught if they are to be successful.

Further reading

There is a great deal of helpful information and good practice in

Sukhnandan, L., Lee, B. and Kelleher, S. (2000) *An Investigation into Gender Differences in Achievement Phase 2*. Slough: NFER.

Murphy, P.F. and Gipps, C. (1999) *Equity in the Classroom*. London: Institute of Education/Unesco present research findings and offers detailed practice changes.

The male perspective is developed in

Martino, W. and Pallotta-Chiarolli, M. (2002) *So What's a Boy: Addressing Issues of Masculinity and Schooling*. Buckingham: Open University Press.

And to start the internet trail, and in addition to the DfES sites we suggest that http://www.scre.ac.uk/rie/n142bamford.html will provide information on considerable gender-related work within Scotland. Considerable bibliographic material exists at www.ed.gov/offices/ODS/g-equity.html but much of this stems from work in the USA.

10 Making a difference

Change in the classroom

The contrast between the questionnaire results in the ten schools in the sample and the comparison of these with other outcome indicators suggests that the teachers are facing two groups of management issues. Simply, these are the factors that can be changed, and those which can't. Resourcing, the limitations of classrooms built in an earlier period, and the curriculum demands which inhibit more adventurous teaching and stimulating learning fall into the first category, but by far the greatest number of features of teaching and learning commented upon can be managed within the classroom. These can be addressed by leadership within the school, by the enhancement of the teacher as leader in the classroom and through staff development activity. These external and internal factors are illustrated by the recent history of Birch Grove School.

> Birch Grove was opened as a purpose-built secondary comprehensive school in the late 1960s and quickly established a local reputation as the school that got results. The school recruited from a wide area of a metropolitan district including a balance between the suburban green fringe and extensive council estates. Industrial decline in the area led to migration of many of the families who had developed a link with the school and the advent of grant-maintained schools within easy travelling distance put further pressures on recruitment. Within a decade the school roll has halved and the local concentration has increased to the extent that 87 per cent of the students come from two areas of social housing. The school has experienced severe financial problems as the roll has fallen, part of the buildings has been leased to an industrial group, and the general atmosphere is one of dereliction. During the 1990s the proportion gaining five or more GCSE A–C grades has dropped from 36 per cent to 5 per cent and the school now has a severe truancy

problem. Not surprisingly the school has been described as needing 'special measures' as a result of a recent Ofsted inspection.

A newly appointed headteacher has led efforts to change the culture from one of fatalistic acceptance to one of determination to succeed although this is difficult given existence under the special measures regime with frequent visits from LEA advisers and Ofsted inspectors. However, there is now much more open discussion of difficulties between the headteacher and the staff and a feeling of cooperative activity is evident in that policies have been reviewed, subject areas have been grouped to allow for better use of resources and the sharing of expertise, and development plans have evolved cooperatively with whole school and subject objectives reconciled. The school is developing systems of target setting and benchmarking but it is indicative of the slow pace of cultural change that these are not yet shared with the students. Much effort is being put into encouraging greater parental involvement in the life and expectations of the school and efforts are being made to improve community perceptions of the extra-curricular work undertaken by some students.

Nevertheless there is a continuing problem of student disaffection. This arises in part from a hierarchical grouping system, but appears also to be related to the perceived pressures to achieve a higher level of GCSE grades through essentially didactic teaching with a higher than normal level of rote learning. There is also evidence that inter-family problems that have their origin outside the school spill over into school life and create difficulties for the staff. The falling roll has meant that some of the more experienced and effective teachers have taken early retirement; for some staff this is providing leadership opportunities, for others the excuse to do only the minimum until they can move elsewhere.

There are pockets of success within the school – bright and tidy subject rooms, orderly student behaviour, and increased GCSE pass rates in three subject areas. For the headteacher the problem is one of 'ensuring that all do as well as the best'.

DISCUSSION POINT

- How can a subject teacher achieve change within this context?
- How can the views of the external community be changed?

Your response to this may be less than positive but there are indications that change can be achieved. To do so involves consideration of

- self-awareness of the teacher as the learning leader in the classroom
- the availability and nature of continuing professional development to support this work
- the ability to reflect on the use of pedagogy and practice in different learning contexts.

New leadership in the classroom

In Chapter 1 we briefly outlined some of the theories of leadership and mentioned the tension between the transactional – 'if you do this then I will do that' – and the transformational – 'let's get this done together', approaches. These do not apply just to the way in which a headteacher works with the staff. It also applies to the relationships within the classroom. Stoll and Fink (1996) argue that in a period of change and in an uncertain external context, when policies and resource allocation can be affected by developments outside the organization, transformational leadership that concentrates on the people rather than the task is more likely to be successful. This certainly fits into the classroom situation where the personalities and known capabilities of up to 30 participants have to be taken into account in the planning and completion of tasks. This requires a people-centred approach, the sharing of objectives, and the building of relationships to secure these. It also requires that those being led know the way in which the leader is working. This leads to consideration of what has become called 'invitational' leadership.

Purkey and Novak (1990) speak of positive interactions between one person and another as invitations, and negative interaction as disinvitations. Effective teachers use invitational leadership – possibly without realizing it – in the messages they give to their students. Stoll and Fink (1996) suggest that these invitational messages should be characterized by

- *optimism*: recognizing and encouraging the achievement of potential
- *respect*: recognizing individuality but encouraging differing viewpoints
- *trust*: developing relationships based upon openness and integrity.

In analysing the professional characteristics of successful teachers Hay McBer (2000) refer to 'the deep seated patterns of behaviour which outstanding teachers display more often, in more circumstances, and to a greater degree of intensity than effective colleagues'. While we are not concerned with assessing the difference between the outstanding and the effective teacher we are concerned with the development of work habits that strengthen an invitational climate. The Hay McBer characteristics of respect for others, challenge and support, and confidence reflect this. We saw it at work at Sycamore High School when a PGCE student was asked to comment on two lessons that had also been watched by her tutor.

Jim Hodges had been regarded as a highly successful teacher at the school for the past twenty years and was considered to be a good choice as a history subject mentor for students in training from the local university department of education. Penny Grieves, one of the PGCE group in the school, observed Jim at work teaching a Year 9 group that 'necessity was the mother of invention' in the Industrial Revolution. Jim had all the appearances of an old-style didactic teacher. The lesson proceeded with some reading from a textbook, through discussion of the way in which Newcomen's steam engine worked, and the listing of significant dates on the board, to the distribution of a worksheet with a diagram of the steam engine and a brief verbal description. Jim then gave the students five minutes 'looking and learning' time and proceeded to a set of quickfire questions on the content of the lesson. He then asked the students to answer the eight questions on the worksheet for homework and added that there would be a test 'on the Industrial Revolution so far' on the following Friday morning and in his fiery Welsh brogue he reminded them 'that the true fire of the Gods would descend on those who fail to achieve correct answers to seven of the ten questions'.

Penny was worried by what she had seen. To her the lesson was didactic, the style transmissive, differentiation was achieved only by the skilful use of questioning and the apparently threatening tone could have inhibited those who did not find factual retention easy. She was also concerned that the link between Newcomen and 'the mother of invention' had not been forcefully made at that stage. She then went to observe a lesson on the same topic by Rahena Khan, one of Jim's departmental staff.

This time the lesson began with some questioning about the diagram on the worksheet, and then Rahena asked the class to move into their work groups. Three girls made a fuss about this saying that they were 'tired of being made to work in groups when the boys didn't want to get down to work and they took over anyway' and it took some minutes for the class to settle. Her immediate response was that 'if they behaved and got down to the job they would get house points for effort'. Rahena ensured that each of the groups got down to their task – this was to build a model steam engine using the pre-drawn cardboard pieces contained in the envelopes that had been distributed. The task for the groups of five was to colour the parts, cut them out, label them, and then stick them together as shown in the diagram. Rahena then attempted to ensure that each of the three girls who had objected were fully involved in the work of their teams but while she was doing this two groups were calling out that they had finished their work and were told to read some pages in their textbook. After a further five minutes Rahena called the class to order and moved them back to a formal classroom situation. She then asked the class to choose one of four pieces of work – a wordsearch followed by a definition of the words that had been highlighted; a description of the working of the engine for an eighteenth-century technical journal; the question 'how was Newcomen's steam engine an answer to needs at the time'; and after a piece of reading, 'what was it like working with machinery in the eighteenth-century compared with our factories today'.

Penny appreciated the variety of activities, the way in which Rahena worked with individuals, the differentiation by encouragement to follow specified activities, and the use of empathy in history teaching. She was less happy about the apparent mayhem as students changed activities, and found the challenging of the teacher by the three girls disturbing.

DISCUSSION POINT

- What was the nature of the leadership used by the two teachers?
- Which approach appeared to be more effective in the short term, and in the longer term?

One of the most important features of successful teaching is the ability to recognize the dynamics of the interaction between teacher as leader and students as learners. 'Off days', a sudden change in administrative arrangements, even the placing of a lesson immediately after a very windy break, all have their impact on what actually happens in the classroom. Goleman (1996) offers the concept of emotional intelligence as part of the armoury which, if understood by teachers, can enhance the learning experience. By this is meant the ability to recognize the place of emotions in interrelationships, and the contribution this makes to the culture of an organization. One of our interviewees spoke of 'the place feeling good – I like being at school because I feel that the teachers want me to do well' (Year 8 boy, Oak Grove School); another referred to the 'prospect of a witch hunt if the results from the subject area don't conform to what the boss thinks we are or should be achieving' (member of staff, Oak Grove School).

These comments show that emotions can be operating at three levels: student–student, student–teacher and teacher–teacher. It is possible that we have differing emotional intensities in our interactions according to the context, but if we are able to recognize the components of the emotional dimension it is possible to control or develop their use. It is the ability to discern not only one's personal emotional complex, but also those of students that appeared fundamental to the invitational style used by Jim in the vignette described above. Goleman (1996) offers five possible domains within our emotional intelligence:

- the ability to know one's emotions
- the ability to manage emotions
- the ability to motivate oneself
- the ability to recognize the characteristics of emotion in others
- the ability to handle relationships.

O'Hanlon (2000) shows how the tension between the need to develop cognitive intelligence and the suppression of emotional intelligence in order to secure compliance with transmissive learning approaches is inhibiting holistic development. In those schools where emotional intelligence is recognized, used as the vehicle for behaviour management and personal development, and then incorporated as an 'awareness' in the structure of learning, stable and responsive cultures are more likely to develop. This is not, however, possible without sustained professional development and the current climate is one of emphasis on the acquisition of cognitive rather than emotional skills.

Professional development

The teaching force is now well used to the idea that they need to train and retrain in order to cope with the demands of a national agenda for school improvement (Hargreaves 1994). The process of professional development has undergone considerable change in the 1990s with a move from LEA-led 'pick and mix' courses that are planned, offered and organized externally to the school, to school-organized, specific and coherent development experiences designed to meet the needs of individual, subject area and school at any particular time (Law and Glover 1995; Law 1999). The faltering steps to link teacher appraisal to professional development needs in the early 1990s were generally frustrated because limited funding meant that development experiences could not be offered and subsequent reappraisal foundered on the failure of schools to meet their obligations to their staff. Part of the response was for schools to develop their own in-house activities. These were often poorly taught and based upon a form of cascaded learning following attendance by the school's 'expert' at an externally provided course. Our research shows that some of the early professional development work in schools aiming to secure a wider acceptance of differentiation, gender issues, bullying and behaviour management was unsuccessful. This was, as the headteacher of Elm High School explained, because 'the staff were not ready to be told what we should be doing by those who had had time out of school. We had to learn that we got nowhere until we began by identifying a need or an idea that might have some impact and then responding to what the staff thought they needed rather than what we felt they ought to want'.

Those schools that showed successful and acceptable continuing professional development were hooked into a system for providing

- an annual review of school, department and individual needs
- a synoptic view of all that was being sought matched to the aims and objectives of the school
- a programme that addressed both the generic and the subject based skills
- a programme that provided opportunities for reflection and development without the pressure to introduce change until it had been tried, evaluated, refined and adequately explained.

In this way the cognitive and emotional needs of staff were being met. In doing so Oak Grove School attempted to use the national frameworks of standards for teachers and subject leaders (TTA 1998a, 1998b). The headteacher felt that 'the system is very good ... it tells us what we ought to be doing and where we should be aiming but it seems to be too much a matter of "can do, can't do" rather than about quality – we need to remember that we are in a profession, not a job'.

Current arrangements for pay and performance management (DfEE 2000) reinstate the link between performance review and development opportunities and provide an opportunity for the development of personal portfolios. These are intended as a developmental record in which the performance targets are established and then evidence of appropriate courses, experiences, and assessed activities is maintained. Teachers in training are now required to complete their Career Entry Profile giving an agreed statement of strengths and weaknesses at the point of entry to the profession, and it is envisaged that this will be the starting point for a career-long portfolio of professional progress. But this raises deeper questions – are teachers required to identify particular competences and then proceed to develop those skills that allow them to assume confidence in their use, or are they just part of the armoury of being a professional?

The belief that the process of teaching could be seen as a set of competences – the ability to do certain tasks, and to be trained to undertake these success-fully, has underpinned much of the teacher training and professional develop-ment work of the TTA. There is a difference between competence (plural competences) as a generic term reflecting an ability in an area of professional work, and competency (plural competencies) which is more specific and related to a component of that work, such as the ability to mark work in a way which is both diagnostic and a foundation for future improvement. The use of competence-based approaches as the foundation for initial and con-tinuing teacher education has been widely criticized. Hager (1994) felt that while there was no basic argument against a competence basis for profes-sional training, there was concern that these should be integrated into an holistic view of development. Tomlinson (1995) argued that the profiling of capabilities, rather than simplistic 'yes/no' assessment, would enable them to be used to promote continuing professional development and Gibbs and Aitken (1996) urged a return to judgement of professional capability which included the beliefs, knowledge and understanding which support effective-ness in the classroom. Brown (1996) expressed the view that approaches based upon the definition and achievement of pedagogic competencies could lead to

- simplistic constructs of professional worth
- the loss of critical and evaluative approaches to the assessment of profes-sional capabilities
- concentration on pass–fail outcomes rather than the process of profes-sional development
- questions about the source of the information and knowledge of subject and pedagogy required for competence analysis.

However, pressures from the teaching force have not led to changes of policy but rather an attempt to merge the highest ideals of professionalism with those of competence analysis and the development of specified competen-cies. This is illustrated in the standards for initial teacher education outlined by the DfEE in 1998. These attempt to bridge the extremes of viewpoint by referring to 'standards' against which all future qualified teachers would be assessed. In brief these standards reflect the previous debate but use the competencies and competences previously detailed as part of an assessment of capacity for acceptance as a qualified teacher. Teachers know what is expected of them but for the benefit of other readers the four areas are as follows:

- knowledge and understanding – the subject basis for teaching
- planning, teaching and class management – subsuming the strategies for effective pedagogy within the social and educational context of the school

- monitoring, assessment, recording, reporting and accountability – stressing the developmental and partnership nature of teaching
- other professional requirements including social and health and safety legislation, and the maintenance of professional standards of appearance and relationships.

Dinham and Scott (1998) who argue that there has to be some reconceptualization of teachers' work to enable them to concentrate on their so-called 'core business' for which they are suited by virtue of the values they hold and the motivation which springs from satisfaction with helping pupils to learn. Teachers need to see that their work is more than the successful transmission of knowledge. Our research has shown that external pressures such as inspection by Ofsted, the development of standards for subject leaders and for headteachers by the TTA, and increased emphasis on school and LEA target setting have led to a shift from management issues back to teaching and learning issues in school-based professional development work. At the same time internal pressures within schools have also prompted concern with developing teaching skills and this appears to be consonant with meeting professional needs outlined by teachers within schools (Glover and Law 2000).

DISCUSSION POINT

- Are teachers more concerned with professional or competence issues in seeking and planning their professional development?

Rowan High School has evolved a means of ensuring coherent professional development by establishing a major priority for the year and then linking subject and individual needs to this. The school is a small 11–18 comprehensive school facing the problems of maintaining a full sixth form curriculum offer within the resource constraints operating with a sixth form roll of 105 students. It was decided that the main theme of 'learning styles' would offer a framework for work at all stages within the school. The detail is beyond the scope of this vignette but typical activities were:

- an investigation of the way in which supported self-study could replace conventional teaching at sixth form level – undertaken by the sixth form tutors
- an investigation of the effectiveness of supported self-study at Key Stage 4 and the preparation of a bank of materials to help individual work plans in all subjects for Years 10 and 11
- attendance by five subject mentors at a local college of higher education in a shared teacher training arrangement with college support for a taught course on learning styles and the preparation of a group report on 'alternative to the standard classroom'

- the use of the individual research days (two per member of staff during the Summer term) to develop a set of lesson plans for the coming term aimed at the use of computerized learning for Years 7 and 8.

At the end of the Summer term each year the school holds an evening review session at which staff complete their professional portfolios and reflect on activities. The outcomes of the activities outlined above have been:

- introduction of a reduced period allocation for all subjects in Years 12 and 13 but enhanced access at non-timetabled times including laboratory access, the use of ICT and library facilities
- the development of a bank of materials for Years 10 and 11 in all subjects. These are topic based but available under staff supervision for individual learning to minimize the effects of absence, and for revision and extension work
- the redesign of the ICT programme for Years 7 and 8 and a move away from designated ICT lessons to integrated ICT in all subject areas
- the development of a study skills component for the PHSE programme in Years 8 to 12 based upon a learning styles analysis.

In this way the professional development activities have been used to benefit teaching and learning across the school. The system enhances staff ownership because it has its roots in a real problem. Had it not been met, there is no doubt that the offer to the sixth form would have been reduced by three subjects and a consequent move by potential students to a nearby large urban comprehensive or the college of further education might have resulted in the loss of all sixth form provision. When interviewed about the activity, the headteacher commented that 'it is most significant that we have begun to find our collective answers to our problems – staff do not realize how professional they have become at their own self-evaluation as effective teachers and learners'. In doing so she was highlighting an important school-based strategy that had lost its momentum in the years following the development of Ofsted. It is re-emerging as a vital tool affecting the culture of teaching and learning in schools.

Self-evaluation

It would be wrong to convey the impression that schools have only been concerned with effectiveness and improvement because of pressures from external influences such as target setting and Ofsted inspections. Many LEAs had become involved in the process of school self-evaluation as early as the mid-1980s and schools were becoming accustomed to producing school self-evaluation reports as part of a cyclic programme of review and development planning (Glover 1990). These appear to have been largely superseded by the Ofsted inspection process after 1992 but there is evidence that the process is now being revived in a different way. MacBeath (1999), Ofsted (1999) and

Saunders and Stradling (2000) all offer mechanisms by which self-evaluation can be sustained in schools and classrooms. Significantly, the swing from external inspection to internal developmental review is now part of official guidance and could indicate that the evolution of externally moderated internally organized inspection is under consideration.

The first round of Ofsted reports indicated that many schools were following only weak development planning procedures and that many departmental reports indicated pragmatic rather than planned use of resources and minimal monitoring and evaluation at all levels (Levačić and Glover 1997). As schools became more aware of the ways in which they could develop more effective planning processes (Hargreaves and Hopkins 1991, 1994) they used enhanced monitoring and evaluation techniques. At the same time the growth of accreditation for professional development based upon action-research offered class teachers more techniques for reflection on the success of their work.

At Sycamore High School there is an annual cycle of meetings aimed at monitoring and evaluating previous performance and using this as the basis of future planning. After the publication of external examination results each subject leader meets with the staff involved in teaching the subject and considers the results against three sets of data:

- the Cognitive Ability Test data developed at the point of entry to the school for all students taking GCSE at 16
- the forecast pass levels for all students produced by subject staff after the 'mock' examinations
- the performance of students in the subject compared with performance in other subjects.

This is a time-consuming process but it enables the subject staff to identify areas of strength and weakness and to identify three areas of action for the coming year, for example, targeted teaching of borderline students, the development of revision strategies on a subject wide basis or planned revision of the course at Key Stage 4 in order to meet identified problems.

In October the subject leader reports to the headteacher with the deputy headteacher responsible for finance and staff development, with a commentary on the results and detail of the actions proposed for the coming year. At this meeting the headteacher also reviews the development plans for the subject department in the light of progress made since these were last determined and agreement is reached on any changed objectives. At this meeting subject leader and head also agree priorities for financial resourcing and staff development in the coming year and the implications for overall planning are recorded by the deputy headteacher.

By January the headteacher is able to provide a report to governors with a commentary on external examination performance and an overall

strategy for securing improvement together with a suggested target
of pass levels at GCSE and A level for the coming year. At the start of
February the headteacher provides a statement of overall objectives and
priorities for resourcing for the coming academic year. Once approved
by governors this becomes the basis of the development plan and is
then revisited when budgetary figures are known.

    The staff of the school were recently asked to comment upon the
system used. While they appeared to be pleased with their involvement
in the review process they highlighted three issues that they felt were
not being addressed. These were:

- over-dependence on Cognitive Ability Tests and underuse of the test
  results from Key Stages 2 and 3 in assessing student potential
- over-dependence on external examination results without
  consideration of the less measurable indicators such as student attitude
  and school ethos
- lack of flexibility in short-term planning because of the way in which
  subject areas become locked into the annual cycle of review and
  planning.

This cameo shows how some self-evaluation can be stimulated by whole
school organization. Our interview evidence demonstrates that most teachers are constantly considering the effectiveness of the strategies under use
within their individual teaching programmes.

DISCUSSION POINT

- What is the difference between review and self-evaluation and how is it
  shown at Sycamore High?

Your conclusion is possibly that there is little difference between the two
terms but we would argue that the only true self-evaluation is that undertaken
by the subject staff at the beginning of this process when they reflect on what
has been achieved in their classrooms during the past year. At all subsequent
stages data collected from primary sources is used as the starting point for a
developmental review. Is there any significance in this distinction?

    Joyce (1991) offers five 'doors' to school improvement. These are

- the development of collegiality as the basis of personal relationships within
  the school
- the development of action research within the school as a means of
  development
- the consideration of the implication of results of research for the school
- the introduction of monitored curriculum initiatives
- the practice of sharing the results of changed teaching strategies.

All these involve the staff in thinking about the way in which they contribute to the process of applying ideas, developing strategies and evaluating the resulting change. This is more active than the process of self-review and likely to be of great value in linking the entire staff into school improvement.

This collegiality and shared involvement in change has been at the heart of TQM processes of continuing self-evaluation within schools. At Oak Grove School this has been developed as the alternative to the once a year examination focused development. They followed the structures outlined by Murgatroyd and Morgan (1992) and began their process by assessing the relationship of the school to its client base – the students and their parents at the heart of the local community. This showed that there were some areas of school development that had been pursued without strategic planning in mind – 'the perpetuation of old practice because we have always done it'. The staff and governors then established a strategic plan for the school and moved on to consider how they would know whether it was working or not. This led them to consider what was meant by 'quality' in the educational context and enabled a movement away from examination data as the sole criterion of success. It was agreed that the way in which all work teams within the school would consider their future performance should be based upon three sorts of data:

- the measurable including exam results at all levels, attendance figures, participation in activities and external events, and records of student behaviour
- the less immediately measurable indicators of quality in the delivery of educational objectives including parental comment and contact with the school, employer and governor observation and the functioning of subject and pastoral teams in securing changes in the school ethos
- the immeasurable but nevertheless important, perceptions of responsiveness of the school to its community undertaken on a rolling basis by a researcher from a neighbouring university.

As part of the 'contract' for change to a quality based system the head agreed that all targets set for use within the school should be SMART (specific, measurable, achievable, realistic and time-bound), that one of the senior management team would take on the responsibility for all data collection and its use with team groups, that all members of staff would be provided with a lap-top computer to maximize efficiency and that there would be a thorough review of all paperwork processes within the school.

After three years of this form of organization an evaluator was asked to assess the impact of the changes made as a result of TQM. In brief these were that:

- there was a much more evident whole-school knowledge of and focus on development and the rationale for change
- there had been an all-round improvement in student–staff relationships, and an increased willingness on the part of staff to listen to parents

- there had been a significant increase in the contribution of the school to the local community and a corresponding increase in community participation in school resourcing and support
- there had been a marked improvement in student behaviour because of the extent of monitoring and the early involvement of parents
- staff felt that the system needed to be constantly reinforced so that the TQM message was known to new staff and students.

One of the problems that subsequently developed at Oak Grove School was that staff felt that they were delivering a system rather than continuing to be part of the strategic and developmental process. In the words of a subject leader: 'I feel that I am delivering the goods but I am not being seen as a person'. This has been countered by the use of the 'Investors in People' (Bell and Harrison 1998) assessment procedure to reinforce the TQM principles. This has been achieved by extending the training and development opportunities for all staff. Hall (1997: 155) queries whether such systems 'change culture only at the level of visible behaviour while values and assumptions remain intact'. It has been suggested that more deep-seated school-based self-evaluation can occur only if ownership of the process is more firmly rooted in the staff as a whole. Saunders and Stradling (2000) offer a set of schedules for use within classrooms, staff meetings and governors' meetings to identify the ways in which staff can

- manage motivation
- review the effectiveness of teaching and learning styles
- provide effective feedback to students
- develop systems to alert the school to problems that militate against achievement.

These objectives may be similar to those used within the TQM and similar systems but they offer a resource for development according to the needs of the school or the teacher. Saunders and Stradling (2000) also stress the importance of school self-evaluation as a technique to support:

- changing culture – and even the use of self-evaluation techniques itself is an indication of a more open attitude on the part of staff
- professional development that is grounded in the shared experience of teaching colleagues working and assessing together
- organizational change to secure enhanced effectiveness
- the development of an agenda for change within the school that is owned by the participants.

DISCUSSION POINT

- Can an individual teacher pursue a policy of productive self-evaluation within a school that is currently hostile to such ideas?

Culture – back to the future

The concept of culture has underpinned much of the discussion throughout this book. It tends to be an indefinable 'something' that is felt by participants, and considered by some to be immutable. School and classroom self-evaluation offer both a starting point and a process for the management of cultural change. Throughout the core chapters of this book we have offered check points that are intended to help with the process of self-evaluation. It will be obvious to any reader that there is a progression from the positive use of the attributes of teaching and learning to what can be described at best as a neutral approach which does not actually harm but does little to enthuse learning in our students. As you have noted where you think you are on this spectrum with regard to each of the attributes, you will also have been nudged to consider how change might be accomplished.

Stoll (1999) summarizes the current notions of culture in organizational terms – and the organization can be as small as a working group at a table, or a class within a school. Hargreaves (1999) offers semi-quantifiable measures of elements of culture. Among these is a simple analysis: the placing of the organization on an eight-point scale from, for example, the warm and friendly to the cold and hostile, or from the collaborative to the individualistic. He also offers a more complex instrument to help analysis of cultures within the formal–hothouse–welfarist–survivalist grid. Both these tools offer the opportunity for asking where are we now, and where do we want to be? In considering the direction and process of movement Hargreaves stresses the importance of a range of structures that can affect cultural outcomes. These are:

- the political structure – formal distribution of power
- the micropolitical structure – the power of informal networks
- the maintenance structure – committees, working groups, procedures
- the development structure – support systems for developmental change
- the service structure – the basic social relationships that underpin the organization.

In thinking about our own organizations it is relatively easy to spot these at work in a way that seems to be beyond our control. The responsibility for all that is, or is not, achieved rests with the system or other people! Hargreaves concludes by suggesting that the ability to effectively change culture is dependent upon three capabilities:

- effective monitoring of what is happening
- proactive and enthusiastic support for change
- resource deployment to make change happen.

Returning to the starting point of this chapter we need to ask how far individual teachers can be the driving force for change. In our research, and considering the detailed leadership and management data for each of the ten schools, we conclude that there are three factors variously external to the classroom, that affect the quality of teaching and learning:

- The quantity and quality of *resources* within the classroom. The external influences on this include the allocation systems within the school, the micropolitical pressures militating against equity, and the prioritization accorded to developmental work. The internal influences include the previous resource history for the subject, creativity in collecting and developing teaching resources, and the systems in place to secure their proper use.
- The *systems* within the school to support effective teaching and learning. These can be seen as maintaining teaching and learning at whole school level through the establishment of the curricular framework, the assessment, recording and reporting systems, and the provision of support through student support systems and professional development opportunities. Within the classroom teachers have their own systems to facilitate effective teaching and learning including classroom routines, seating arrangements, and health and safety procedures.
- The *values* that underpin relationships as part of the climate of teaching and learning. These may be determined outside the classroom by the extent to which there is a shared understanding and vision for the school and what it stands for, rewards and expectations and acceptance of a way of involvement of staff in considering problems and lines of development. Within the classroom these values are most commonly seen in the interaction between teacher and student, between students and in the attitudes that are evident as 'the way in which we work'.

The combination of these elements results in a quality of learning which can be described as:

- *Basic Learning*: where there is evidence of sufficient resources; where there is some attempt to match learning needs and teaching styles and where students are challenged to work at a group level. Teaching aimed at a whole-class level usually marks this.
- *Developing Learning*: where there is evidence of resource development to support learning needs; where a variety of approaches is used in subject teaching and where students are individually challenged according to assessment of prior progress. This is usually marked by awareness of individual learning need within whole-class teaching.
- *Stimulating Learning*: where there is evidence of the availability and use of alternative learning resources and classroom equipment, where the theory of learning style preference and teaching response based upon concepts such as multiple intelligences is being developed, and where the individual achievement is monitored using refined techniques. It is only in the latter that techniques of progress from subject learning to awareness of the total learning experience (metacognition) and of individualized learning on a school-wide scale are being developed.

But do teachers recognize such variations? Self-evaluation is of value only if it prompts change to secure successful teaching and learning outcomes. The extent to which an individual teacher can bring about change is affected in part by his or her ability to affect the resources, systems and values of the school and the classroom. It is possible for a visionary teacher to influence what happens in his or her classroom establishing what the headteacher of Oak Grove describes as 'an oasis of good practice and secure relationships that is an example to all the other staff but which cannot be simply duplicated by providing resources or good working practices in other rooms – it is the known values that make the difference'. The development of good practice as the norm appears to require a willingness on the part of all participants to secure cultural change.

Conclusion

Throughout this book we have attempted to prompt thinking with questions about practice. We have also sought to offer a framework for analysing what is happening in the teaching and learning process. If we bring together those aspects of our structure – environment, challenge, teaching and learning, relationships, and the achievement of the broader curriculum, and then consider these against the resource base, the maintenance of interest and the interaction between the classroom participants it is possible to construct a matrix for the assessment of teaching and learning at classroom and whole-school level. The attainment of all descriptors at the highest level would indicate perfection!

	Resources	Maintained interest	Interaction
Environment	Quality and availability of books, equipment	Classroom state and stimulation	Standards of care as common concern
Challenge	Individualized, differentiated and suited to the learner	Realistic targets to balance coping and pace	Known and agreed expectations and effective monitoring
Approach and planning	Variety of learning tools in the lesson and over time	Changed activities, pace and differentiation if needed	Appropriate learning support where matching teaching and learning style may require this
Relationships	Time and space opportunities for refection and interaction	Assessment, encouragement and involvement in varied learning situations	Support and encouragement for both groups and individuals
Broader curriculum	Opportunities for discussion and practice	Through use of skills, debate of issues, and awareness of relevance of learning to life	Using mutuality and key skills to secure maturation of capacity to reflect and present a view

The evidence from the first group of schools suggests that while many of these objectives may be inhibited it is possible through teacher awareness and planning, to offer consistently challenging and interesting learning experiences.

Further reading

Further reading suggestions in previous chapters underpin school improvement and effectiveness work. For those seeking to explore these issues in detail

Teddlie, C. and Reynolds, D. (eds) (2000) *The International Handbook of School Effectiveness Research*. London: Falmer offers a rich source book.

The redevelopment of school self-evaluation within current political thinking is outlined in

MacBeath, J. (1999) *Schools Must Speak for Themselves*. London: Routledge.

Those seeking more work on the management of change are referred to

Morrison, K. (1998) *Management Theories for Educational Change*. London: Paul Chapman.

Bell, J. and Harrison, B.T. (1998) *Leading People: Learning from People*. Buckingham: Open University Press

The internet trail will have been either a source of help, or a source of irritation! You will now know most trails. Exploration of research materials via BIDS, ERIC and similar search engines will lead you to work from the international community. There is good work on self-evaluation from the educational web sites of the Australian State governments and the New Zealand government. Good hunting!

Appendix

Percentage responses rating statements recorded as 'usually true' of teaching in the subjects or year groups listed

Topic	Overall	Male	Female	Eng.	Math.	Sc.	His.	Geo.	MFL	Tech.	Yr. 7	Yr. 8	Yr. 9	Yr. 10	Yr. 11
Cohort size	2895	1409	1433	499	889	446	157	125	131	227	610	389	549	598	727
Environment															
Lot to look at in room	51	51	49	56	50	36	43	39	65	73	62	47	49	45	51
Can see teacher's desk and board	76	76	76	78	77	79	84	62	68	73	77	72	75	77	74
Layout helps work	54	52	56	51	57	53	49	44	41	69	58	53	58	47	52
Well equipped for subject	69	67	73	68	68	70	55	59	62	80	78	75	62	65	63
Books available for homework	50	49	49	46	66	49	41	53	63	28	47	45	58	50	48
Challenge															
Can cope with work set	73	73	75	73	68	77	78	83	66	73	70	74	76	75	68
Different tasks to meet ability	18	18	17	31	36	15	21	17	61	13	22	21	28	18	33
Teacher helps my concentration	32	36	30	27	31	29	38	44	40	39	38	30	35	32	27
Activities changed to help understanding	60	59	61	54	57	50	66	62	49	61	68	61	56	54	47
Teacher checks understanding	69	68	70	59	66	58	75	85	52	77	84	67	68	60	52
Teaching and learning approaches															
Opportunities to work in groups	31	29	34	30	5	64	31	13	31	19	22	27	16	35	32
Notemaking as a record	26	26	28	20	17	46	27	11	18	33	24	12	20	34	25
We use ICT in this subject	9	9	10	9	6	3	4	7	4	36	11	17	6	5	5
Individual work opportunities	53	53	54	61	69	28	59	64	8	63	57	57	64	48	57
Variety of resources available	37	37	36	42	19	41	63	65	65	11	37	35	25	39	35
Homework instructions are clear	65	63	70	62	66	58	71	75	60	73	73	61	68	59	59
Understand how lessons fit together	56	56	57	51	49	53	59	63	47	68	58	56	52	54	49
Variety of activity in lessons	26	28	25	18	17	21	35	31	39	23	27	31	21	31	16
Subject learning maintained in notebook	74	71	79	62	78	76	80	87	74	65	78	68	72	75	64
Balance between talking and doing	56	53	60	54	55	56	59	61	46	61	58	54	57	51	56

Teacher–student relationships															
Made to work hard	55	55	53	59	60	45	62	53	45	51	53	54	54	56	59
Reports used to help plan progress	35	35	35	32	30	32	43	47	35	42	40	37	35	26	28
Teacher knows what is happening in room	64	64	66	70	45	67	73	68	56	55	66	71	58	59	51
We know how well we are doing	54	55	54	50	52	46	66	67	48	60	61	44	53	53	48
Encouragement for individuals/groups	62	62	64	64	52	58	70	69	60	60	64	62	61	59	54
The total curriculum															
Have to learn a lot of facts	56	56	56	31	55	69	76	72	42	52	58	49	53	55	50
Relevance of learning to life	16	17	15	17	11	17	30	28	52	20	18	13	14	13	20
Practice what we have learnt	47	48	48	37	39	37	36	44	45	72	50	43	44	48	38
Discuss work-related issues	49	49	50	46	35	45	58	63	43	54	56	50	40	43	33
Teacher goes back through things	54	54	55	48	57	51	57	57	53	52	61	55	52	51	47

References

Adey, K. and Jones, J. (1997) The professional development co-ordinator: obstacles to effective role performance, *Educational Management and Administration*, 25(2): 133–44.

Altrichter, H. and Elliott, J. (eds) (2000) *Images of Educational Change*. Buckingham: Open University Press.

Argyris, C. and Schön, D. (1981) *Organizational Learning: A Theory of Action Perspective*. London: Addison-Wesley.

Arnold, R. (1997) *Raising Levels of Achievement in Boys*. Slough: National Foundation for Educational Research.

Arnot, M., Gray, J., James, M., Rudduck, J. and Duveen, G. (1998) *Recent Research on Gender and Educational Performance*. London: Ofsted/Stationery Office.

Atkinson, S. (1998) Cognitive style in the context of design technology project work, *Educational Psychology*, 18(2): 183–94.

Atweh, B., Kemmis, S. and Weeks, P. (1998) *Action Research in Practice*. London: Routledge.

Avis, J., Bloomer, M., Esland, G., Gleeson, D. and Hodkinson, P. (1996) *Knowledge and Nationhood: Education, Politics and Work*. London: Cassell.

Bailey, A. and Johnson, G. (1997) How strategies develop in organizations, in M. Preedy, R. Glatter and R. Levačić (eds) *Educational Management: Strategy, Quality, Resources*. Buckingham: Open University Press.

Ball, S.J. (1994) *Education Reform: A Critical and Post-structural Approach*. Buckingham: Open University Press.

Barber, M. (1996) *The Learning Game: Arguments for an Education Revolution*. London: Victor Gollancz.

Barth, R. (1990) *Improving Schools from Within: Teachers, Parents and Principals can Make a Difference*. San Francisco, CA: Jossey-Bass.

Beare, H., Caldwell, B. and Millikan, R. (1989) *Creating an Excellent School: Some New Management Techniques*. London: Routledge.

Bell, J. and Harrison, B.T. (1998) *Leading People: Learning from People*. Buckingham: Open University Press.

Bennett, N. (1976) *Teaching Style and Pupil Progress*. London: Open Books.

Bennett, N. (1997) *Managing Professional Teachers: Middle Management in Primary and Secondary Schools*. London: Paul Chapman.

Bennett, N., Desforges, C., Cockburn, A. and Wilkinson, B. (1984) *The Quality of Pupil Learning Experiences*. London: Lawrence Erlbaum.

Beresford, J. (1999) *Target Setting and Classroom Practice: A Secondary School Case Study*. Waltham Abbey, Herts: King Harold School.

Bernstein, B. (1977) *Class, Codes and Control, Vol. 3: Towards a Theory of Educational Transmissions*. London: Routledge and Kegan Paul.

Blake, R. and Mouton, J. (1964) *The Managerial Grid*. Houston, TX: Gulf.

Blatchford, P. and Martin, C. (1998) The effects of class size on classroom processes, *British Journal of Educational Studies*, 46(2): 118–37.

Blaxter, L., Hughes, C. and Tight, M. (1996) *How to Research*. Buckingham: Open University Press.

Bloom, B. (1956) *Taxonomy of Educational Objectives*. London: Longman.

Bowe, R., Ball, S.J. and Gold, A. (1992) *Reforming Education and Changing Schools*. London: Routledge.

Bowring-Carr, C. and West-Burnham, J. (1997) *Effective Learning in Schools*. London: Pitman.

Bray, R., Gardner, C., Parsons, N., Downes, P. and Hannan, G. (1997) *Can Boys Do Better?* Leicester: Secondary Heads Association.

Broadhead, P., Cuckle, P., Hodgson, J. and Dunford, J. (1996) Improving primary schools through school development planning, *Educational Management and Administration*, 24(3): 277–90.

Brookfield, D. (1987) *Developing Critical Thinkers*. Milton Keynes: Open University Press.

Brookhart, S.M. (1997) A theoretical framework for the role of classroom assessment in motivating student effort and achievement, *Applied Measurement in Education*, 10(2): 161–80.

Brown, G.A. and Edmondson, R. (1984) Asking questions, in E.C. Wragg (ed.) *Classroom Skills*. London: Croom Helm.

Brown, S. (1996) Assessing student teachers: the implications of competence and school-based models, *New Zealand Council for Teacher Education June Conference Proceedings*: 24–34.

Bruner, J.S. (1966) *Towards a Theory of Instruction*. Cambridge, MA: Harvard University Press.

Bush, T. (1995) *Theories of Educational Management*. London: Paul Chapman.

Bush, T. (2000) Management styles: impact on finance and resources, in M. Coleman and L. Anderson (eds) *Managing Finance and Resources in Education*. London: Paul Chapman.

Caine, R.N. and Caine, G. (1997) Maximising learning, *Educational Leadership*, 54(6): 11–15.

Caldwell, B. and Spinks, J. (1988) *The Self-managing School*. London: Falmer.

Caldwell, B. and Spinks, J. (1992) *Leading the Self-managing School*. London: Falmer.

Caldwell, B. and Spinks, J. (1998) *Beyond the Self-managing School*. London: Falmer.

Cameron, R.J. (1998) School discipline in the U.K.: promoting classroom behaviour which encourages effective teaching and learning, *Educational and Child Psychology*, 15(1): 40–5.

Canter, M. and Canter, L. (1999) Lighten up, *Managing Schools To-day*, 8(6): 28–30.

Clark, A. and Trafford, J. (1995) Boys into modern languages: an investigation of the discrepancy in attitudes and performance between boys and girls in modern languages, *Gender in Education*, 7(3): 315–25.

Cohen, V.L. (1997) Implications for learning in a technology rich school, *Journal of Interactive Learning Research*, 8(2): 153–74.

Coldstream, P. (1994) Training minds for to-morrow: a shared responsibility, *Higher Education Quarterly*, 48(3): 159–68.

Coleman, J., Coser, L.A. and Powell, W.W. (1966) *Equality of Educational Opportunity*. Washington, DC: US Government Printing Office.

Coleman, M. and Anderson, L. (eds) (2000) *Managing Finance and Resources in Education*. London: Paul Chapman.

Colley, A., Comber, C. and Hargreaves, D. (1998) IT and music education: what happens to boys and girls in co-ed and single sex schools, *British Journal of Music Education*, 10(2): 123–4.

Collins, J. and Cook, D. (2000) *Understanding Learning: Influences and Outcomes*. London: Paul Chapman.

Cooper, P. and McIntyre, D. (1994) Patterns of interaction between teachers' and students' classroom thinking and their implications for the provision of learning opportunities, *Teaching and Teacher Education*, 10(6): 633–46.

Cooper, P. and McIntyre, D. (1996) *Effective Teaching and Learning: Teachers' and Students' Perspectives*. Buckingham: Open University Press.

Coopersmith, S. (1967) *Antecedents of Self-esteem*. San Francisco, CA: W.H. Freeman.

Cordellichio, T. and Field, W. (1997) Seven strategies that encourage neural branching, *Educational Leadership*, 64(6): 33–6.

Crombie-White, R. (1997) *Curriculum Innovation: A Celebration of Classroom Practice*. Buckingham: Open University Press.

Cullen, R. (1998) Teacher talk and the classroom context, *English Language Teaching Journal*, 52(3): 179–87.

Cullingford, C. (ed.). (1999) *An Inspector Calls: Ofsted and its Effect on School Standards*. London: Kogan Page.

Cuthbert, R.E. and Latcham, J. (1979) *Analysing Managerial Activities, no. 1410*. Blagdon, Som.: Further Education Unit.

Dale, R. (1997) The State and the governance of education: an analysis of the restructuring of the state–education relationship, in A.H. Halsey et al. (eds) *Education: Culture, Economy, Society*. Oxford: Oxford University Press.

Dalin, P., Rolff, H. and Kottkamp, R. (1993) *Changing the School Culture*. London: Cassell.

Davis, I.K. (1976) *Objectives in Curriculum Design*. London: McGraw-Hill.

Deal, T. (1985) The symbolism of effective schools, *Elementary School Journal*, 85(5): 601–20.

Dearing, R. (1997) *National Committee of Inquiry: Higher Education for the 21st Century*. London: Stationery Office.

Dennison, B. and Kirk, R. (1990) *Do, Review, Learn, Apply: A Simple Guide to Experiential Learning*. Oxford: Basil Blackwell.

Department for Education and Employment (DfEE) (1997) *Excellence in Schools*, Cm 3681. London: DfEE.

DfEE (1998) *Requirements for Courses of Initial Teacher Training*, Circular 4/98. London: DfEE.

DfEE (1999) *Reviewing Performance and Pay of Heads and Deputy Heads: Guidance to Governors*. London: DfEE.

DfEE (2000) *Performance Management: Guidance for Governors*. London: DfEE.

Department for Education and Science (DES) (1988) *Education Reform Act*. London: HMSO.

Diaz, R.M., Neal, C.J. and Amaya-Williams, M. (1991) The social origins of self-regulation, in L.C. Moll (ed.) *Vygotsky and Education: Instructional Implications and Applications of Sociohistorical Psychology*. New York: Cambridge University Press.

Dimmock, C. and Walker, A. (2000) Cross-cultural values and leadership, *Management in Education*, 14(3): 21–4.

Dinham, S. and Scott, C. (1998) Reconceptualising teachers' work, *Australian College of Education National Conference September Proceedings*. Canberra: Australian College of Education.

Dixon, T. and Woolhouse, M. (1997) Secondary school teachers and learning style preferences: action or watching in the classroom, *Journal of Further and Higher Education*, 20(3): 15–22.

Dore, R. (1976) *The Diploma Disease: Education Qualification and Development*. London: Allen & Unwin.

Duignan, P. (1989) Reflective management: the key to quality leadership, in C. Riches and C. Morgan (eds) *Human Resource Management in Education*. Milton Keynes: Open University Press.

Duke, D.L. (1998) Does it matter where our children learn? White Paper presented to an invitational meeting, Washington, DC, 18 February.

Egan, S.K., Manson, T. and Perry, D.G. (1998) Socio-cognitive influences on change in aggression over time, *Developmental Psychology*, 34(5): 996–1006.

Elliott, J. (1991) *Action Research for Educational Change*. Buckingham: Open University Press.

Elliott, J. (1999) Factors affecting educational motivation: a study of attitudes, expectations and behaviour of children in Sunderland, Kentucky and St. Petersburg, *British Educational Research Journal*, 25(1): 75–94.

Eraut, M. (1994) *Developing Professional Knowledge and Competence*. Lewes: Falmer.

Esland, G. (1996) Education, training and nation-state capitalism; Britain's failing strategy, in J. Avis, M. Bloomer, G. Esland, D. Gleeson and P. Hodkinson, *Knowledge and Nationhood*. London: Cassell.

Ferguson, M. (1982) *The Aquarian Conspiracy*. London: Granada.

Feuerstein, R. (1980) *Instrumental Enrichment: An Intervention Programme for Cognitive Modifiability*. Baltimore, MD: University Park Press.

Fidler, B. (1996) School development planning and strategic planning for school improvement, in P. Earley, B. Fidler and J. Ouston (eds) *Improvement through Inspection: Complementary Approaches to School Development*. London: David Fulton.

Fielding, M. (1997) Beyond school effectiveness and school improvement: lighting the slow fuse of possibility, in J. White and M. Barber (eds) *Perspectives on School Effectiveness and School Improvement*. London: Institute of Education, University of London.

Finnan, C. and Levin, H.M. (2000) Changing school cultures, in H. Altrichter and J. Elliott (eds) *Images of Educational Change*. Buckingham: Open University Press.

Fisher, D.L., Fraser, B.J. and Bassett, J. (1995) Using a classroom environment instrument in an early childhood classroom, *Australian Journal of Early Childhood*, 20(3): 10–15.

Fisher, D., Kent, H. and Fraser, B. (1998) Relationships between teacher–student interpersonal behaviour and teacher personality, *School Psychology International*, 19(2): 99–119.

Fitz-Gibbon, C.T. (1996) *Monitoring Education: Indicators, Quality and Effectiveness*. London: Cassell.

Follman, J. (1995) Elementary public school rating of teacher effectiveness, *Child Study Journal*, 25(1): 57–78.

Foskett, D. (1998) Schools and marketization: cultural challenges and responses, *Educational Management and Administration*, 26(2): 211–19.

Fraser, D. (1997) Ethical dilemmas and practical problems for the practitioner researcher, *Educational Action Research*, 5(1): 161–71.

Fullan, M. (1991) *The New Meaning of Educational Change*. Columbia, NY: Teachers College Press.

Fullan, M. (1992) *What's Worth Fighting for in Headship*. Buckingham: Open University Press.

Gardner, H. (1983) *Frames of Mind: The Theory of Multiple Intelligences*. New York: Basic Books.

Gardner, H. (1993) *The Unschooled Mind*. London: Fontana.

Gardner, H. (1999) Multiplicity of intelligences, *Scientific American*, 9(4): 19–23.

Gardner, J. and McMullan, T. (1990) Computer literacy in UK education – an evolving strategy. Paper presented to European Conference on Technology and Education, Denmark, 23–7 April.

Garrett, V. and Bowles, C. (1997) Teaching as a profession: the role of professional development, in H. Tomlinson (ed.) *Managing Continuing Professional Development in Schools*. London: Paul Chapman.

Gibbs, G. and Aitken, G. (1996) The competent teachers: beyond competencies, *New Zealand Council for Teacher Education June Conference Proceedings*, Auckland: 93–8.

Gilroy, P. and Wilcox, B. (1994) Ofsted, criteria and the nature of social understanding: a Wittgensteinian critique of the practice of educational judgement, *British Journal of Educational Studies*, 45: 22–38.

Glover, D. (1990) Towards a school development plan: process and practice, *Educational Management and Administration*, 18(3): 22–7.

Glover, D. (1992) An investigation of criteria used by parents and the community in the judgement of school quality, *Educational Research*, 34(1): 35–44.

Glover, D. and Cartwright, N. (1998) *Towards Bully-free Schools: Interventions in Action.* Buckingham: Open University Press.

Glover, D. and Law, S. (1996) *Managing Professional Development in Education.* London, Kogan Page.

Glover, D. and Law, S. (2000) Perceptions of pressure: external and internal influences on secondary school policy-making directed at enhanced teaching and learning, *Westminster Studies in Education*, 24(1): 45–60.

Glover, D., Levačić, R., Bennett, N. and Earley, P. (1996) Leadership, planning and resource management in four very effective schools, *School Organization*, Part One, June: 135–48; Part Two, September: 247–61.

Glover, D., Gleeson, D., Gough, G. and Johnson, M. (1998) The meaning of management: the development needs of middle managers in secondary schools, *Educational Management and Administration*, 26(3): 279–92.

Goleman, D. (1996) *Emotional Intelligence: Why It Matters More than IQ.* London: Bloomsbury.

Gray, J., Jesson, D., Goldstein, H. et al. (1995) A multi-level analysis of school improvement: changes in schools' performance over time, *School Effectiveness and School Improvement*, 6(2): 97–114.

Gray, J., Hopkins, D., Reynolds, D. et al. (1999) *Improving Schools: Performance and Potential*, Buckingham: Open University Press.

Gregorc, A.F. (1982) *Gregorc Style Delineator: Development Technical and Administrative Manual.* Columbia, CT: Gregorc Associates.

Habermas, J. (1972) *Knowledge and Human Interests.* London: Heinemann.

Hager, P. (1994) Is there a cogent philosophical argument against competency standards?, *Australian Journal of Education*, 38(1): 3–18.

Hall, S. (1981) Schooling, state and society, in R. Dale et al. (eds) *Education and the State: Vol. 1, Schooling and National Interest.* London: Falmer.

Hall, V. (1997) *Choices for Self-managing Schools: Autonomy and Accountability.* London: Paul Chapman.

Hallam, C. and Cowan, R. (1999) *What do We Know about Homework? Viewpoint no. 9.* London: Institute of Education, University of London.

Halpin, D. and Troyna, B. (1995) The politics of education policy borrowing, *Comparative Education*, (31)3: 303–10.

Halsall, R. (ed.) (1998) *Teacher Research and School Improvement: Opening Doors from the Inside.* Buckingham: Open University Press.

Hammond, T. and Dennison, B. (1995) School choice in less populated areas, *Educational Management and Administration*, 23(2): 104–13.

Handy, C. (1989) *The Age of Unreason.* London: Pan.

Handy, C. (1993) *Understanding Organizations*, 4th edn. Harmondsworth: Penguin.

Handy, C. and Aitken, R. (1987) *Understanding Schools as Organizations.* Harmondsworth: Penguin.

Hannay, L.M. (1996) The role of images in the secondary school change process, *Teachers and Training*, 2(1): 105–22.

Hargreaves, A. (1994) *Changing Teacher, Changing Times: Teachers' Work and Culture in the Post-modern Age.* London: Cassell.

Hargreaves, D. (1982) *The Challenge for the Comprehensive School*. London: Routledge and Kegan Paul.

Hargreaves, D. (1995) School culture, school effectiveness and school improvement, *School Effectiveness and Improvement*, 61(1): 23–46.

Hargreaves, D. (1999) Helping practitioners explore their school's culture, in J. Prosser (ed.) *School Culture*. London: Paul Chapman.

Hargreaves, D. and Hopkins, D. (1991) *The Empowered School*. London: Cassell.

Hargreaves, D. and Hopkins, D. (1994) *Development Planning for School Improvement*. London: Cassell.

Harris, A. (1996) Raising levels of achievement through school improvement, *Support for Learning*, 11(2): 62–7.

Hartman, V.F. (1995) Teaching and learning style preferences: transition through technology, *VCCA Journal*, 9(2): 18–20.

Hasan, A. and Wagner, A. (1996) The school of the future, *OECD Observer no. 199*.

Hay McBer (2000) *Research into Teacher Effectiveness: A Model of Teacher Effectiveness*. London: DfEE.

Hersey, P. and Blanchard, K.H. (1988) *Management of Organizational Behaviour: Utilising Human Resources*. London: Prentice Hall.

Hitchcock, G. and Hughes, D. (1995) *Research and the Teacher*, 2nd edn. London: Routledge.

Honey, P. and Mumford, P. (1986) *Manual of Learning Styles*. Maidenhead: Peter Honey.

Hopkins, D. (1993) *A Teacher's Guide to Classroom Research*. Buckingham: Open University Press.

Hopkins, D., Ainscow, M. and West, M. (1994) *School Improvement in an Era of Change*. London: Cassell.

House of Commons Select Committee on Education and Employment (1999) *Ninth Report: The Role of Headteachers*. London: Stationery Office.

Howe, C. (1997) *Gender and Classroom Interaction: A Research Review*. Edinburgh: Scottish Council for Research in Education.

Hoy, W.K. and Miskel, C.G. (1987) *Educational Administration: Theory, Research and Practice*. New York: McGraw-Hill.

Hultgren, A. and Stephen, P. (1999) Class management in senior high schools during teaching practice: the Norwegian experience, *Mentoring and Tutoring*, 6(3): 18–30.

Hurrell, P. (1995) Do teachers discriminate? Reactions to pupil behaviour in four comprehensive schools, *Sociology*, 29(1): 59–72.

Hutton, P. (1990) *Survey Research for Managers: How to Use Surveys in Management Decision-making*, 2nd edn. London: Macmillan.

Jack, S., Shores, R.E., Denny, R. et al. (1996) An analysis of the relationship of teachers' reported use of classroom management strategies on types of classroom interaction, *Journal of Behavioural Education*, 6(1): 67–87.

James, S. (1998) Whole class teaching, democratic skills and improving performance, *Management in Education*, 12(1): 22–4.

Jester, C. and Miller, S. (2000) *Introduction to DVC Learning Style Survey*. http:silcon.com Pleasant Hill, CA.

Johnson, M. (1998) *Report on the Implementation of Change Related to the Social Regeneration Budget in Lancashire Schools*. Keele, Staffs: Department of Education, University of Keele.

Joyce, B. (1991) The doors to school improvement, *Educational Leadership*, 48(8): 59–62.

Joyce, B., Calhoun, E. and Hopkins, D. (1997) *Models of Learning – Tools for Teaching*, Buckingham: Open University Press.

Joyce, B., Calhoun, E. and Hopkins, D. (1999) *The New Structure of School Improvement: Inquiring Schools and Achieving Students*. Buckingham: Open University Press.

Kaye, S. (1998) Pupils' achievement and school management. Unpublished PhD thesis, University of Leeds.

Keep, E. and Mayhew, K. (1996) Economic demand for higher education – a sound foundation for further expansion?, *Higher Education Quarterly*, 50(2): 89–109.

Kelly, A. (1989) *The Curriculum: Theory and Practice*, 3rd edn. London: Paul Chapman.

Kemmis, S. (1983) Action research, in T. Husen and T. Postlethwaite (eds) *International Encyclopedia of Education: Research and Studies*. Oxford: Pergamon.

Kemmis, S. and McTaggart, R. (1988) *The Action Research Planner*, 3rd edn. Geelong, Victoria: Deakin University Press.

Kinder, K., Harland, J., Wilkin, A. and Wakefield, A. (1995) *Three to Remember: Strategies for Disaffected Pupils*. Slough: National Foundation for Educational Research.

Kolb, D., Rubin, I. and McIntyre, J. (1971) *Organizational Psychology: An Experiential Approach*. Hemel Hempstead: Prentice Hall.

Lackney, J.A. (1999) Reading a school building like a book. Speech to the Program of Research and Evaluation for Public Schools Conference, Jackson, Missouri, 28 January, http://www.edi.msstate.edu/prepsintro.html

Land, S.M. and Hannafin, M.J. (1996) Student centred learning environments: foundations, assumptions and implications. Proceedings of the 1996 National Convention of the Association for Educational Communications and Technology, 18 April. Indianapolis, IN.

Law, S. (1999) Leadership for learning: the changing culture of professional development in schools, *Journal of Educational Administration*, 37(1): 66–80.

Law, S. and Glover, D. (1995) The professional development business: school evaluations of LEA and higher education INSET provision, *British Journal of In-service Education*, 21(2): 181–92.

Law, S. and Glover, D. (1999) Does Ofsted make a difference?, in C. Cullingford (ed.) *An Inspector Calls*. London: Kogan Page.

Law, S. and Glover, D. (2000) *Educational Leadership and Learning: Practice, Policy and Research*. Buckingham: Open University Press.

Lawn, M. and Grace, G. (1987) *Teachers: The Culture and Politics of Work*. London: Falmer.

Lawrence, M. and Veronica, M. (1997) Secondary school teachers and learning style preferences: action or watching in the classroom, *Educational Psychology*, 17(1–2): 157–70.

Lawton, D. (1983) *Curriculum Studies and Educational Planning*. London: Hodder and Stoughton.

Lawton, D. (1990) *Education, Culture and the National Curriculum*. Lewes: Falmer.

Leask, M. and Terrell, I. (1997) *Development Planning and School Improvement for Middle Managers*. London: Kogan Page.

Lee, K. (1996) A study of teacher responses based on their conceptions of intelligence, *Journal of Classroom Interaction*, 31(2): 1–12.

Levačić, R. (1995) *Local Management of Schools*. Buckingham: Open University Press.

Levačić, R. and Glover, D. (1994) *OFSTED Assessment of Schools' Efficiency: An Analysis of 66 Secondary School Inspection Reports*. Milton Keynes: Centre for Educational Policy and Management, Open University.

Levačić, R. and Glover, D. (1997) Value for money as a school improvement strategy: evidence from the new inspection system in England and Wales, *School Effectiveness and School Improvement*, 8(2): 231–54.

Levačić, R. and Woods, P. (2000) The impact of quasi-markets and performance regulation on socially disadvantaged schools. Paper presented at American Educational Research Association, New Orleans, 24–8 April.

Lewin, K. (1946) Action research and minority problems, *Journal of Social Issues*, 2: 34–46.

Lightfoot, S. (1983) *The Good High School: Portraits of Character and Culture*. New York: Coleman Basic Books.

Lofthouse, M. (1994) Managing learning, in T. Bush and J. West-Burnham (eds) *The Principles of Educational Management*. London: Longman.

Louis, K.S. and Miles, M.B. (1990) *Improving the Urban High School: What Works and Why*. London: Cassell.

McAleese, K. (2000) Budgeting in schools, in M. Coleman and L. Anderson (eds) *Managing Finance and Resources in Education*. London: Paul Chapman.

MacBeath, J. (1999) *Schools Must Speak for Themselves: The Case for School Self-evaluation*. London: Routledge.

MacBeath, J. and Mortimore, P. (eds) (2001) *Improving School Effectiveness*. Buckingham: Open University Press.

MacDonald, A., Saunders, L. and Benefield, P. (1999) *Boys' Achievement, Progress, Motivation and Participation: Issues Raised by the Recent Literature*. Slough: National Foundation for Educational Research.

MacGilchrist, B., Myers, K. and Reed, J. (1997) *The Intelligent School*. London: Paul Chapman.

McGregor, D. (1960) *The Human Side of Enterprise*. New York: McGraw-Hill.

McGuinness, C. (2001) *Core Concepts for Teaching Thinking*. London: Paul Chapman.

McIntyre, D. and Hagger, H. (1992) Professional development through the Oxford internship model, *British Journal of Educational Studies*, 3: 264–83.

McNiff, J., Lomax, P. and Whitehead, J. (1996) *You and your Action Research Project*. London: Routledge.

McPherson, A. (1992) Measuring added value in schools, *National Commission on Education (NCE), Briefing no. 1*. London: NCE.

McSporran, E. (1997) Towards better listening and learning in the classroom, *Educational Review*, 49(1): 13–20.

Maker, C.J. (1982) *Curriculum Development for the Gifted*. Austin, TX: Popular Education.

Martino, W. and Pallotta-Chiarolli, M. (2002) *So What's a Boy: Addressing Issues of Masculinity and Schooling*. Buckingham: Open University Press.

Melba, T. (1997) Learning styles, *Inquiry*, 1(1): 45–8.

Merry, R. (1997) *Successful Children, Successful Teaching*. Buckingham: Open University Press.

Meyer, D.K. (1997) Challenge in the mathematics classroom: students' motivation and strategies in project based learning, *Elementary School Journal*, 97(5): 501–21.

Meyerson, D. and Martin, J. (1997) Cultural change: integration of three different views, in A. Harris, N. Bennett and M. Preedy (eds) *Organizational Effectiveness and Improvement in Education*. Buckingham: Open University Press.

Mintzberg, H. (1990) The design school: reconsidering the basic processes of strategic management, *Strategic Management Journal*, 11(3): 171–95.

Mintzberg, H. (1994) *The Rise and Fall of Strategic Planning*. London: Prentice Hall.

Moore, R. and Hickox, M. (1994) Vocationalism and educational change, *The Curriculum Journal*, 5(3): 281–9.

Morrison, K. (1998) *Management Theories for Educational Change*. London: Paul Chapman.

Mortimore, P. (1991) School effectiveness research: which way at the crossroads?, *School Effectiveness and School Improvement*, 2(3): 213–29.

Mortimore, P. and Whitty, G. (1997) *Can School Improvement Overcome the Effects of Disadvantage?* London: Institute of Education, University of London.

Mortimore, P., Sammons, P., Stoll, L., Lewis, D. and Ecob, R. (1988) *School Matters: The Junior Years*. Wells: Open Books.

Moss, G. (1999) Drawing on personal resources, *Managing Schools To-day*, 8(5): 27–8.

Muijs, D. and Reynolds, D. (2001) *Effective Teaching, Evidence and Practice*. London: Paul Chapman.

Murgatroyd, S. and Morgan, C. (1992) *Total Quality Management and the School*. Buckingham: Open University Press.

Murphy, P.F. and Gipps, C. (1999) *Equity in the Classroom*. London: Institute of Education/Unesco.

Myers, K. (1996) *School Improvement in Practice: The Schools Make a Difference Project*. London: Falmer.

Nadler, D.A. (1993) Concepts for the management or organizational change, in C. Mabey and B. Mayon-White (eds) *Managing Change*. London: Paul Chapman.

National Commission on Education (1993) *Learning to Succeed*. London: Heinemann.

Nias, J., Southworth, G. and Campbell, P. (1992) *Whole School Curriculum Development in the Primary School*. London: Falmer.

Nisbet, J. and Shucksmith, J. (1986) *Learning Strategies*. London: Routledge.

Nixon, J., Martin, J., McKeown, P. and Ranson, S. (1996) *Encouraging Learning: Towards a Theory of the Learning School*. Buckingham: Open University Press.

Nuttall, D. and Stobart, G. (1994) National Curriculum Assessment in the UK, *Educational Measurement: Issues and Practice*, 13(2): 24–7 and 39.

Office for Standards in Education (Ofsted) (1992) *Framework for the Inspection of Schools*. London: HMSO.

Ofsted (1995) *Guidance on the Inspection of Secondary Schools*. London: HMSO.

Ofsted (1996) *The Gender Divide: Performance Differences between Boys and Girls at School*. London: HMSO.

Ofsted (1998) *Further Guidance to Inspectors*. London: Stationery Office.

Ofsted (1999) *Annual Report: Standards and Quality in Education*. London: Stationery Office.

O'Hanlon, C. (2000) The emotionally competent school: a step towards school improvement and raising standards, *Management in Education*, 14(2): 22–5.

Olson, D.R. and Torrance, N. (eds) (1998) *The Handbook of Education and Human Development*. Oxford: Blackwell.

Paechter, C., Preedy, M., Scott, D. and Soler, J. (eds) (2000) *Knowledge, Power and Learning*. London: Paul Chapman.

Parker, J. (2000) One step at a time, *Managing Schools Today*, 9(6): 34–9.

Payne, G., Payne, J. and Hyde, M. (1996) Refuse of all classes? Social indicators and social deprivation, *Sociological Research On-line*, (1): 1–19.

Peters, T. (1987) *Thriving on Chaos: A Handbook for a Managerial Revolution*. London: Macmillan.

Piaget, J. (1950) *The Psychology of Intelligence*. London: Routledge and Kegan Paul.

Pickering, J. (1997) *Raising Boys' Achievement*. Stafford: Network Educational Press.

Pollard, A. and Triggs, P. (1997) *Reflective Teaching in Secondary Education*. London: Cassell.

Postman, N. and Weingartner, C. (1971) *Teaching as a Subversive Activity*. Harmondsworth: Penguin.

Potter, T. and Duenkel, N. (1996) Key ingredients to meaningful educational experiences, *Ontario Journal of Outdoor Education*, 8(4): 18–21.

Power, S. and Whitty, G. (1999) New labour's education policy: first, second and third way, *Journal of Educational Policy*, 14(5): 535–46.

Powney, J. (1996) *Gender and Attainment: a Review*. Edinburgh: Scottish Council for Research in Education.

Powney, J. and Hall, S. (1998) *Closing the Gap: the Impact of Student Feedback on Students' Subsequent Activity*. Edinburgh: Scottish Council for Research in Education.

Preedy, M. (1989) *Managing Schools: Managing Curricular and Pastoral Processes*. Milton Keynes: Open University Press.

Prosser, J. (ed.) (1999) *School Culture*. London: Paul Chapman.

Purkey, W.W. and Novak, J. (1990) *Inviting School Success*, 3rd edn. Belmont, CA: Wadsworth.

Ramsden, P., Martin, E. and Bowden, J. (1989) School environment and sixth form pupils' approaches to learning, *British Journal of Educational Psychology*, 59(2): 129–42.

Randall, P. (1996) *A Community Approach to Bullying*. Stoke-on-Trent: Trentham.

Ranson, S. (1994) *Towards the Learning Society*. London: Cassell.

Reavis, C.A., Vinson, D., Fox, R. (1999) Imparting a culture of success via a strong principal, *Clearing House*, 72(4): 199–203.

Reid, K., Hopkins, D. and Holly, P. (1987) *Towards the Effective School*. Oxford: Blackwell.

Reynolds, D. (2000) Can and should pedagogic change be mandated at times?, *Journal of Educational Change*, 1(2): 193–8.

Rismark, M. (1996) The likelihood of success during classroom discourse, *Scandinavian Journal of Educational Research*, 40(1): 57–68.

Rosenberg, M. (1965) *Society and the Adolescent Self-image*. Princeton, NJ: Princeton University Press.

Rosenholtz, S. (1989) *Teachers' Workplace: The Social Organization of Schools*. New York: Longman.

Rosier, M. (1988) Survey research methods, in J. Keeves (ed.) *Educational Research, Methodology and Measurement: An International Handbook*. Oxford: Pergamon.

Rutter, M., Maughan, B., Mortimore, P., Ouston, J. and Smith, A. (1979) *Fifteen Thousand Hours: Secondary Schools and their Effects on Children*. Cambridge, MA: Harvard University Press.

Samdal, O., Wold, B. and Bronis, M. (1999) Relationship between students' perceptions of school environment, their satisfaction with school and perceived academic achievement: an international study, *School Effectiveness and Improvement*, 10(3): 296–320.

Sammons, P., Reynolds, D., Stoll, L., Barber, M. and Hillman, J. (1995) *A Country Report: School Effectiveness and School Improvement in the United Kingdom*. London: Ofsted.

Saunders, L. and Stradling, B. (2000) *Raising Attainment in Secondary Schools*. Slough: National Foundation for Educational Research.

Scanlon, M. (1999) *The Impact of Ofsted Inspections*. Slough: National Foundation for Educational Research.

Scheerens, J. (1992) *Effective Schooling*. London: Cassell.

Schein, E.H. (1985) *Organizational Culture and Leadership*. San Francisco, CA: Jossey-Bass.

Schön, D. (1983) *The Reflective Practitioner: How Professionals Think in Action*. New York: Basic Books.

School Curriculum and Assessment Authority (SCAA) (1996) *Boys and English*. London: SCAA.

Scott, P. (1995) *The Meanings of Mass Higher Education*. Buckingham: Open University Press.

Shipman, M. (1990) *In Search of Learning*. Oxford: Blackwell.

Shore, R. (1998) Personalising the school environment, *Thrust for Educational Leadership*, 28(1): 30–1.

Simkins, T. (1989) Budgeting as a political and organizational practice, in R. Levačić (ed.) *Financial Management in Education*. Milton Keynes: Open University Press.

Simkins, T. (1995) The equity consequences of educational reform, *Educational Management and Administration*, 23(4): 221–32.

Simpson, M., Payne, F., Munro, R. and Lynch, E. (1998) Using information and communications technology as a pedagogical tool: a survey of initial teacher education in Scotland, *Journal of Information Technology for Teacher Education*, 7(3): 431–46.

Skillbeck, M. (1989) A changing social and educational context, in B. Moon (ed.) *Policies in the Curriculum*. Milton Keynes: Open University Press.

Slee, R. and Weiner, G. (eds) (1998) *School Effectiveness for Whom: Challenges to the School Effectiveness and School Improvement Movements*. London: Falmer.

Smith, A. (1996) *Accelerated Learning in the Classroom*. Stafford: Network Educational Press.

Smyth, J. (1995) Devolution and teachers' work: the underside of a complex phenomenon, *Educational Management and Administration*, 23(3): 168–75.

Stefani, L.A. (1999) Assessment in partnership with learners, *Assessment and Evaluation in Higher Education*, 23(4): 339–50.

Stenhouse, L. (1975) *An Introduction to Curriculum Research and Development*. London: Heinemann.

Stoll, L. (1999) School culture: black hole or fertile garden for school improvement culture, in J. Prosser (ed.) *School Culture*. London: Paul Chapman.

Stoll, L. and Fink, D. (1996) *Changing our Schools*. Buckingham: Open University Press.

Stradling, R. and Saunders, L. (1993) Differentiation in practice: responding to the needs of all pupils, *Educational Research*, 35(2): 127–37.

Sukhnandan, L. (1999) *An Investigation into Gender Differences in Achievement Phase 1*. Slough: National Foundation for Educational Research.

Sukhnandan, L., Lee, B. and Kelleher, S. (2000) *An Investigation into Gender Differences in Achievement Phase 2*. Slough: National Foundation for Educational Research.

Tabberer, R. (1995) The only way is up, *Education*, 185(23): 15.

Task Group on Assessment and Testing (1988) *Three Supplementary Reports*. London: DES.

Teacher Training Agency (TTA) (1998a) *National Standards for Headteachers*. London: TTA.

Teacher Training Agency (1998b) *National Standards for Subject Leaders*. London: TTA.

Teacher Training Agency (1998c) *National Standards for Qualified Teacher Status*. London: TTA.

Teddlie, C. and Reynolds, D. (eds) (2000) *The International Handbook of School Effectiveness Research*. London: Falmer.

Thomas, S., Smees, R., Sammons, P. and Mortimore, P. (2001) Attainment, progress and added value, in J. MacBeath and P. Mortimore (eds) *Improving School Effectiveness*. Buckingham: Open University Press.

Tobin, P. (1998) New technology and curriculum change, *Teaching Mathematics and its Applications*, 17(3): 97–103.

Tomlinson, P. (1995) Can competence profiling work for effective teacher preparation? Part II: pitfalls and principles, *Oxford Review of Education*, 1(3): 219–314.

Tooley, D. (1999) New versus old Barber: an unfinished revolution, *British Journal of Educational Studies*, 47(1): 28–42.

Topping, K. (1986) *Parents as Educators: Teaching Parents to Teach their Children*. London: Croom Helm.

Tuohy, D. (1999) *The Inner World of Teaching: Exploring Assumptions which Promote Change and Development*. London: Falmer.

Tuomey, J. (1998) An investigation of the relationship between learning styles, the preferred teaching style and the academic ability of leaving certificate pupils in a secondary school in Ireland, *Irish Educational Studies*, 17: 370–6.

Tyler, R. (1949) *Basic Principles of Curriculum and Instruction*. Chicago: University of Chicago Press.

Vygotsky, L.S. (1978) *Mind in Society: The Development of Higher Psychological Processes*. Cambridge, MA: Harvard University Press.

Warrington, M. and Younger, M. (1996) Goals, expectations and motivation: gender differences in achievement at GCSE, *Curriculum*, 17(2): 80–93.

Weindling, D. (1997) Strategic planning in schools: some practical techniques, in M. Preedy, R. Glatter and R. Levačić (eds) *Education Management, Quality and Resources*. Buckingham: Open University Press.

West-Burnham, J. (1992) *Managing Quality in Schools*. London: Longman.

Whitaker, P. (1995) *Managing to Learn*. London: Cassell.

Williams, C. (1997) Managing motivation, *Managing Schoools To-day*, 6(9): 28–30.

Willms, J.D. (1992) *Monitoring School Performance*. London: Falmer.

Wilson, J. and Haugh, B. (1995) Collaborative modelling and talk in the classroom, *Language and Education*, 9(4): 265–81.

Wilson, L. and Easen, P. (1995) Teachers' needs and practice development: implications for in-classroom support, *British Journal of In-service Education*, 21(3): 325–41.

Wragg, E.C. (1997) Oh Boy!, *Times Educational Supplement*, 16 May: 4220.

Younger, M., Warrington M. and Williams, J. (1999) The gender gap and classroom interactions: reality or rhetoric?, *British Journal of Sociology*, 20(3): 325–41.

Name index

Subject index

EDUCATIONAL LEADERSHIP AND LEARNING
PRACTICE, POLICY AND RESEARCH

Sue Law and Derek Glover

. . . it sets out both the theory and the everyday realities that lie behind the Government's 'improving leadership' agenda.

T. E. S. Friday

Educational leaders – whether in schools, colleges or higher education – are challenged with steering unprecedented change; educational management has never been more demanding. Within the context of a new 'learning age' and the Teacher Training Agency's National Standards, this book explores many of the key issues facing those both aspiring to and already involved in leadership and management, whether at middle or senior levels.

While focusing particularly on schools and colleges, this book evaluates issues increasingly central to leadership in a variety of professional educational settings, for example, school improvement, innovation, teamwork, organizational culture, professional development, motivation and the nature of leadership. In identifying key concepts, it scrutinizes possible management strategies within a changing policy context that is increasingly focused around standards, accountability and reputation.

The book utilizes research evidence to illuminate the practices, challenges and problems facing educationists and endeavours to overcome the perceived gap between practice and research to create an integrated approach to leadership and management development: one which both supports and stimulates managers' professional development aspirations.

Contents
Part I: Leading and managing – The context for educational leadership – Developing leadership and management effectiveness – Managing ourselves and leading others – Motivating and managing others – Leading effective teams – Part II: Changing and learning – Effective communication – Organizational cultures – Managing change and creating opportunities – Educational improvement, inspection and effectiveness – Leading and managing in learning organizations – Part III: Tasks and responsibilities – Managing staff and promoting quality – Managing resources and finance – Managing stakeholder relationships and partnerships – Leading and managing for professional development – Postscript – Bibliography – Name index – Subject index.

320pp   0 335 19752 3 (Paperback)   0 335 19753 1 (Hardback)

IMPROVING SCHOOL EFFECTIVENESS

John MacBeath and Peter Mortimore (eds.)

- What have we learned after three decades of research into school effectiveness?
- What are the messages for policy makers, for schools, for classroom teachers, for parents and their children?
- What can we say with confidence about how schools improve?
- What do we want from our schools in the future and how can we achieve it?

This book sets out to answer these questions, reviewing findings from seminal international work and from a major study conducted recently in Scotland, the Improving School Effectiveness Project. It builds up a fascinating picture of what effectiveness is, how it can be measured, and what it means for teachers, parents and pupils. It provides key quantitative data that shows just how schools can and do make a difference, but that their effects tend to be more powerful at different stages in a child's school career, and with differing effects for girls and boys, and for different school subjects. From in-depth work with twenty-four 'case study' schools we are also given much rich qualitative evidence about, for instance, the links between attitudes and attainment within a school, about the ethos of a school and its capacity for change, about the significance of a school development plan in bringing about changes, and about the role and impact of 'critical friends' in pursuing improvement in schools.

Improving School Effectiveness is an important book for everyone who is interested in valuing the effectiveness of and securing improvement in schools: for teachers, heads, inspectors, policy makers, and students and scholars of school effectiveness and improvement.

Contents

Introduction – School effectiveness and improvement: the story so far – The policy context – The research design and methods – Attainment, progress and added value – Views of pupils, parents and teachers: vital indicators of effectiveness and for improvement – Extending the quality framework: lessons from case study schools – Change leadership: planning, conceptualization and perception – Do schools need critical friends? – A profile change – The change equation: capacity for improvement – Beyond 2000: where next for effectiveness and improvement? – Bibliography – Index.

240pp   0 335 20687 5 (Paperback)   0 335 20688 3 (Hardback)

openup

ideas and understanding
in social science

www.**openup**.co.uk

 **Browse, search and
order online**

 **Download detailed
title information and
sample chapters***

*for selected titles

www.**openup**.co.uk